# THE WORLD WITHIN

*Also by Guy Stagg*

The Crossway

# THE WORLD WITHIN

*Why Writers, Artists and Thinkers Retreat*

## GUY STAGG

SCRIBNER

London · New York · Amsterdam/Antwerp · Sydney/Melbourne · Toronto · New Delhi

SCRIBNER

First published in Great Britain by Simon & Schuster UK Ltd, 2025

1 3 5 7 9 10 8 6 4 2
Simon & Schuster UK Ltd
1st Floor
222 Gray's Inn Road
London WC1X 8HB

www.simonandschuster.co.uk
www.simonandschuster.com.au
www.simonandschuster.co.in

Simon & Schuster Australia, Sydney
Simon & Schuster India, New Delhi

The authorised representative in the EEA is Simon & Schuster Netherlands BV, Herculesplein 96,
3584 AA Utrecht, Netherlands. info@simonandschuster.nl

Image credits:
Photo booth portrait of Ludwig Wittgenstein, c. 1930 © Mila Palm Collection, Vienna /
Photo: Leopold Museum, Vienna/Manfred Thumberger
Vintage postcard of Klosterneuburg Monastery, provenance unknown / Photo: Creative Commons, CC0
Portrait of David Jones c.1930 by an unknown photographer / Photo: Peter Wakelin
Caldey Abbey c.1907 by William Richard Shepherd / Photo: Creative Commons, CC0
Portrait of Simone Weil by unknown photographer / Photo: Editorial Trotta
Postcard of Abbaye Saint-Pierre de Solesmes, provenance unknown / Photo: Creative Commons, CC0

The author and publishers have made all reasonable efforts to contact copyright-holders
for permission, and apologise for any omissions or errors in the form of credits given.
Corrections may be made to future printings.

A CIP catalogue record for this book is available from the British Library

Hardback ISBN: 978-1-3985-3350-9
eBook ISBN: 978-1-3985-3351-6
eAudio ISBN: 978-1-3985-3392-9

Typeset in Bembo Std by Palimpsest Book Production Limited, Falkirk, Stirlingshire

Printed and Bound in the UK using 100% Renewable Electricity at CPI Group (UK) Ltd

One morning in May, I woke before dawn and stepped out into a flawless day. The air was bright and breezeless, the sky untroubled by a single cloud. I walked on pavements and roads, on the glossy lawns of a golf course and the ragged slopes of a heath. Then I joined a track turning south and walked straight into the sun.

The path was pale chalk, soapy from recent rain. For an hour I followed its course through fields planted with wheat and rye. The trees by the track were thickening, their branches stippled with leaves, while blossom hung from the hawthorn like a late fall of snow. There were no cars to busy the roads, however, nor any planes to pierce the taut silence of the sky. There were no strangers dressed in hiking gear and striding slowly towards me.

This was the first spring of the pandemic, when half the world was locked in their homes. Each night I watched the news, learning about hospital wards filled with patients and the elderly dying without family beside their beds. But here the crisis left little mark, except for the muted villages and unpeopled paths, and the birdsong sounding like distant sirens.

I walked until I came to a woodland clearing with bluebells pooling among the undergrowth. There was something enchanted about this space, the flowers seeming to float from the floor, their purple petals like the trace of a spell. For a while I waited among the trees, not blinking, not breathing, but standing without moving and listening to the birds that called from every branch.

All the world was in retreat and my own life felt suspended too. Yet I found a curious relief in those absent weeks, when my plans were paused and my future cast in doubt. Despite the crisis overwhelming the country – the jobs ended, the families separated – there was an unreal quality to each stalled day. A calm that resulted from knowing history had been put on hold. A serenity that came from needing only to survive.

Purple poured across the woodland floor. Meadows spreading to the edges of the sky. Nothing to stir the leaves on the trees, and time made powerless in that sheltered space. For a moment I wanted only to remain in the clearing, as if this was where I belonged. But soon the chorus of birds was sounding again, the branches becoming crazed with song. So then I began to trace my route, walking out of the woodland and stepping again into that immaculate morning.

# Introduction

All my life I have dreamed of retreat. Of leaving behind my ambitions. Of saying goodbye to family and friends. Of turning my back on the places I know and escaping to some secret hideaway. Whenever I feel unequal to the world, that vision plays once more in my mind. Why not give up all you have and withdraw from society?

It's not simply the cliché of solitude I seek. Nor the holiday calm that comes from closing the laptop and switching off the phone. It's not even the relief of letting go of every obligation and forgetting each one of my responsibilities. Instead, I imagine finding my own home in this world, the place that, once reached, I need never leave.

This wish is not attached to any specific location. Rather, it's an idea I always carry in my mind. One day I will settle down and be satisfied with what I have. One day I will no longer need to pretend.

I know I'm not the only one. The dream of retreat is shared by countless people. A bothy built by a lakeside, or a cabin buried in the woods. A cottage hidden in the fold of a valley, only reached via an unsurfaced road. Occasionally

I will chance upon one of these refuges and imagine another life for myself: simpler and smaller, quieter and more self-contained. The days spent growing food in the garden and the evenings passed reading books by the fire. No company but the whispering wind and the clouds making muted journeys through the sky.

This is a book about retreat. It looks at three people — writers, thinkers and artists — who decided to withdraw from the world. In some cases, they did so in order to work; in others, they were seeking a cure for sickness or trauma; but each of them hoped to remake themselves. It asks what they gained and what they lost by stepping back from this life, and it wonders why so many share the desire to retreat, calling to us through busy routines and crowded commitments, promising a sanctuary of our own.

God was the very first solitary. Once the pagan empires passed and the heavens emptied out, the only deity that remained was alone. Perhaps he made the world for want of company, created the heavens and the earth to escape from isolation. Which would make God the very first artist, too, seeking relief from solitude by imagining something new.

When the prophets wanted to speak with God, they went into the desert to share that solitude. Moses spent forty days on Mount Sinai, alone on the smoking mountaintop. Elijah spent forty days on Mount Horeb, until a still, small voice asked, 'Why are you here?' Jesus likewise went into the wilderness, fasting in the Judean desert, but instead of the creator he was visited by the devil, another lonely soul who haunts the waste places of this earth. Three times he was tempted, and three times he refused, because none of the world's prizes could equal his ambition. So then the devil departed and a chorus of angels dropped down from the sky, surrounding the young man with song.

Retreat has been practiced in all the major religions. In Tibetan Buddhism, a yogi withdrew into a lightless cave and meditated until the darkness became bright with visions. In Sufi Islam, a *murid* passed forty days in seclusion, repeating the name of Allah until given a glimpse of heaven and hell. In certain Hindu teaching, retreat was the third *ashrama* or stage of life, when the believer abandoned their home and family, retiring into the forest to spend their days in prayer. The methods were diverse, but the aims were the same: forsaking this world to meet with God.

Of course, there have always been religious communities who separated themselves from society. But retreat was not reserved for monks and nuns; it was a practice every believer could share. Because it did not require saying goodbye forever, only withdrawing for long enough to examine your faults, discern your future, pray for a change of heart. What made it different from a holiday was the desire to become someone new.

Today, the word retreat means something else entirely. It means women's retreats and men's retreats, couples' retreats and singles' retreats, silent retreats and detox retreats, nature retreats and breathwork retreats. It means reeling round a wooden lodge, the air becoming thick with sweat and smoke, and then plunging into a mountain pool, skin prickled with the sudden gasp of pain. It means forest glades, or rewilded glens, or manicured expanses of desert – withdrawing to discover ourselves rather than the divine.

Nonetheless, retreat is on the rise once more. The word often recurs in newspaper supplements and social media feeds. Health spas and holiday rentals and summer festivals all advertise themselves as some kind of refuge. At times they're selling nostalgia: living off grid and foraging for food, pushing back against the pressure to produce and consume. Other times they're selling self-care: rising to meditate in the dawn light, or performing yoga on an empty beach, or falling asleep to the sound of waves sighing back and forth along the shore. But always they seem to promise that paradise can be found here and now.

What's the reason for this revival? Why are so many people stepping back from cities and careers and crowded lives? For some, it's the fear of environmental collapse and the wish to return to nature. For others, it's the relentless pace of the digital age and the desire to leave behind technology. A few might be seeking shelter from economic anxiety or political upheaval; a few more want to recover from heartbreak or burnout; the rest are searching for a sense of purpose. In each case, they retreat in the hope that another life might be possible.

All this is easy to critique. The inflated prices and elaborate menus. The whispered voices and vacant smiles. The random mix of fitness, therapy and spirituality, blending into a New Age blur. At times, retreat resembles nothing more than a self-righteous holiday, inviting people to escape their privilege by ignoring normal life for a while. It's only available to those who can afford to pause their lives, turning their focus inwards as the world begins to burn. And it makes a virtue of apathy, of idleness, of indulgence even; no flight from the ego but sinking deeper into ourselves.

Yet there is another kind of retreat. Less escaping from crises than finding the strength to endure them. Less abandoning responsibility than understanding its limits. A refuge for those without homes, or a sanctuary for those without hope. A way of stepping back far enough to see the world with perspective. This was the retreat that interested me.

Faith played little part in my childhood. I never went to Sunday school, let alone confirmation classes. Instead I was a teenage atheist, telling anyone who would listen that I did not believe.

In early adulthood, things began to change. The first half of my twenties was marred by heavy drinking and deep depression. After I recovered, I became interested in the more ascetic forms of religion: the believers who willingly turned their back on temptation and welcomed misfortune as a test of faith.

I suspect the monastic calling has a special draw for those who have struggled with depression. Those who think emotion is something to endure rather than enjoy, who think happiness can never lift so high as disappointment brings crashing down. For them, the sacrifice of religious life is a simple wager: forfeiting the chance of pleasure to protect yourself from pain. Certainly, my own fascination with monks and nuns came from wanting to escape the feelings I could not endure.

Then, aged twenty-five, I spent ten months walking across Europe and the Middle East. My route followed medieval pilgrim paths and most nights I stayed in churches, or else in monasteries and convents. Though I did not believe, I was impressed by the communities who cared for me, because they seemed to share a contentment that was lacking in the wider world. Perhaps it was the willed simplicity of their existence, with little interest in wealth or fame, material possessions or physical pleasures. Or perhaps it was the ordered calm of their daily routine, shaped around the seasons and the hours of prayer.

Once the walk was over, I had no wish to return to the city where I had rented or the office where I had worked. I was looking for a new way to live, so I tried learning what I could from those who have withdrawn. For the next five years I helped care for a family member after a serious accident and wrote a book about the walk. Relationships and friendships, job offers and professional opportunities – all of these were ignored.

To begin with, the solitude made me feel superior. I imagined there was something heroic about giving up things society seemed to value. And something virtuous about committing completely to this stripped-back life, as if the world would reward me for asking so little. I also hoped that, by whittling down my wishes to the smallest possible size – no partner or family, no settled job or permanent home – I could guard myself against disappointment.

After a while, I started to talk about writing as a vocation. In other words, I believed my work was a duty, one I had to obey whatever the outcome. By removing the illusion of choice, I removed any responsibility too, which meant the only mistake I could make was failing to commit completely. And I was inspired by the idea of writing as a burden I must endure no matter how heavy it became, because I believed the test of genius was the willingness to sacrifice everything for the sake of one's work. If I made my own life punishing enough, I would surely create something that lasted.

Long after the book was finished, I kept up these solitary routines. It was not until the pandemic forced us all into retreat that I began to doubt my approach. In the long lull of those vacant days, I started wondering whether solitude was enough to sustain an entire creative career. Lockdown made clear the things our lives lacked, and for me it was the commitments and relationships I once thought a distraction. On those lonely lockdown walks, a single question began burning in my mind: How much should a writer remain in the world and how much should they withdraw?

I was fifteen when I first read Rainer Maria Rilke's *Letters to a Young Poet*. One line made a lasting impression: 'What is necessary, after all, is only this: solitude, vast inner solitude. To walk inside yourself and meet no one for hours – this is what you must be able to attain.' From that point on, solitude and writing were synonymous in my mind.

When a writer or artist withdraws, two journeys are taking place. The first is the physical retreat: seeking some isolated setting to work without disruption. The second is the mental retreat: stepping into the imagination to wander through rooms furnished from fantasy. Both create a protected place where ideas and images become more vivid than the departed world.

Many authors have biographies made up of love affairs and tragic losses and time spent travelling in distant lands. However, the moments of stillness are no less important for understanding their lives, because this is where the writing occurs. The sudden chancing on a metaphor, the slow perfecting of a verse, or the little insight that finally finishes a paragraph – these events occur in private. Similarly, though retreats are often seen as interludes in writers' lives, they can craft their characters as deeply as any adventure beyond the study.

After reading Rilke's letters, I began collecting examples of authors who had sought out lonely locations to write. Montaigne, Hölderlin and Vita Sackville-West, looking down on the world from their towers. Or Henry David Thoreau building a wooden cabin next to Walden Pond, or Carl Jung building a miniature castle beside Lake Zurich. Then there was Gustave Flaubert in his pavilion on the banks of the Seine, watching the fishermen work by the light of the moon. And Virginia Woolf in a potting shed at the end of her Sussex garden, writing in an armchair with a plywood board balanced on her lap. And Dylan Thomas in a green-painted garage in Carmarthenshire, the window framing a view of the Taf Estuary, the desk strewn with boiled sweets. Not to mention the recluses: Emily Dickinson refusing to leave her home, dressing in white and talking to visitors from behind a door; Marcel Proust lying in bed for the last three years of his life, the walls padded with cork to dampen the sounds of the Paris streets; Emily Brontë becoming mute to everyone except family members and moorland animals; J. D. Salinger writing endless unread novels while hiding in the New Hampshire woods.

Most interesting to me were the writers who spent time with religious communities. T. S. Eliot once planned to end his life at an Art Deco abbey in Buckinghamshire. Graham

Greene returned each year to a bare cell at a medieval monastery in Galicia. Iris Murdoch and Rumer Godden stayed at the same convent in Worcestershire, both writing a book inspired by their retreats. Christopher Isherwood joined a Vedanta Centre in Hollywood to spend his days translating the Bhagavad Gita. Katherine Mansfield's last weeks were passed in George Gurdjieff's Institute for the Development of Harmonious Man.

I was curious whether these writers glimpsed an echo of their work in the strict routines of monastic life. The patient practice repeated each day and the quiet devotion to a single cause. The discipline, the isolation, and the sacrifice too, carried out for the sake of something intangible. Why else do we use the word contemplation to describe both thought and prayer, or the word calling for religious and creative pursuits? Why else do we compare artists to prophets and priests?

There were three figures who might help me to answer these questions. Three writers and thinkers from between the wars whose lives were shaped by retreat. All three spent time with religious communities and all three were changed by the experience.

Ludwig Wittgenstein was born in Vienna in the last decades of the Austro-Hungarian Empire, a member of one of Europe's wealthiest families. He wrote the twentieth century's most influential work of philosophy, only to desert his subject and find employment as a soldier, a teacher, an architect too. He also retreated several times in his life, withdrawing to labour in the gardens of monasteries, as well as remote corners of Norway, Austria and Ireland. To his mentor Bertrand Russell he was 'the most perfect example I have known of genius as traditionally conceived'. To his Russian teacher Fania Pascal, he was 'above all a person in search of spiritual salvation'.

David Jones was an artistic prodigy, born to a working-class Welsh family in London in 1895. Aged fourteen, he entered Camberwell College of Art, but his studies were interrupted by the outbreak of war. As a soldier, he endured longer in the trenches than any other poet, inspiring his great account of the conflict, an epic called *In Parenthesis*. This poem was started years after the fighting, while living among religious and creative communities; T. S. Eliot believed it 'a work of genius' and W. H. Auden called it 'the greatest book about the First World War'. However, Jones became ever more withdrawn over the course of his life, spending his final decades as a near-recluse in a North London boarding house.

Simone Weil was born in Paris midway through the First World War and died midway through the Second. From adolescence she campaigned as an anarchist and pacifist, but grew disillusioned after fighting in Spain. Then, following a Holy Week retreat, she began to produce a stream of essays, letters and journal entries discussing morality, metaphysics and mysticism. Few of these writings were published during her life, yet in the decade after her death she was recognised as one of the most original thinkers of the century. To Albert Camus, she was 'the only great spirit of our time', while Simone de Beauvoir envied her for 'having a heart that could beat right across the world'.

These three never met one another, yet their biographies often ran in parallel. None of them married, or had children, or acquired their own homes. None of them had settled careers either, living in deliberate poverty and seeking out lonely places to work. And, though none of them were traditional believers, each one entered the Catholic Church after their experiences of conflict. Furthermore, each one went to stay with a religious community at around the age of thirty: either becoming a gardener at a monastery outside Vienna, or spending several months on an island off the coast of Wales, or passing a fortnight at a great gothic abbey in north-west France.

The retreats were made at moments of crisis in their lives. Wittgenstein was mourning the loss of the man he loved and struggling to publish his first book. Jones was escaping the collapse of his engagement and scraping a living from engravings. Weil was on permanent sabbatical from her teaching career, with migraines so severe that she even considered suicide. But, during the time they spent with these communities, they found a shelter from disappointment and despair.

Over the course of the lockdown, I kept returning to the work of these three. I hoped their writing might give a hint of the role retreat played in their creative and intellectual careers. Most biographies described their retreats as blank spaces in the story, but I was convinced they had a more lasting influence, convinced the weeks they spent withdrawn gave birth to their later lives. Because these journeys took place before any of them were celebrated figures, yet set them on a path they would follow until the end.

The communities where these three stayed were still intact. What's more, their ways of life had changed little over the last century. So I decided that, once the lockdown lifted, I would visit the monasteries where Wittgenstein, Jones and Weil stepped back from society. I would stay in their guest houses and speak with their monks. And I would try to reckon with the cost of leaving the world behind.

Wittgenstein's sister once called him an unhappy saint. Jones was compared to a holy man hiding in his cell. Weil wrote in letters about her longing to become a martyr. These descriptions offered three models for retreat: as a moral project, as a flight from society, as a form of self-sacrifice. Saint, hermit and martyr: the symbols I would use to understand their beliefs and make sense of their biographies.

# The Saint

*Ludwig Wittgenstein (1889–1951)*

Each night he prayed for courage. The courage to face the fighting. The courage to endure the enemy assault. The courage to trust his life to God. Then he stepped out into the darkness, lit by the blossoming flames of mortar fire.

It was 1916, halfway through the war. Ludwig Wittgenstein was stationed in Galicia, modern-day Ukraine. The Austrian and Russian armies were facing one another in a long line that ran north from the River Dneister. This was where Wittgenstein came to learn the lessons philosophy could not teach.

He joined the army soon after war was declared, enlisting as a soldier and assigned to an artillery regiment. Medically he could have been spared compulsory service; socially he could have applied for an officer's commission. However, he wanted to come close to death, hoping it would reveal the truth about his character.

His first two years were spent in a workshop, growing impatient with his fellow soldiers – the crude jokes, the stupid comments, the total lack of solitude. Then, in the spring of 1916, he transferred to the front line and volunteered for an observation post, guaranteeing he would come under enemy fire. 'Tomorrow perhaps I shall be sent out, at my own request, to the observation post,' he wrote in his diary. 'Then and only then will the war begin for me. And possibly life too! Perhaps nearness to death will bring light into my life.'

Soon Wittgenstein was put on night duty: the period of heaviest shelling. Every evening, setting off to his post, he wondered whether he would return. He told himself that fear was an intellectual error, showing too much attachment to this life. But still his mouth would dry and his stomach clench, his whole body becoming tense with terror.

Within weeks the Russian army had launched its major assault, known as the Brusilov Offensive. During one of these battles, Wittgenstein was positioned in front of a gun emplacement being hammered by artillery fire. Again and again his companions shouted for him to take cover, as the shelling and mortar thundered down from the skies. But Wittgenstein refused to duck out of sight, standing with binoculars pressed to his eyes until he could identify the source of the mortar rounds. The ground shaking, the earth scattering, the deafening crashes all around – yet still he remained calm in the face of danger, his fear defeated at last.

In June, the front line was breached and the Austrian army withdrew. Wittgenstein joined the long retreat into the Carpathian Mountains, sitting slumped on the back of

a horse and trying not to fall from the saddle. On reaching
the mountains, he returned to his diary, but the entry he
made that day was neither logical analysis nor an account
of his experiences at the front. Instead, it was the breakthrough he had been waiting for, the reason he came to
war:

What do I know about God and the purpose of life?
I know that this world exists.
That I am placed in it like my eye in its visual field.
That something about it is problematic, which we
call its meaning.
This meaning does not lie in it but outside of it.
That life is the world.
That my will penetrates the world.
That my will is good or evil.
Therefore that good and evil are somehow
connected with the meaning of the world.
The meaning of life, i.e. the meaning of the world,
we can call God.

Wittgenstein was forever withdrawing. From the wealth and
fame of his family. From the privileged societies of Vienna
and Cambridge. From the settled career of an academic
philosopher and the ideas he had authored, the reputation
he had made.

Sometimes he retreated in search of answers, trying to

solve the fundamental questions that troubled his mind. Other times he retreated to improve himself, hoping to confront his faults and correct his flaws. And sometimes he retreated to hide away, overcome by a sense of defeat he could no longer endure.

These retreats were the reason I became curious about the philosopher, because they seemed to express a paradox at the centre of his character. After all, Wittgenstein was the heir of an Austro-Hungarian steel magnate, but gave up his inheritance to live in poverty. He studied logic under the sceptic Bertrand Russell, but became a committed Christian during the First World War. He wrote the *Tractatus Logico-Philosophicus*, and then abandoned philosophy for more than a decade.

Even the *Tractatus* shared something of this paradox. The first time I attempted to read the book, one sentence made a lasting impression on me: *Nicht wie die Welt ist, ist das Mystische, sondern dass sie ist*. 'Not how the world is, is the mystical, but that it is.'

Mystical? What was a word like mystical doing among pages of language and logic? The *Tractatus* was meant to be the Bible of the analytic philosophers, rationalist thinkers from the early twentieth century who tried to turn their subject into a science. According to the analytic tradition, philosophy should consist of nothing but concrete facts connected by chains of reasoning. Ethics, aesthetics, and metaphysics were all mistrusted, not to mention the claims of religion. As far as I knew, Ludwig Wittgenstein was one of the movement's leading members, and the few photographs I had seen of the philosopher seemed to confirm this impression. The pointed features, the piercing gaze, the flesh pulled tight across the face: here was genius as a reasoning machine, immune to the confusion the rest of us experience.

Once I began learning about Wittgenstein's biography, my understanding changed. I discovered that his life was interrupted several times by depression, and during the worst periods he would withdraw from the world, seeking out the sparsely populated landscapes of Norway and Ireland, as well as the mountain villages of Austria. He was not some chilly caricature of unfeeling logic, but a familiar mix of doubt and despair.

To me, one story proved this point better than any other. During the summer of 1920, Wittgenstein spent a couple of months as an assistant gardener at Klosterneuburg, a monastery in the hills north of Vienna, where he worked in the nurseries during the day and slept in a potting shed each night. His letters around this time were filled with mentions of suicide, but he experienced some relief while employed as a gardener.

I was bewitched by the idea of this brilliant mind busying himself with manual labour. And the idea that tending a garden might have rescued Wittgenstein from despair. So, I decided to visit Klosterneuburg myself, to spend a week in the place where the philosopher sought refuge and try to understand how it saved him.

High summer when I came to the city, and the heat hit its peak as I reached Klosterneuburg. The airport had the anxious crowding of the months after the pandemic, yet the slow train that carried me to the suburbs was almost empty. It was the same when I climbed from the station to the old town: a single street rising between chalet-style houses, the road bare and the pavements deserted. Nobody was loitering in the town square, either, or sitting at the tables outside the inns – as if all the locals were hiding from the heat.

A pair of iron gates sealed the far corner of the square. Beyond lay a cobbled area like a cathedral close, surrounding the monastery buildings. To the left was a gothic church with pointed spires and a pitched roof, its latticed tiles green and gold in the bright afternoon. To the right rose a dome of clouded copper with a copper crown balanced on top, like a curious kind of weathervane. Straight ahead stood the monastery façade, three storeys of shuttered windows and a pair of double doors set into an arcing porch. Its walls were the rich yellow of egg yolk and the whole place looked recently painted, the old render shining as if brand new.

Inside I found a rounded entrance hall, the air cool and the space shaded. I sat on a bench in the porter's lodge, waiting for the guest-master to find me. A coved ceiling was suspended two storeys above the hall, high enough for a horse and carriage to pass underneath, while the floor was paved with wooden tiles to create a muffled quiet. No footsteps echoed from the flanking corridors, no voices sounded from the inner courtyard, and even the ringing of a phone seemed subdued in the lofty chambers of the porter's lodge.

Fr Clemens was the name of the guest-master. He was an American priest who moved to Klosterneuburg two decades ago. From the emails we had exchanged, I expected someone tall and gaunt, but the man who met me was stocky, with his cheeks plucked into a sardonic smile. He was not wearing a habit either; only a polo shirt and a pair of swimming trunks.

'Just heading for a swim,' he explained. 'Want to come?'

'No swimming kit,' I replied. 'Never thought to pack it.'

'Best thing to do in this heat.' He checked the glinting watch on his wrist. 'In that case, I should show you the room.'

He led the way down a corridor with floors of pale stone and walls of moulded plaster. Lace curtains were drawn across the windows and the doors had brass handles set at shoulder height. My cell was likewise designed with giants in mind: a suite of rooms filled with heavy items of furniture, including a wardrobe the size of a telephone box and a table large enough to host a dinner party.

The guest-master circled the suite, pointing out the single

bed, the corner desk, the kitchenette. 'How long did you say you were staying?' he asked, and when I reminded him that I was here for a week, he replied, 'You'll probably be sick of us by Friday.'

A pair of windows looked out on the main courtyard, my view obscured by the scaffolding supports of a stage. 'Opera festival,' Fr Clemens added. 'Klosterneuburg hosts one every summer. This year they're performing Puccini, so I hope you like *La bohème*.' Then he left me for his swim, promising a tour of the gardens after dinner.

Paintings and icons were pinned to the walls and the rich reek of varnish lingered in the air. I was expecting to find a timetable on the desk listing the regular church services, but instead there was a sticker giving the Wi-Fi code, along with a telephone connected to the internal network. Above hung a print of Klosterneuburg from a century ago, its edges speckled and its corners foxed.

For a while I lapped round the room, unpacking my clothes and hanging them in the wardrobe. My first retreat was underway, yet I had no idea what to do with myself. I did not want to check my phone or go online, but it seemed too early to visit the chapel and pretend to pray. Instead I sat at the desk, making notes from the morning and waiting for the guest-master to rescue me from my own company.

Before leaving, Fr Clemens had said something about half the community being away on holiday. I was reminded of visiting school after the end of term: the slight feeling of

futility in the corridors and classrooms, as well as the stillness that haunted every public space. Those unoccupied
buildings designed for crowds of people; those empty
expanses of unscheduled time. Occasionally I heard a shrill
sound from the courtyard as the backstage team tested their
speakers, or else the shouts of workmen assembling the
stepped seating: *Komm! Warte! Halt!* Otherwise the monastery was quiet.

Wittgenstein arrived at Klosterneuburg in the summer of
1920. Nature felt near here, the monastery separated from
Vienna by the Kahlenberg and Leopoldsberg hills, their
slopes strung with vines and their summits stippled with
woodland. Formal gardens surrounded the monastery's main
buildings, sinking down towards the Danube. For the next
six weeks, those gardens were Wittgenstein's home.

He had been to Klosterneuburg once before, on a
weekend trip in the early months of the war. Then, the
branches of the woods were bare and the twisted vines were
naked, too, while the pointed spires of the monastery clawed
the winter sky. Now the skies were clear and the breeze
was still, the temperature rising towards thirty degrees. Now
he had come here to stay.

The philosopher spoke like a Viennese gentleman, but
did not look like one. He dressed in loose jackets and baggy
trousers, and rarely ever wore a tie. Sometimes he put on
his military uniform, though the war had ended two years

ago, its green-grey fabric faded with use and its collars and cuffs beginning to fray. Otherwise, his cheeks were hollow and his eyes deep set, the sunken pupils staring without blinking as if appalled by what they saw.

At the time, the city was filled with former soldiers. Some were maimed, others deranged, and all of them searching for work. In the aftermath of the war, Austria's new neighbours set up trade blockades, cutting off the grain from Hungary and the coal from Bohemia. Half the population was unemployed, but the government had to print money to finance their debts, making inflation much worse. The cost of living almost tripled over the course of 1919, and by the end of the year the weather was so cold that the wealthy were burning their furniture, while the poor chopped down trees in the Vienna Woods in a desperate effort to keep warm.

But in Klosterneuburg these hardships felt far away. The monastery was founded in 1114 and rebuilt in a grandiose style during the eighteenth century. Its southern range contained a palace, the façade carved with pediments, columns and crests, while a squad of sculpted Atlases held high the entrance hall. The other monastic buildings housed the largest private library in Austria, along with paintings and statues and priceless treasures, too. And the most important religious figure in Austria – Cardinal Friedrich Gustav Piffl – was a former member of the community.

Before the war, Klosterneuburg was the favourite monastery of the Austro-Hungarian monarchs. Each year, the royal family visited the church for the feast day of St Leopold, watching the service from an ornate chamber above the choir stalls. After mass, they would process to the Imperial apartments, where the walls were hung with tapestries and the ceilings celestial with murals. Floors of polished parquet, cabinets of delicate marquetry and a wooden throne surrounded by a canopy of crimped gold – all the majesty of the Holy Roman Empire. But, by the time Wittgenstein came to stay, the emperor was dead and the royal family living in exile. Furthermore, the empire was shattered and its territories shared among half a dozen different states. However, Wittgenstein was not here to explore the library, let alone tour the imperial apartments. Instead he had been hired as an assistant gardener to work in the grounds each day.

At this point Wittgenstein was thirty-one years old. The first half of his twenties had been spent studying philosophy, the second half fighting in the Great War. Now he planned to work as a primary school teacher and was waiting to be posted to a mountain village. In the meantime, he needed a job.

Wittgenstein was supposed to spend the summer months visiting his closest friend, Paul Engelmann. But the nearer the time came, the more he felt dismayed by this idea, and in the middle of July he wrote to cancel the plan. 'I was longing for some kind of regular work,' he explained, 'which, of all the things I can do in my present condition, is the most nearly bearable, if I am not mistaken.'

That condition was one of deep depression. His correspondence from the late spring and early summer returned again and again to the idea of ending his own life. 'I have sunk to the lowest point,' he told Engelmann in a previous letter. 'May you never be in that position. Shall I ever be able to raise myself up again?'

Klosterneuburg was a kind of sanctuary. Wittgenstein hoped the regular work would lift his spirits, or at least distract from suicide. But this does not explain why he chose a job in the gardens of a monastery, nor account for the community he had come to live among.

That story starts in the desert, some two hundred years after the death of Christ. Here, in the unpeopled expanses of Egypt and Syria, the first hermits began to gather. In tombs and caves and the ruined remains of human settlements, they made their lonely homes. Then they waited for the devil to visit.

These hermits went into the desert to flee the world, but their fame soon spread among the cities of the Levant. Before long, the eastern edge of the Sahara was filled with anchorites, spending their days in prayer. In between they would collect rainwater to drink, eke out their sparse supplies of food, or lay down on the rocks to sleep. All this attracted more fame, more followers.

The Bible contains no command to retreat. However, these hermits believed they were imitating Christ, their solitary calling a kind of crucifixion. The most well-known was Anthony the Great, who retreated to the Nitrian Desert between Alexandria and Cairo in the first half of the fourth century. During his life, Anthony was celebrated for miraculous cures and the bruising battles he fought against demons, while the biography written after his death became a bestseller by ancient standards. It also spread the idea of monasticism across the Western and Eastern Churches, and inspired the conversion of St Augustine at the age of thirty-one.

Augustine spent his early years in Carthage, Rome and Milan, where he fathered a child and dabbled in Manicheanism. Then, on learning about the life of Anthony the Great, he converted to Christianity and returned home to North Africa. Soon he had sold the land attached to his father's farm and started a community in the leftover buildings.

By this point, the desert hermits were separated into two distinct groups. Those who lived and worshipped in isolation were called eremites, while those who formed communities of solitaries – praying together and following the same set of rules – were called cenobites. Augustine taught that true contentment was not a consequence of human relations: only love of the divine brought lasting happiness. But his own rule guarded against the isolation of the eremites by encouraging a balance between solitude and community. And his followers lived in simplicity rather than austerity, prioritising the work of the Church above acts of endurance.

Over the course of the Middle Ages, Augustine's rule was

adopted by groups of priests who combined prayer with pastoral obligations. Known as Augustinian Canons, they would often settle near a town or city, living in common and serving the local parishes. The great humanist scholar Erasmus of Rotterdam was a member of the order, calling the canons a midway point between monks and clergy. Though they still took vows of poverty, chastity and obedience, their lives were less regimented than the contemplative orders, better suited to preaching and teaching in urban societies.

The canons at Klosterneuburg had followed the Rule of St Augustine ever since the monastery's founding. They were not separated from the town, nor was their community cloistered from the world. This meant there was little sense of withdrawing into isolation, let alone the forbidding solitude of the desert. Rather, Klosterneuburg resembled a public institution like a town hall or county court, positioned at the centre of the society it served.

Wittgenstein did not come to Klosterneuburg on account of Augustine. Still, he quoted from the saint several times in his own work and thought *Confessions* 'the most serious book ever written'. That book narrates the author's wayward early life and conversion to Christianity, offering a model of the self-reckoning Wittgenstein admired. In fact, it was the kind of experience he hoped to realise in retreat.

In the late afternoon, Fr Clemens returned. First we went to Vespers, then to the canons' dining hall. This looked like a ballroom, with plaster pilasters lining the walls and gilt-framed mirrors set in between. Tiered chandeliers hung down from the ceiling and a marble fountain occupied a niche on the far side, all scalloped curves and folds of stone. And a set of dining tables framed the floor, laid with cloths of starched white and bowls of bright flowers.

The windows faced east towards the Danube, but the river was hidden from view. Instead I could see the road and the railway leading back to the city, as well as the flat-roofed buildings sprawling along the bank. Standing in the silence before grace, I could also hear the distant throb of traffic and the passing clatter of a freight train.

There were eight of us that evening, gathered on the table nearest the windows. The canons wore black cassocks with white collars and cuffs, as well as long white bands that looped round their necks like oversized ties. Two of them wheeled a trolley from the next-door kitchen, before placing half a dozen dishes on the table: an anonymous soup tasting of salt, with a single dumpling floating in the middle; gnocchi mixed with mushrooms and ham, served in a cream-coloured sauce; a salad of sliced courgette with a sour dressing; and jugs of tepid water to drink.

During the meal, the sun sank through the sky and the room became tranquil in the early evening light. But the conversation at the table was stilted, as if nobody knew whether we were allowed to speak. At one point, the canon sitting opposite asked why I was visiting and, when I mentioned my interest in Wittgenstein, he folded his arms and furrowed his brow, saying that he did not realise the philosopher had spent time at the monastery. Then I explained that he was a gardener here, and my companion looked disappointed.

'The community was quite scholarly at the time,' he replied. 'I doubt they would have mixed much with a gardener.'

Once we finished eating, the trolley of dishes was taken next door. Then Fr Clemens offered to show me the grounds, so I followed him down to the monastery cellars. A doorway opened onto a gravel path, edging along the base of the building before descending to the bottom of the hill. The path led between bands of pine and broadleaf trees, the shade from their branches adding to the sense of depth, like we were dropping several more storeys below ground. At the bottom, a pair of lozenge-shaped lawns surrounded an ornamental pond, with different sections created by the stepped terraces, the scattered flowerbeds, the screens of bamboo. Taken together, the arrangement suggested an English garden, as if this haphazard layout of bushes and trees was an accident of nature.

The place was much smaller than I had expected, occupying an acre of hillside at most. However, on the south side of the enclosure, another garden spread over the hill's lower slopes. This was once an orchard, but most of the trees were gone, leaving a wide ramp of grass rising up to the royal apartments. Fr Clemens explained that a carpark had been dug beneath the grass, with a tarmac road tunnelling into the earth. 'The enclosure was meant as somewhere for the canons to relax, but we don't really use it enough. We ought to start having barbeques again, except there's the noise from the road, the railway too . . .' His voice faltered for a moment and fell silent. 'Before the pandemic, I guess.'

We crossed to the northern side of the enclosure, where low brick walls skirted a third garden. Miniature hedgerows bordered squares of grass and felled tree trunks lined the flowerbeds. These beds were planted with palms and cacti, or else decorated with flat stones stacked in uneven pillars, like the gardens of a Mediterranean villa.

A painted greenhouse occupied the far end. In the late light, its windowed walls were panes of dusk, the last colour seeping from the sky. Out front, picnic tables and wooden benches had been arranged on the gravel, their chairs tipped forwards and their parasols drawn. Fr Clemens explained that this building was called the orangery, designed by the same architect who built the monastery's nineteenth-century extension.

'Just beyond there's a couple of outbuildings,' he added, pointing to the structures that lined the far wall. 'They must have been replaced over the years, but there's no reason the location changed. I'm guessing that's where Wittgenstein slept.'

There was little to see: a single-storey lodge, a hut with

clapboard walls and a tiled roof, and a set of gates that led out to a parking lot. Not the sanctuary I had been hoping for.

'Were there any other sheds?' I asked, glancing round the garden to find a more scenic spot, as the traffic churned beyond the gate and another train went rattling by. But Fr Clemens shook his head. 'None that I know of.'

Wittgenstein was not a tourist. All the same, when compared with the monastery's magnificent buildings – the gothic church, the royal apartments, the double-height entrance hall – this hut was a disappointment. Before visiting Klosterneuburg, I had conjured an image of wooded hills and river views and crumbling medieval cloisters. My potting shed was weathered and worn into somewhere unique, like the hermit's grotto from an Arthurian legend. But the reality was much more drab: a paved courtyard, a painted green-house and a few pieces of picnic furniture laid out like the smarter kind of garden centre. This was where Wittgenstein came to disappear.

The last of the daylight was dimming and the garden growing vague in the dusk. I thanked Fr Clemens for showing me round and we began climbing a staircase up the hillside together. By the time we stepped back into the monastery, the lights were switched off in the cells and our footsteps made no sound in the corridors, like we were walking weightless on the bed of the sea.

★

This was not the first time Wittgenstein had withdrawn. Seven years earlier, after the death of his father, he retreated to Norway. The retreat was not made for religious reasons, yet it marked the first step of his journey towards Klosterneuburg.

Three out of Wittgenstein's four grandparents were Jewish. However, his father Karl converted to Lutheranism and his mother Leopoldine was raised a Catholic. Their eight children were baptised in that religion too, though Wittgenstein later claimed to have lost his faith as a boy.

By the time he arrived at Cambridge to study philosophy, he shared the critical view of religion expressed by authors like Arthur Schopenhauer. But, in the winter of 1910, he returned to Vienna for the holidays and saw a play called *Die Kreuzelschreiber* by Ludwig Anzengruber. The play was forgettable, the performance too, but at one point a character said something that lodged in the young man's mind. According to this character, no matter what happened in the world, nothing bad could happen to *him,* because he had faith.

This line transformed Wittgenstein's understanding of belief from a series of doctrines and creeds to a sense of complete security. For the rest of his life, this search for security was the fundamental religious impulse, offering a consolation that could not be found in philosophy.

In 1912, Wittgenstein wrote to his tutor Bertrand Russell that he had been reading William James's *The Varieties of Religious Experience.* 'I think that it helps me to get rid of the *Sorge,*' he explained, quoting the word used by Goethe to mean worry, anxiety and dread. Soon after sending this letter, he decided to leave Cambridge, convinced the distractions of university life prevented original thinking. For the sake of his work, he would spend two years living alone in Norway and settle the foundations of logic.

Russell thought the plan insane, writing in his diary: 'I said it would be dark & he said he hated daylight. I said it would be lonely & he said he prostrated his mind talking to intelligent people. I said he was mad & he said God preserve him from sanity.' Wittgenstein placed his furniture, papers and possessions into storage, before catching the boat to Bergen. From there it was two more days of travel, steaming up the length of Norway's longest fjord, until he reached the village of Skjolden. Here, the dark sea waters gave way to the bright blues of inland lakes, with farmers' houses scattered over the shallow hills between.

Wittgenstein rented a pair of rooms and spent each day working on philosophy. He also went for long walks, enchanted by the 'quiet seriousness' of the scenery: the orchards rising to forests of conifers, or the mountains dropping down to the water's edge. To Russell he wrote: 'Being alone here does me no end of good, and I do not think I could bear life among people.'

In fact, the village had a busy lemonade factory, a bustling port and a hotel popular with summer tourists. But

Wittgenstein did not resent the presence of other people and even learned enough Norwegian to speak with the locals. What he resented were the obligations placed on him by family and colleagues, dissipating the energy that should be saved for thinking.

His closest friend at Cambridge, David Pinsent, called Wittgenstein's retreat 'a hermit's life'. That spring he exiled himself even farther, buying a plot of land a mile or more from the village with a view of nearby Eidsvatnet Lake. There he had a cabin built on a high crag of rock, visible from across the lake but separated by the wide expanse of water. This cabin was constructed in the Alpine style, its gable braced with a balcony looking back towards the village. So it was a conspicuous kind of isolation: a show of solitude rather than real anonymity, or an ornamental version of the anchorite's life.

While living in Skjolden, Wittgenstein completed an early draft of the *Tractatus*. In fact, the months he spent in Norway were among the most productive of his life, and he later claimed it was the only time when his thoughts were entirely his own. For Wittgenstein, originality and autonomy depended on one another, which meant that freeing himself from people also provoked new ideas. But, for his sister Hermine, there was a more obvious explanation: 'he was in a heightened state of intellectual intensity,' she wrote, 'which verged on the pathological.'

Too much solitude, like too much money, can turn people

into tyrants. The compromises required to live in company temper the worst parts of our characters. Wittgenstein was already abrupt, impatient, selfish even – and living alone made these tendencies worse. In seven months at Skjolden, he fell out with Russell and another colleague from Cambridge, as well as his early mentor, the mathematician Gottlob Frege. Years later, Russell identified this period as the beginning of a breakdown that turned Wittgenstein towards religion: 'It all started from William James's *Varieties of Religious Experience* and grew (not unnaturally) during the winter he spent alone in Norway before the war, when he was nearly mad.'

Wittgenstein himself recognised that a violent change was taking place. As he explained in another letter to Russell: 'Deep inside me there's a perpetual seething, like the bottom of a geyser, and I keep hoping that things will come to an eruption once and for all, so that I can turn into a different person.'

In the end, his retreat was cut short by the assassination of Franz Ferdinand. It was not Wittgenstein but the seething continent of Europe that erupted first. And, with the coming of that conflict, the second stage of his transformation started.

Soon after the First World War was declared, Wittgenstein volunteered to join the Austro-Hungarian army. Within weeks he was stationed in Tarnów, a city on the empire's eastern edge, searching for something to read. But the city's only bookshop was almost empty, with a single text on sale: Leo Tolstoy's *The Gospel in Brief.*

*The Gospel in Brief* tells the story of Christ's life by combining the four accounts in the Bible. As well as cutting the repeated material, Tolstoy removes everything he considers improbable. So, out go the birth and the miracles, the death and the resurrection, and any reference to prophecies fulfilled. All that remain are the parables and teaching – the radical moral doctrine of Christianity, as summarised in the Sermon on the Mount.

Tolstoy's book drew on the work of nineteenth-century scholars, who applied critical historical methods to Biblical texts. As the introduction to the *Gospel* explains, they cast doubt on the miracles and Messianic claims, less for reasons of scientific scepticism than a lack of verifiable sources. Many of these scholars were pious men, trying to rescue their religion from superstition, yet their conclusions were condemned by church authorities for questioning Christian dogma.

*The Gospel in Brief* went further: not only removing material, but adding new lessons too. Tolstoy's Christ warned his followers against anger and sexual pleasure, against swearing oaths and seeking legal judgement, as well as making any distinction between nationalities. If the author was opposed to political institutions, his Christ was a proto-anarchist, rejecting religious dogma as strongly as imperial might. In Tolstoy's introduction, he even singled out the Russian Orthodox Church for special criticism. The church responded by excommunicating him.

Wittgenstein read the text several times, carrying a copy wherever he went and learning entire passages by heart. Later he would claim that 'this book virtually kept me alive' during the war. He was attracted to Tolstoy's vision of Christ, liberated from the trappings of Christianity. But he was also attracted to the author: the wealthy aristocrat who gave up his estate; the celebrated novelist who abandoned literature; the privileged intellectual who tried to live like a peasant.

As Tolstoy explained in the book's introduction, he returned to Christianity in despair, seeking a system of values that could overcome life's lack of meaning. This echoed Wittgenstein's own situation, and, soon after finishing *The Gospel in Brief*, he began writing out prayers in his diaries: 'God help me . . . God give me strength . . . God be with me . . .' One entry from May 1916 simply read, *Gott mit mir*, 'God with me'.

The diaries present a very different picture of Wittgenstein to the author of the *Tractatus*. Studying the journals from the war, it's hard not to feel pity for this frightened young man and the heavy burden of his belief. Faith was less a set of dogmas and creeds than an intense awareness of his own sinful state.

By this point Wittgenstein had been sent to the Eastern Front, which helps explain the desperation of his diary entries. The prayers became a way to endure this helplessness, as he makes clear in an entry from June 1916:

> To pray is to think about the meaning of life.
>
> I cannot bend the happenings of the world to my will: I am completely powerless.
>
> I can only make myself independent of the world — and so in a certain sense master it — by renouncing any influence over my happenings.

To live independent of the world means escaping one's own circumstances. This independence is paradoxical: it does not come from greater control, but from surrendering the will. In this paradox, Wittgenstein discovered the courage to survive the conflict. However, once the fighting ended, he needed a new method of overcoming his ego.

Approaching the final weeks of the war, Wittgenstein was captured in northern Italy. He spent the next nine months at a camp in the southern corner of Lazio, alongside 35,000 German, Austrian and Hungarian prisoners. Some of them occupied brick huts; the rest were housed in barn-sized structures with beds packed close together. The barns had little insulation, so in winter the soldiers would sleep beneath their rucksacks for want of heat. Then, in summer months, the air would bake and fill with the stench of sweating men.

Wittgenstein's camp covered the open ground below the sixth-century abbey of Montecassino. From the boundary of the camp you could glimpse the abbey walls, balanced on an outcrop of rock some 500 metres above sea level. The walls were constructed from sand-coloured stone, like sunlight catching a mountain summit, and the chiming bells of the campanile could be heard in the valley below. This was where St Benedict had written the rules for religious life that would influence Western monasticism more than any other.

Unlike the loose guidelines composed by St Augustine, the Rule of St Benedict made a strict account of every hour. Benedictine monasteries divided the day between *ora et labora*, 'worship and work', with an emphasis on stability and obedience. The camp below followed a similar routine, with the prisoners expected to attend mass each morning, before lectures and classes, choirs and football clubs.

During his internment, Wittgenstein became friends with a Catholic teacher named Franz Parak. Together, they walked arm-in-arm round the borders of the camp, discussing the novels of Dostoevsky. At one point, Wittgenstein claimed to feel 'reborn', and Parak thought this echoed the language of St Paul – 'He that is renewed with Christ is another man' – as well as the final pages of *Crime and Punishment*. Once Raskolnikov has been sent to Siberia, he looks forward to the life awaiting him after seven years of exile. 'But that is the beginning of a new story – the story of the gradual renewal of a man, the story of his gradual regeneration, of his passing from one world into another, of his initiation into a new unknown life.'

If Wittgenstein's former self died during the war, his new self was still emerging. Tolstoy had taught him the value of poverty, humility and peasant-like simplicity, but now he wanted to remake his life in that image. Returning to Vienna or Cambridge would mean resuming his former habits; instead, he decided to become a primary school teacher in a remote Alpine village. As he explained to Parak, he 'would have preferred to become a priest, but as a teacher I shall also read the Bible with the children.'

Wittgenstein never made clear what exactly he believed. However, years later he told a former student, Maurice O'Connor Drury, 'If you and I are to live religious lives, it mustn't be that we talk a lot about religion, but that our manner of life is different. It is my belief that only if you try to be helpful to other people will you in the end find your way to God.' In other words, the true measure of faith was not the way you thought but the way you acted.

Klosterneuburg was the place where Wittgenstein came the summer before his teaching career. It was both a stepping stone towards his new life and a shelter from his former self. A refuge from his past and a glimpse of his fate.

Next morning I woke to sunlight seeping between the shutters in my room and stifled movements in distant parts of the monastery. But there were no chiming bells calling the community to prayer, and after washing and dressing I made my way to the dining hall. Though the room was empty that morning, a spread of food had been laid out on one table: wicker baskets piled with buns, lidded dishes loaded with eggs and metal trays cluttered with yoghurts in coloured cups, as well as folded slices of ham and cheese.

Entering the room, I felt like the only person awake in a stranger's house, wandering round the kitchen on tiptoe, trying not to make too much noise. There was little monastic about the meal, however, with its tins of Fortnum & Mason tea and the stainless-steel coffee pots placed on little saucers. Instead, I was reminded of the breakfast room in an expensive hotel.

Eventually I was joined by a pair of stern-seeming Austrian priests. They said good morning in careful English and started reading folded copies of *Die Presse*. The priests only came to breakfast after performing mass in the local parishes, so the next day I decided to attend one of their services.

Morning prayers took place at eight o'clock in the main church. The building dated back to the twelfth century, but this too had been reconstructed and restored over the years. Its exterior was a mix of medieval Romanesque and nineteenth-century Gothic; its interior a profusion of Baroque. The emblems of the Habsburg Empire adorned the choir stalls — shields from the duchies of Styria and Bohemia, Dalmatia and Illyria — while the high altar was a horde of marble pillars, carved figures, painted scenes of salvation.

For all the richness of the setting, the service was underwhelming. A few locals made their way into the church early, gathering in the pews near the altar. On the hour, one of the priests began reciting the German liturgy in a functional fashion: no choirs or chanting or shafts of sunlight piercing the clouds of incense, the whole ceremony taking place without any display. Thirty minutes later the service was done, the congregation hurrying out to make way for the tour groups.

Later that day I joined one of the tours. My group consisted of half a dozen elderly couples from the American Midwest. We were shown round the church, the chapels and the royal apartments, before visiting the treasury together. This was a museum containing the monastery's most precious items: a mix of vestments and chalices, reliquary caskets and royal regalia. One room had a glass case housing the Austrian archducal crown, its velvet cap braced in gold, with tufts of ermine ringing the band. Another case held a monstrance shaped like a starburst, spears of silver light decorated in diamonds, emeralds and rubies, as well as 1,395 pearls. Within the monstrance was a scrap of sacred veil that told the story of Klosterneuburg's founding.

That story began with Leopold III, the twelfth-century Margrave of Austria. On the day he married Agnes von Waiblingen, a gust of wind carried the wedding veil from his wife's face and dragged it into the sky. For the next nine years the veil was lost, until Leopold went hunting in the forest of Klosterneuburg and chanced upon the missing item in the branches of an elder tree. Not only was the fabric perfectly preserved, but as he came closer it opened wide to reveal a vision of the Virgin Mary.

So Leopold built a monastery on the site of the miracle. Its first stone was laid in 1114, and by 1136 a church had been consecrated too, dedicated to the Virgin. That was the year Leopold died, his body buried in the church and his tomb becoming a place of pilgrimage. The pilgrims to Klosterneuburg increased when he was canonised in the fifteenth century, and again halfway through the seventeenth, when he was proclaimed the patron saint of Austria.

However, the modern history of Klosterneuburg began with Charles II of Spain, the most inbred of the Habsburg emperors. Short and lame, epileptic and bald, Charles II lived in almost constant pain until his death in 1700 at the age of thirty-eight. The physician attending the emperor noted that his corpse did not contain a single drop of blood; his heart was the size of a peppercorn, his lungs corroded, his intestines rotten, his single testicle black as coal, and his head filled with water.

The emperor's body was laid to rest in the Royal Pantheon at the Escorial Palace. Because he died without an heir, the nations of Western Europe spent the next decade at war, trying to decide the succession. Eventually Philip of Anjou took control of the Spanish Empire, while the rival candidate, Charles of Austria, became ruler of the Holy Roman Empire.

With the loss of any claim to Spain, Charles VI (as he

was now known) vowed to build his own Escorial. He chose the site of Klosterneuburg, perched on a hill outside the capital, just like the original palace. Of course, the medieval monastery would have to be torn down, replaced with a majestic assembly of Baroque buildings designed by an Italian architect named Donato Felice d'Allio. The architect proposed a grid of grand courtyards balanced above the Danube, but his plans were too modest for the emperor's taste, so they were revised to include a series of monumental domes topped with the crowns of the House of Habsburg.

Charles VI was weighed down with debt and his exchequer contained just 100,000 florins, so he insisted the canons fund the rebuilding and even furnish the monastery with a suite of royal rooms. But, one damp October day in 1740, the emperor fell ill while hunting in Hungary. Within weeks he was dead and the building work ceased.

By this point, only the north and east wings of the main courtyard were complete – an eighth of the original design. Charles's heir Maria Theresa had little interest in her father's Austrian Escorial, and his grandson Joseph II was an Enlightenment monarch opposed to the overreach of the Catholic Church. Nonetheless, Klosterneuburg survived Joseph's reform of religious houses, as well as Napoleon's occupation of Vienna in 1809. Then, in the period of relative peace that followed the French emperor's defeat, the main courtyard was finally finished.

All this history was related as we toured round the royal

apartments. Our guide showed us a concert hall, an audience chamber, and a chapel containing the monastery's most famous artefact: a twelfth-century altar by Nicholas of Verdun, its fifty-one enamelled panels illustrating the entire Biblical narrative. At times there was too much splendour to take in — an overwhelming collection of carvings and murals, marble and gilt — making it easy to forget that this grandiose setting was still a religious institution. And only once did I glimpse a member of the community marching past in his black cassock, as if posing for the tourists to photograph.

Towards the end of the tour, we visited the medieval monastery on the northern side of the church. Its buildings were set around a slanted courtyard with none of the wings quite even. Some of the architecture dated back to the original foundation: the palace of St Leopold from the twelfth century and a gothic gatehouse from the fourteenth century. Planted beds bordered the buildings' bases, while the fountain at the centre was set on a mound of grass, with flowers on each side arranged to resemble a crest: the yellow emblem of an eagle repeated five times, recalling the five kingdoms of the Habsburg monarchs.

Everything in religious life is a symbol. For instance, most medieval abbeys contained a cloister with a garden at its centre. This was a monastery in miniature, a haven walled off from the wider world, where the gaze turns inward to cultivate the self. In addition, there might be a kitchen garden planted with vegetable beds, or a herb garden growing remedies for the infirmary, or a burial ground with flowers budding besides the graves, or an enclosure filled with orchards. Settings where, with patience and care, the disorder of nature could be disciplined. These settings also connected the community to the Biblical gardens where the central scenes in the Christian story were performed: Eden, Gethsemane and Golgotha, as well as a fourth garden that is the paradise promised to the faithful.

For all these religious resonances, there was nothing symbolic about the work. Monks and nuns would often labour in their gardens for several hours a day, turning the earth, planting the seeds, pruning and trimming and tending the beds. Idleness was the enemy of religious life, no less a temptation than lust or greed, so it was vital that communities were kept busy with chores. As well as making monasteries self-sufficient, a manual job was a way of piercing any pride, learning humility by surrendering your will in the service of others. In the process, a contemplative could rediscover their body: back aching from an afternoon bent over a shovel, neck sore from hours exposed to the sun, forearms numb from nettle-rash and shins bloody from kneeling on the gravelled ground. There was also something contemplative about the work, the repetitive routines of physical labour providing the kind of disciplined boredom that creates a space for reflection.

However, none of this was true for Klosterneuburg, where the canons spent their time preaching and studying. Instead, gardeners were employed to look after the grounds, which was why they hired Wittgenstein for the summer. The philosopher had little gardening experience, but a natural talent for manual tasks, and though there was enough time to write letters and read the papers, otherwise his days were occupied.

The gardens at Klosterneuburg have changed over the years, but we can still guess how Wittgenstein filled his days. Each morning in July and August, one of the staff had to open the vents of the orangery to regulate the heat behind the glass. They also had to water the rows of plants, with more water splashed over the orangery floor to keep the space humid. The rest of the gardens needed watering too: the flowerbeds and fruit trees and planted borders lining the courtyards.

Some days Wittgenstein would have spent trimming the vegetation, dead-heading the flowers, or laying woodchip on the soil to prevent new weeds from taking seed, as well as digging the strands of couch grass, bittercress and chick-weed from the soil. Other days he might have worked in the orchard, gathering the damaged apples from the earth, sweet and reeking with decay. Always there were mildewed leaves for him to remove, as well as dead fruit hanging on the branches, leaking the pulpy residue of larvae. Most of the diseased material would have to be pruned, along

with the insect nests and peeling bark, and the trees themselves often needed trimming. Tall branches were chopped
to keep the fruit near the ground; crossing branches were
clipped to let light into the bough; bunches were thinned
to stop the apples from rubbing.

The new gardener had little contact with the canons, and
there's no record of whether he attended mass. According
to one account, Wittgenstein's potting-shed was close to the
canons' cemetery, and, when asked if he minded sleeping
near the graves, he replied: 'The dead don't talk.'

The head chef took pity on the new gardener, giving
him pastries for breakfast and meat from the dining hall.
But only one member of the community knew his identity,
the provost Dr Josef Eduard Kluger. At some point the
provost passed by Wittgenstein while at work. 'So,' he
commented, 'I see that intelligence counts for something
in gardening too.'

Otherwise the philosopher was anonymous, which was
part of the job's appeal, the strict routines of religious life
becoming a way to erase himself. And there was relief in
concentrating on a single task, with no thought for the past
or the future either. After all, the twelve months before
Wittgenstein came to Klosterneuburg were perhaps the least
happy in his life.

One year earlier, Wittgenstein had returned home from the
prison camp at Montecassino, reaching Vienna in the late

summer of 1919. His family's main residence was a neoclassical mansion at No. 16 Argentinierstrasse known as the Palais Wittgenstein. Its front hall contained a fountain, the music room had a built-in organ, and seven grand pianos were scattered round the house, along with sculptures by Rodin and paintings by Klimt.

Wittgenstein's late father was known as the Andrew Carnegie of the Austro-Hungarian Empire. A steel magnate who became a patron of the arts, his house was a centre of Viennese culture. The capital's most celebrated musicians performed there in private, with Mahler and Brahms both regular guests. What's more, the family's fortune was little damaged during the war, their money transferred to investments in Holland and America before the fighting started. So, when Wittgenstein came back to No. 16 Argentinierstrasse, he was still met by the liveried servants, the gaudy ballroom, the seven grand pianos. However, he now felt uneasy with the ostentatious wealth that had surrounded him since birth.

Within a few weeks of returning, Wittgenstein visited the family's bank manager to renounce his inheritance. At first, the manager suggested some money should be kept aside, in case he changed his mind. But Wittgenstein told him no. Then the manager explained that the money was tied up in property and stocks, meaning it was difficult to simply separate his share. Once more Wittgenstein told him no. Every penny must be given away – no secret stash, no emergency fund – and he repeated this condition again and again until eventually the manager conceded defeat. According to the notary authorising the decision, Wittgenstein was committing financial suicide.

For Franz Parak, the friend from Montecassino, this decision was no surprise. After all, Christ's challenge to the rich young man had been simple: if you want to be perfect, go sell your possessions and follow me. But Wittgenstein did not actually sell his possessions, only transferred them to his brothers and sisters. He was not worried about the lives of the poor; the act of sacrifice was what mattered.

Wittgenstein's siblings were appalled when they found out he was planning to teach in a primary school. His sister Hermine argued that he was wasting his intelligence on country folk, like using a precision instrument to open a wooden crate. 'You remind me of somebody who is looking out through a closed window and cannot explain to himself the strange movements of a passer-by,' her brother replied. 'He cannot tell what sort of storm is raging out there or that this person might only be managing with difficulty to stay on his feet.'

Midway through September, Wittgenstein packed up his possessions and left the palace. To begin with he stayed in lodgings; then he moved to the home of some family friends. From this point on, he lived in rented rooms or college accommodation, never returning to the opulent properties of his youth. He even began denying that he was related to the family of the famous industrialist.

Though Wittgenstein intended to teach, he first needed a diploma. By the end of September he was sitting in a classroom at the *Lehrerbildungsanstalt*, the teacher-training college, surrounded by adolescents who had just finished high school. As a university graduate, he was spared from studying academic subjects, but still had to take the pedagogic ones: music, calligraphy and rural economy. So he learned the basics of agriculture and practiced playing the clarinet, writing in a letter to Paul Engelmann, 'the humiliation is so great for me that often I think I can hardly bear it!'

The following month Wittgenstein wrote to Engelmann again, confessing that he had thought several times of taking his own life. 'Not from my despair about my own badness but for purely external reasons.'

Loneliness was the most obvious reason. Wittgenstein had not lived in Vienna since he left the city in 1906 to attend university in Berlin. He had few friends in the capital and was cut off from the cultural circles at No. 16 Argentinierstrasse. As he explained to Russell later that year, he was no longer able to acquire new friends, because 'I'm too stupid for nearly everybody.'

This pattern recurred across his life: spurning companionship only to end up lonely. It was a paradox repeated in the biographies of David Jones and Simone Weil – now longing to separate themselves, now lamenting their isolation. Solitude can be a balm for loneliness, but even a willing exile might sometimes wish for company, or regret all the contacts they have cut. Perhaps the full cost of solitude cannot be counted until every bond has been broken, or perhaps our deepest instincts are capricious and our desires always pull in opposite directions.

Set against these humiliations, teaching was a modest comfort. During the practical lessons, Wittgenstein read fairy tales with his class, telling Engelmann that this was 'the one good thing in my life'. But, on earning his certificate before coming to Klosterneuburg, he felt no sense of achievement, telling Russell: 'How things will go for me – how I'll endure life – God only knows. The best for me, perhaps, would be if I could lie down one evening and not wake up again.'

When Wittgenstein spoke of suicide, it was not some idle boast. He had been thirteen when his brother Hans went missing in the Chesapeake Bay in an unexplained boating accident. He had been fifteen when his brother Rudolf ended his life by drinking cyanide mixed with milk in a fashionable Berlin bar. Then, in the final weeks of the war, his brother Kurt also took his own life when his soldiers mutinied during the retreat from Italy. The two intellectual heroes of his youth also died by their own hands: the philosopher Otto Weininger shot himself in 1903 and the physicist Ludwig Boltzmann hanged himself in 1906.

Schopenhauer, the other major influence on Wittgenstein's early thinking, denied that suicide was immoral. In his celebrated essay on the subject, the philosopher rejected the Christian command against self-slaughter, arguing that religious thinkers tell us 'suicide is the greatest piece of cowardice . . . when it is quite obvious that there is nothing in the world to which every man has a more unassailable title than to his own life and person.'

During the war, Wittgenstein returned several times to the idea of self-slaughter, writing in his journal: 'If suicide is allowed then everything is allowed. If anything is not allowed then suicide is not allowed. This throws a light on the nature of ethics, for suicide is, so to speak, the elementary sin. And when one investigates it is like investigating mercury vapour in order to comprehend the nature of vapours.'

As Schopenhauer pointed out, suicide is rarely considered a sin among the pagan philosophers. Only when God becomes sole creator does the act appear immoral, usurping the divine role as the giver and taker of life. Hence Wittgenstein's claim that, if suicide is allowed, there can be no other moral limits, because God is no longer the author of all creation. But Wittgenstein was also aware that too much time spent thinking about suicide can seduce the philosopher. Mercury is a toxic metal that poisons the body and deranges the mind: anyone who studies its vapour risks destroying themselves in the process.

The war gave Wittgenstein a sense of purpose, but the end of the fighting marked another crisis in his life. By the early summer of 1920 — a few weeks before coming to Klosterneuburg — the idea of suicide filled his thoughts once more. 'I have had a most miserable time lately,' he told Engelmann. 'Of course, only as a result of my own baseness and rottenness. I have continually thought of taking my own life, and the idea still haunts me sometimes.'

In response, Engelmann argued that suicide was surely a mistake. The feeling of hopelessness that inspires the act is temporary, yet the solution it offers is a permanent one. This argument Wittgenstein conceded: suicide presents itself as the answer to an unbearable situation, but, rather than fix the situation, it simply destroys the person who is suffering. Or, as Wittgenstein phrased it: 'I know that to kill oneself is always a dirty thing to do. Surely one *cannot* will one's own destruction, and anybody who has visualised what is in practice involved in the act of suicide knows that suicide is always a *rushing of one's own defences*.'

So, what's the alternative? Schopenhauer's essay not only shows how the giving and taking of life became a divine prerogative, but also makes the case that Christianity teaches believers to submit to their misery with gratitude. 'The inmost kernel of Christianity is the truth that suffering — the Cross — is the real end and object of life. Hence Christianity condemns suicide as thwarting this end . . .'

Suicide promises freedom from pain and humiliation, but what if pain and humiliation are the point? Wittgenstein never made this argument — unlike Simone Weil, who grounded her faith in suffering – yet he felt some sympathy towards it. Years later he told his close companion Maurice Drury: 'Of this I am certain, that we are not here in order to have a good time.'

We are not here to have a good time. At first this seems a bleak philosophy, but it also offers some consolation. Pain does not necessarily mean we have followed the wrong path; pain might be the true texture of existence, no failure or flaw but the cost of experience. In which case, suicide becomes a denial of our duty to endure.

If suicide is forbidden, what about withdrawing another way? For someone who wanted to kill themselves, retreat might offer a substitute of sorts. While at Klosterneuburg, Wittgenstein could cut ties to his former life, even say goodbye to the person he had been. So, retreat was not only a symbol of this inner transformation, but a practical way of protecting it.

In the middle of the week I was shown round the library by another American canon called Fr Ambros. After meeting near the entrance hall, I followed him to the top floor, where a series of book-lined rooms led towards a large rotunda. The first few rooms had the cramped closeness of an attic, warm despite the shutters drawn across the windows. Shelves were racked up to the ceiling, filled with texts cased in leather and cloth, light brushing their spines like loose shavings of copper and brass. Meanwhile, shadows clotted in the corners and the air had a powdery texture like the chaff of harvested wheat.

Assistants worked at the tables, some photographing the pages of old volumes, others searching the slim drawers of the catalogue system. One young woman was even restoring a book's broken binding in a workshop between the eaves, threading a needle with a cord of spun silver.

These assistants were mostly students: some studying medieval history, others taking courses to become librarians. As Fr Ambros explained, that summer they were creating digital versions of the entire collection – 1,256 manuscripts, 836 incunabula (the earliest printed texts) and 748 antique books – all scanned and uploaded online.

My guide marched ahead, speaking in an exaggerated whisper. 'Medieval monasteries were manuscript factories, copying out works of theology, legal codes, scientific treatises too.' Much of the collection at Klosterneuburg was made in their scriptorium, while other pieces were purchased from Italy and France, like the constellation catalogue from the early thirteenth century, or the astronomical manuscript from the mid-fifteenth century, or comedies by the Roman playwright Terence. 'That's what they used to teach Latin,' my guide added. 'All the monks in all the monasteries of Christendom, reading Terence to learn the language.'

Fr Ambros had a rubbery face that gave his expression a cartoonish quality. His manner was cartoonish too, the conversation made up of puns and word games and playful imitations. He was dressed in the familiar black cassock with white collar and cuffs, and from time to time he would tug on the long white band around his neck, like someone ringing the rope of a bell, before flicking the fabric back over his shoulder. The religious texts were what interested him most, such as a four-volume choir book commissioned in the fifteenth century, each volume the size of a briefcase. One of these we pulled from the shelves, opening its leather case to reveal psalms written out in gothic script above lines of musical notation. A few of the pages were illuminated, too, the music bordered in blue and green vines, their tendrils rainbow streamers and their leaves like the flourishing colours of some hallucinated garden.

It was midday when we reached the rotunda suspended above the entrance hall. This was a circular space with an inner ring of arches supporting a vast dome. Double-storey bookcases were installed in the arches, and a second level of shelves set into the outer ring. Long windows let in light from each side of the room, and more light poured down from the cupola, its edges covered in decorative mouldings, the rosettes foaming with ornament and the cornice swarming with classical detail.

'After the Renaissance, the library started acquiring non-theological texts,' Fr Ambros went on. 'So there's history, geography, medicine, but also things you would never expect to find. Like the complete works of Martin Luther, or the encyclopaedias of the French Enlightenment.'

Display cabinets were laid out on the marble floor, along with globes in cages of carved walnut. One globe recorded the sky at night, with all the massed constellations struggling for space – crabs and bears the size of continents, crawling over the parchment-coloured seas. When I asked my guide if the community came here often, he replied, 'In the past, the canons were professors at the University of Vienna, which meant the library had to contain the latest works. Over time the community got smaller and the number of scholars shrank.' He paused. 'So nowadays it's mostly used for events. Afraid the conversation at the dinner table's not quite what it used to be.'

Lunchtime prayers were at quarter past twelve, and lunch was fifteen minutes later. I presumed Fr Ambros knew this, but he kept wandering between the bookshelves, whispering about the contents of the collection. At times his mouth dropped open and his eyes appeared to shine, as if the past were a fantasy designed to delight. Once or twice I tried to hurry him, but he kept finding new items of interest, like a child let loose in a toy shop. Here the catalogues of the medieval monastery's lands, and there the collection of texts on numismatics, and over there the antique mantel clocks that divided the rows of leather-backed books.

By the time our tour was finished, it was a quarter to one. When Fr Ambros looked at his watch, his face stretched wide in a show of surprise. 'Oh dear. Silly me. We've managed to miss prayers.' Then the surprise became an embarrassed frown, as he tugged on his tie and pretended to think. 'Well, if you could bear to have lunch with me instead—'

We both knew the mistake was deliberate, but the show was performed in such an innocent manner it seemed unkind to refuse. Besides, I did not want to skip the meal simply to prove a point, so I followed my guide down from the rotunda and we stepped out into the sun.

The restaurant lay beyond the monastery gates, in a court-yard to one side of the town square. Awnings and parasols were strung above the tables, with views over the wooded hills to the north. The contrast between the shaded library and the brightness of the square left me stunned, and for a moment I sat staring at the menu without reading a word, threads of light drifting across my eyelids and strobes of white floating before my face.

Lunchtime was busy. Young mothers with children in pushchairs, middle-aged men with phones vibrating on the tables, and elderly ladies eating in pairs. Most of the guests were well dressed, wearing trousers of cream-coloured linen and blouses of powder-blue cotton, or else pressed shirts with rolled sleeves and monogrammed pockets. I tried to remind myself that I was not here on holiday, but it appeared that nobody in Klosterneuburg had much to do and all the time in the world to do it.

Fr Ambros ordered for the two us: chicken schnitzel with potato salad and glasses of lemonade. Then he began talking about his family, explaining that his ancestors lived in Scotland before joining the Quakers in Philadelphia. Later they moved to Virginia and converted to the Episcopalian Church, which was the religion of his childhood. But from a young age Fr Ambros knew he wanted to become a Catholic.

'I was a graduate student at Cambridge when I heard about Klosterneuburg. It was a skiing holiday in Austria – some friend with too much money – and he suggested we visit for the day. It turned out the novice-master had studied at Oxford: he was the one who encouraged me to come back.'

Up to that point, monastic life had little appeal for Fr Ambros. For all the romance of Catholic ritual, he could take no pleasure in cold cells, plain meals, denying all the pleasures of this world. 'I'm a child of comfort, you see.' But there was nothing severe about Klosterneuburg, where the glittering vestments and glorious architecture suited his tastes. 'Have you ever seen such lofty ceilings? Such preposterous plasterwork?' That said, coming here meant giving up any professional ambition, because an outsider could never reach a position of authority in the Austrian Church.

'A few years ago, I went to a dinner party in England with that friend I mentioned from the skiing trip. He owns a large house in Oxfordshire now and one of the guests was somebody important – a member of the cabinet, maybe.

There was a time when I would have tried to impress him, or worried what he thought about me, but I care much less these days. Maybe age has taught me humility.'

What he cared about instead was feeling content. He had never been melancholy by nature, yet his life in Austria was a lonely one. He missed intelligent conversation, missed people who could make him laugh, and longed to be in a relationship.

'What about the vow of celibacy? I thought that came with the job?'

'Something else that has changed with time,' he replied. 'I've got more sympathy for human failings.'

When the meal was finished, Fr Ambros suggested we go for a swim. I mentioned the lack of swimming trunks, but he replied that boxer shorts would be fine. Again I wondered whether to play along with this game, but my skin felt sticky in the midday heat and the thought of the water was too tempting to refuse.

The swimming pool lay on the western edge of the close, behind a pair of barn-like buildings that belonged to the monastery's wine business. We passed through a wooden gate and a walled garden slatted with solar panels, before reaching a paved terrace with a pool on the far side. Plastic loungers were arranged over the paving stones and the water looked jewelled in the afternoon sun.

'Did Charles of Austria insist on the swimming pool too?' I asked.

Fr Ambros laughed. 'The monastery used to contain a school. This was where the boys came to exercise.'

'Doesn't fit with the image of monks in my mind. Vow of poverty, life of sacrifice, restoring medieval Christendom.'

'But we're priests not monks,' Fr Ambros replied. 'Besides, there's a Benedictine monastery that's much richer than us. Their swimming pool has a retractable roof.'

Over the next hour we talked about Austrian society. My host had spent the previous day at a garden party given by a local Catholic family. He claimed to have little interest in the upper classes, yet he described the guests, the drinks and the garden in detail. And several times he called the Augustinian Canons the gentlemen of the clergy, more educated and urbane than the priests you might find in your average parish.

For a while I swam laps of the pool, before sitting on a lounger in the shade. But I had no wish to lie flat in the sun, let alone surrender to the holiday mood. Somewhere in my mind the figure of Wittgenstein was shaking his head in disapproval: a disapproval that was my own as much as his. What I wanted was solitude, hardship, inner turmoil even – to show I had left the world behind. Instead I was spending my afternoon sunbathing beside a swimming pool, as if a religious life were no different from a secular one.

Most displays of luxury left me a little queasy. Though I liked to think the waste was the reason, the truth was much more complicated. I recognised my own desire for comfort, my own taste for excess, yet such wishes seemed superficial to me. No philosopher had ever praised money, no artist was motivated by wealth; self-denial was the proof of piety and genius a question of discipline.

At least, this was the story I told myself. Now I wonder whether there was something childish about my black-and-white view of the world. Perhaps I insisted on this purity of purpose because I doubted my own commitment to the creative life. Or perhaps I took a perverse pride in temperance because I knew how easily I could succumb to distraction. But, at the time, I thought virtue was a question of saying no enough times, so I remained sitting upright on the sun lounger, refusing to delight in the dappled shade across the lawn or the lapping currents of the pool, each one crested with glints of golden light.

During the summer he spent at Klosterneuburg, Wittgenstein received an invitation to dine at his old Cambridge college. He was delighted by this invite – despite the war, and the years away, he had not been completely forgotten. But it was impossible for him to attend, so he wrote to Bertrand Russell to decline on his behalf.

'When shall we see each other again?' Wittgenstein added. 'Perhaps never. Every day I think of Pinsent. He took half my life away with him. The devil will take the other half.'

David Pinsent was Wittgenstein's closest friend from Cambridge. It was Russell who introduced the two of them, back when Pinsent was a brilliant mathematics student at the same college. Soon after this meeting, Wittgenstein went to a chapel service to hear his new friend reading the lesson. The text was taken from the Gospel of Mark, Chapter 8, 'For what shall it profit a man, if he shall gain the whole world, and lose his own soul?' Later, Wittgenstein told Russell how much he admired this line, saying there were few men who did not lose their souls. Russell recorded the conversation in his correspondence: 'I said it depended on having a large purpose that one is true to. He said he thought it depended more on suffering and the power to endure it. I was surprised – I hadn't expected that kind of thing from him.'

Suffering and the power to endure it. This was what Wittgenstein sought in religion, likewise David Jones and Simone Weil. In some of his last writings, the philosopher argued that 'Life can educate one to a belief in God. And experiences too are what bring this about; but I don't mean visions and other forms of experience which show us the "existence of this being", but e.g. sufferings of various sorts.' Faith was less a question of encountering the divine than enduring disappointment.

Wittgenstein's suffering was most acute in the last months of the war, when he learned about Pinsent's death. His friend was killed in a flying accident near Farnborough in May 1918. Wittgenstein found out in late July or early August, shortly before taking military leave. As he was travelling to Salzburg, he decided to throw himself from one of the summits surrounding the city, or disappear in the silent valleys of the Salzkammergut Mountains. However, by chance he met his uncle at the railway station, who guessed that something was wrong. So Uncle Paul invited Wittgenstein to stay in his villa south of Salzburg, where he finished the final drafts of the *Tractatus*.

When the book was finally published, it was dedicated to the memory of Pinsent. Wittgenstein's diaries make clear the love he felt for his friend, yet he never shared these feelings with anyone else. His brother Rudolf likely committed suicide because of the fear his homosexuality would be made public, and afterwards any mention of Rudi's name was forbidden in the Wittgenstein family. At the time, gay sex was outlawed in both Austria and Britain, considered not only a crime but also evidence of a psychiatric condition. So it was natural for Wittgenstein to assume his sexuality was something to discipline and be drawn towards those forms of faith that promised to temper any longing.

Religion has often been a refuge for those troubled by their own desires. Tolstoy's *The Gospel in Brief* invented the command: 'Do not seek delight in sexual gratification . . . All sensuality destroys the soul and therefore it is better for you to renounce the pleasure of the flesh than to destroy your own life.' Wittgenstein might have been following this command when, in his late thirties, he was briefly engaged to a Swiss woman named Marguerite Respinger, on the condition that they did not share a bed when married, but spent their evenings in Bible study.

Early biographies brushed over Wittgenstein's attraction to other men. Then, in the 1970s, a controversial account of the philosopher's life was published, claiming he would regularly go cruising in the months before Klosterneuburg. It's true that Wittgenstein's correspondence from this period hints at some secret shame: 'In fact I am in a state that is terrible to me,' he wrote to Engelmann in the middle of June. 'I have been through it several times before: it is the state of *not being able to get over a particular fact.*' It's also true that, in later life, Wittgenstein had physical relationships with a mathematician called Francis Skinner and a medical student named Ben Richards. But the author of the book never shared his sources, and the majority of scholars treated this claim with distrust.

Wittgenstein's most thorough biographer, Ray Monk, argued that lust was enough to humiliate the philosopher, because it did not fit his picture of perfection. Engelmann thought something similar, describing the absolute standards Wittgenstein set for himself in a memoir about their friendship. 'An ethical totalitarianism in all questions,' he wrote, 'a single-minded and painful preservation of the purity of the uncompromising demands of ethics, an agonising awareness of one's own permanent failure to measure up to them.'

If temptation alone could torment Wittgenstein, one reason for retreat was to avoid it. Another reason was penance:

making yourself miserable to atone for some imagined sin. And a third reason was grief, because all this time he was filled with regret, for himself as much as his beloved friend. Perhaps the fact that Wittgenstein struggled to overcome was the loss of the future he once imagined for himself, as well as the past that was gone for good. Tears to water the soil. Blooms the colour of blood. The garden was a place of temptation, but a place of resurrection too.

There was one final reason why Wittgenstein came on retreat: to escape the shame he felt after failing to publish the *Tractatus*. The book's text was finished in the summer of 1918, when Wittgenstein was staying with his uncle near Saltzburg. While still a prisoner at Montecassino, he sent a copy to Russell and the two men agreed to meet as soon as he was free.

That meeting took place at The Hague in December 1919. Wittgenstein arrived at Russell's hotel early one morning, knocking on the door until his former tutor was awake. The moment they were reunited, he began talking about philosophy with a 'passionate purity' that Russell had never seen equalled.

After six years apart, Wittgenstein had changed beyond recognition. As Russell wrote to his lover Lady Constance Malleson: 'I had felt in his book a flavour of mysticism, but was astonished when I found that he has become a complete mystic. He reads people like Kierkegaard and Angelus Silesius, and he seriously contemplates becoming a monk . . . He has penetrated deep into mystical ways of thought and feeling, but I think (although he wouldn't agree) that what he likes best in mysticism is its power to make him stop thinking. I don't much think he will really become a monk – it's an idea, not an intention. His intention is to be a teacher.'

That change could be seen in his philosophy too. The *Tractatus* is a book about the relationship between language and reality. Though based on the theories Wittgenstein developed when a student at Cambridge and when living alone in Norway, during the war he added several important ideas from his journal, as his interests 'expanded from the foundations of logic to the nature of the world'.

Most readers of the *Tractatus* will notice this shift. After seventy or so pages spent discussing questions of language and logic, the author introduces a section devoted to ethics, meaning, death and the divine. This final section is made more surprising by the fact that the book seems to be arguing such subjects lie beyond the limits of speech.

Wittgenstein's wartime conversion helps explain the shift, in particular his reading of Tolstoy's *The Gospel in Brief*. The two texts echo one another, both written in a series of numbered statements and composed from gnomic declarations without any contextual arguments. In places Wittgenstein borrows Tolstoy's ideas – such as his discussion of time and eternity – but the real influence goes much deeper.

The *Gospel* largely contains ethical commands from the Bible, while the *Tractatus* casts doubt on the meaning of most moral claims: 'It is clear that ethics cannot be put into words. / Ethics is transcendental.' Nonetheless, in a letter to the magazine editor Ludwig von Ficker, Wittgenstein argued that 'the point of the book is ethical'. This was not because it taught anyone how to live, but rather, like *The Gospel in Brief*, attempted to change the reader's perspective.

For Wittgenstein, scientific facts could be stated, but assertions about ethics, aesthetics, metaphysics – these could only be shown. The borders of language are also the borders of logic; neither is able to resolve our moral or metaphysical questions. On realising this, the questions are not answered so much as dissolved: 'We feel that even if all possible scientific questions be answered, the problems of life still have not been touched at all. Of course there is then no question left, and just this is the answer. The solution of the problem of life is seen in the vanishing of the problem.'

The *Tractatus* does not promise resolution so much as a new way of thinking. Philosophy may be unable to answer fundamental questions, but it can change the frame through which we view the world. Therefore, the work of philosophy resembles the work of therapy – a comparison Wittgenstein would make explicit in his second book, *The Philosophical Investigations*: 'There is not a single philosophical method, though there are indeed methods, like different therapies.'

Wittgenstein refers to the propositions that could not be stated but only shown as mystical – the term that caught my eye when I first read the text. 'There are, indeed, things that cannot be put into words,' he writes. 'They *make themselves manifest*. They are what is mystical.'

Mystical is one of those vague words that changes meaning depending on the speaker. That said, mystical experiences are characterised by the fact that they are inexpressible – some insight has been communicated from beyond the borders of language. In the *Tractatus*, Wittgenstein broadens the meaning from divine revelation to include all the truths that lie outside language. We do not reason our way towards these truths; instead, they demonstrate themselves in our lives.

Which is why, as the book concludes, we should say nothing about such subjects. This does not require discarding ideas of beauty, goodness or truth, but simply protecting them from the misplaced efforts of scientific evaluation. As his friend Paul Engelmann later wrote: '*Wittgenstein passionately believes that all that really matters in human life is precisely what, in his view, we must be silent about* . . . When he nevertheless takes great pains to delimit the unimportant, it is not the coastline of that island which he is bent on surveying with such meticulous accuracy, but the boundary of the ocean.'

Engelmann's account transformed the *Tractatus* for me. Before, the book seemed as cold and precise as a piece of machinery. Afterwards, this technical quality became so much scaffolding, which hid a beautiful building. What mattered in the *Tractatus* were the words that went unwritten, and I was moved by the idea that Wittgenstein cared most about the thoughts he could not express.

All the same, such claims were too woolly for the sceptic Russell. His own major work, *Principia Mathematica*, attempted to provide a logical basis for mathematics by proving its fundamental assumptions. Russell hoped Wittgenstein would do something similar for language, demarcating the boundary between what does and does not make sense. In his view, the things language could not articulate were better off discarded; were, literally speaking, meaningless. All the same, after several days of intense discussion in The Hague, he agreed to write an introduction for Wittgenstein's book.

By this point Wittgenstein had shared the manuscript with several publishers, but each one rejected the text. Jahoda & Siegel, the publishers of the celebrated critic Karl Kraus; Baumüller, the publishers of his childhood idol Otto Weininger; Ludwig von Ficker, who had printed the poetry of Rilke and Trakl. This back and forth was drawn out over many months, Wittgenstein becoming ever more demoralised as the rejections mounted.

Eventually, in early 1920, the Leipzig house Reclam showed some interest. But they would only print the text on the condition it included Russell's introduction. When Wittgenstein received that introduction in spring, he disagreed so strongly with its contents that he refused to let them appear together. Sure enough, Reclam declined the book, and by the early summer Wittgenstein had given up on its ever being published. A few weeks before coming to Klosterneuburg, he wrote to Russell to explain. 'Either my piece is a work of the highest rank, or it is not a work of the highest rank. In the latter (and more probable) case I myself am in favour of its not being printed. And in the former case it's a matter of indifference whether it's printed twenty or a hundred years sooner or later.'

Read in this light, Wittgenstein's decision to abandon philosophy makes more sense. He believed the *Tractatus* had solved the subject's major questions, not with any definitive conclusion, but with the proof that philosophy could offer no answer. At the same time, he was humiliated by the early responses to the book, as even those readers who championed his work struggled to understand its argument.

During the war, Wittgenstein discovered that the best way to overcome disappointment was to detach himself from any outcome. A life without desire is a life without loss; a life without the wish for success is also a life without failure. This was another reason for him to retreat: breaking each bond to the world, until it loses its power to hurt.

Wittgenstein believed in insights that lay beyond the reach of rational thought. But Klosterneuburg was never the place that words cannot access, that logic cannot limit. Rather, it was the setting where speech was rarely needed, where he could silence himself. He did not come here seeking an intellectual breakthrough, but to leave behind the life of the mind.

On Thursday I climbed into the hills above the monastery. A footpath led through the rows of vines, towards woods of hazel and hornbeam. There was nobody out walking the paths or working the vineyards that afternoon, so I had the whole hillside to myself.

It took fifteen minutes of climbing before I was panting in the heat. The summer air was sluggish and the dense sunshine made me dizzy and confused. Several times I turned back on myself, brightness filtering between the branches of the trees and splashing the woodlands with light, while the footpaths were bleached on the open ground.

Eventually I came to a pasture of yellow grass between the trees. A bench was propped on the highest point, looking back towards Klosterneuburg. From here I could see the twin spires of the church piercing the untidy rooftops of the town, and the wooded slopes on the far side of the Danube framing the monastery like the green felt of a billiard table. Half the hillsides were stitched with vines and the river's surface shimmered in the sun, but the roads and train tracks were camouflaged by trees. This view had changed little in the last hundred years, the whole town giving off a rich and satisfied impression of permanence.

For much of its history, wine was the source of Kloster-neuburg's wealth. Its houses were inhabited by winemakers and its high street lined with *Heuriger* taverns. Several of the canons' buildings are still used to make wine, and their four storeys of vaulted cellars stocked with ageing barrels. But, in the middle of the nineteenth century, the Danube was redirected to the east and the road and rail links improved. The town became popular with civil servants who wanted to live outside Vienna, the distance from the capital helping to preserve its subdued character.

That atmosphere was captured in a series of sketches by Egon Schiele, who lived in Klosterneuburg during his teenage years. From 1905, the young artist lodged above a blacksmith's shop and attended a local secondary school, where his love of sketching meant he neglected his studies and had to repeat a year. Thankfully, the school's drawing teacher was a painter who gave him private lessons, while the monastery's custodian of collections, Fr Wolfgang Pauker, encouraged him to apply to the Academy of Fine Arts.

Schiele's sketches offer a picture of the town over a century ago. What's striking is the lack of human presence: empty streets and empty yards and pavements cleared of people. We see bright-tiled roofs and pastel-painted walls, or the ivy spreading over an archway, but we never see inside a building or glimpse the inhabitants of a house. For all Schiele's later fascination with bodies, they are absent from this early work, and instead the spectator is a constant stranger – always outside and always alone.

Looking at these sketches again, the town appears

preserved in the nineteenth century. Certainly, there were few intrusions from the modern world: no newspapers or radios, no telephones or electric wires. Perhaps Schiele felt like his life had stalled, or perhaps Klosterneuburg itself was preserved in time, shaped around the liturgical calendar and the wine-making seasons. Fin-de-siècle Vienna was the 'laboratory of the apocalypse', in Karl Kraus's memorable phrase, but here the clocks had ceased to turn.

I could still feel that atmosphere in the modern town, which had the suffocated perfection of a university campus. Rows of detached houses in the Alpine style, wearing their wide-pitched roofs like overlarge hats. Contemporary properties constructed from timber and glass, with immaculate gardens and electric cars out front. Neoclassical apartment blocks painted pink and cream like the sponge of a Battenberg cake, with hand-written nametags printed above the doorbells – but no litter, or graffiti, or signs of life.

Over the course of the week, I began succumbing to the stilled atmosphere. Most of the time I have little trouble staying busy, but during those days at Klosterneuburg, I struggled to keep myself occupied. It would have been cheating to spend the retreat working, or take the train into Vienna and visit museums all day. Nonetheless, the closeness of the city meant I never really felt removed from the world, and when I asked whether there was any extra work in the gardens, my request was met with polite confusion. But it was hard to do nothing for hours on end, and even harder to trust that idleness might be the first step towards insight, or that boredom was the cordon between the mundane and the transcendent. The one time I sat alone in the chapel, I soon started to feel embarrassed, rising from my seat and hurrying outside, as if someone might be watching me. Otherwise, I roamed round the courtyards of the monastery and the streets of the town, searching for mementos of my subject.

At first, I assumed this attempt to withdraw was a failure. Then I began asking whether I should welcome the boredom. I was so used to distraction in the rest of life — news feeds and group chats and constant email chains — that its removal felt less like relief than a loss. Or maybe this impatience was a gift, not evidence my retreat was mistaken, but proof I was on the right path.

For Wittgenstein boredom was a balm. Entering a place outside of time protected him from the past and the future too. When he came to Klosterneuburg, he was not seeking a space for reflection, but a way to evade his own thoughts. During the summer he spent at the monastery, he worked so hard that his sadness started to lift. Rather than becoming reconciled to unhappiness, he wearied himself to the point that the wish to end his own life was spent.

In late August, Wittgenstein wrote to Engelmann again, saying this was surely the best use of his holiday. When the gardening work was done, he was too tired to feel unhappy, and he retired to his potting shed with the calm that comes from exhaustion. But he would soon begin his teaching job in a remote mountain village, and 'unless all the devils in hell pull the other way, my life is bound to become very sad if not impossible'.

Wittgenstein did not explain what might make his life impossible. All the same, for one summer the monastery offered him a sense of complete security. At Klosterneuburg he had been absorbed in the simplicity, the anonymity, the regular routine, but now he was retreating further, to a place where his convictions would be tested and his wish to become a saint found wanting. The next stage of his transformation had begun.

Tomorrow I was leaving Klosterneuburg, so I went to thank Fr Clemens for letting me stay. Returning to the monastery a little after six, I spotted a small crowd of people gathering on the cobbled close. A row of temporary tables had been set up beneath the trees, laid with champagne flutes and bottles in shining buckets. The men wore dinner jackets and the women evening dresses, while half a dozen staff circled the crowd, carrying trays of canapés. Approaching this crowd, I realised that the opera festival must be underway.

Fr Clemens's rooms occupied the western corner of the main courtyard. The front room had a pair of suitcases open on the floor, half-filled with clothes for the summer holiday. Beyond was a sitting room and study with windows on three sides, light pouring in from the sinking sun.

The two of us sat on opposite chairs, blinking in the

brightness of the early evening. Through the open windows, we could hear the murmur of well-mannered conversation and the melody of expensive laughter, hear silver and ice and the polite popping of corks. At one point, Fr Clemens offered me a glass of wine – 'It will do you good!' – and when I turned him down he looked disappointed. Later, when I offered him a glass of water, it was his chance to refuse, explaining, 'No, no, it will go to my head.'

My host was travelling to America next week. When I asked if it was a holiday, he replied, 'It's my penance.' I then asked whether he was visiting family, and he added, 'That's what they call themselves.' This was the way he liked to speak, every question answered with sarcasm, each comment a blend of the earnest and ironic.

As a boy, Fr Clemens had been sent to a boarding school on Rhode Island called Portsmouth Abbey. The school was started by English Benedictines and modelled on institutions like Ampleforth and Downside. On graduating he hoped to join the English order, even coming to live with a community in Devon, but a few days after arriving he realised his mistake. Waking at quarter past five each morning to the sound of rain on the windowpanes. Breaking for crumpets every afternoon, before watching a television show about sheepdogs. The boredom, the damp, the relentless Englishness – all this for the rest of his life.

So he went back to America, working on Wall Street before deciding to become a priest. After seminary, he spent five years in Washington, but some part of him still longed to join a religious community. By this point he was visiting Klosterneuburg every year, yet he was surprised when the novice-master suggested joining the canons.

'To begin with, I had all kinds of doubts. About leaving America, about moving to Austria, about trying the whole monastic thing again. I was settled in the States – most of my friends were there – and I worried what would happen if my parents got ill. But the novice-master replied, "Well, that's what aeroplanes were invented for." At that moment I knew this was the right community for me, because it meant I wouldn't have to give up my old life.'

I was surprised by Fr Clemens's answer. In my mind a monastic calling required cutting all ties to the past. This sacrifice was part of the point, surrendering everything for the sake of God.

'But I don't think of it as a sacrifice,' he replied. 'For me this is the best place to be. You're fed, you're clothed, given somewhere comfortable to live. I can't understand why everyone doesn't want this!'

I asked Fr Clemens how he felt about the wealth of the institution. After all, this was nothing like the simplicity Wittgenstein sought, nor the asceticism I had expected. Even if it was impossible to leave the world behind completely, why withdraw to an institution so little different from secular society?

'The community has plenty of money, but the canons

don't own very much. Although there's nothing in the Rule of Augustine about making yourself miserable.'

'But what about those religious orders who seek out suffering? Franciscan poverty, Trappist silence, Carthusian isolation – that kind of thing?'

'I once had a friend who wanted to become a Carthusian. He even tried spending time at the charterhouse in Vermont. But a wise abbot warned him that it's very hard to live among the saints. Much easier among the sinners.'

Reaching the end of our conversation, Fr Clemens wondered whether I had found what I was looking for. In response, I explained how Wittgenstein had retreated to escape his privileged upbringing and the obligations of academic society. He felt a strong sense of guilt, and a strong draw towards abstinence, and religion gave a sense of purpose to these feelings. But Klosterneuburg was a setting of such abundant spectacle that I doubted his stay could have lasted beyond the summer. He would never have felt at home here, swapping one palace for another.

Perhaps I should have added that my own week's retreat showed me splendour was not the same thing as beauty, and boredom less the enemy of insight than the first step towards understanding. I had hoped that by simply visiting Klosterneuburg, I might acquire a deeper perspective on myself, but I realised now that to gain any lasting lessons from retreat, I must really leave the world behind.

When I went back to my room, the opera was underway.

As I approached the main courtyard, I heard strains of Puccini sounding round the building. The lights were off in the corridors and the monastery dim in the long summer dusk, yet the glare from the stage seeped through the windows and yellow light spilled across the floor.

Pacing down the corridors to reach my room, I passed several members of the cast watching the performance. A woman was waiting by the windows, dressed in a dishevelled gown, and coming closer I noticed that her face and hair were powdered white, like somebody taking part in a Halloween parade. And each one of her teeth was painted black, with a gaping darkness where her smile should have been.

For a while I stood in my room without switching on the lights, the evening air swelling with music. The woman's spectral outfit did not fit with the cast of characters I remembered from *La bohème*, and I began wondering whether I had imagined this figure. Still, that shadowed smile haunted my thoughts, as I listened to the polite clapping after each aria and the scattered conversation that marked the interval. Listened to the gentle lament of Mimi's last words and the majestic sorrow of Rodolfo's despair, as well as the moment of silence between the performance ending and the first sprinkle of applause, weighted with a thousand hopes and regrets, none of them ever expressed.

The village was four hours from Vienna, yet it felt a world away. Trattenbach was its name, a small settlement in the south-west corner of Lower Austria. The houses were spread along a mountain stream, with forested slopes rising up on either side. In the sixteenth century, the farmers were known for making *feitel*, pocket knives of Scharsach steel, but few workshops remained by the time Wittgenstein arrived. Now, most of the local men were employed in the mines, or else the timber trade.

Unlike Klosterneuburg, this was an isolated place. Wittgenstein had originally been sent to Semmering, a summer resort popular with Viennese society, but he was disgusted by the fashionable crowds and asked to be moved somewhere more remote. Trattenbach was the answer, a village in the mountains to the south of the resort town. During the summer months, it was a three hour walk to Semmering through the woods, but in winter the way was blocked by snow.

Wittgenstein was not only seeking remoteness, but also trying to hide his past. His first job application was made under an alias and, when his identity was discovered, he turned down the teaching role. In Trattenbach he attempted to keep his surname secret, discouraging his siblings from visiting and returning their gifts of money or food. But the villagers soon started asking questions about the Viennese gentleman who was sleeping on a camp bed in the school kitchen. Surely he was a wealthy count, living here on some eccentric whim?

To begin with, Wittgenstein was delighted by his mountain

retreat. In September 1920 he wrote to Russell, reporting that, 'A short while ago I was terribly depressed and tired of living, but now I am slightly more hopeful.' The next month he wrote to Engelmann, describing the village as 'a beautiful and tiny place' where he was 'happy in my work at school'. But, he added, 'I do need it badly, or else all the devils in hell break loose inside me.'

Wittgenstein was a devoted teacher. He delighted in practical demonstrations, such as dissecting an animal or building a steam engine. He also introduced his students to Grimm's fairy tales, *Gulliver's Travels* and Tolstoy's short stories. To favourite pupils, he was generous with his time and attention; but to those less able, he could be very strict, beating the unruly boys and boxing the ears of the slower girls when they struggled to understand algebra.

Before long Wittgenstein's mood started sinking. By January he was writing to Engelmann again, complaining that he had been morally dead for more than a year. 'I had a task, did not do it, and now the failure is wrecking my life. I ought to have done something positive with my life, to have become a star in the sky. Instead of which I remained stuck on earth, and now I am gradually fading out. My life has really become meaningless and so it consists only of futile episodes.'

Why did Wittgenstein keep teaching if it made him miserable? One clue lies in the letters he wrote to Dr Ludwig Hänsel, another Catholic teacher from Montecassino. During this period, the two men corresponded often, with Wittgenstein asking his friend for advice and teaching material. Dr Hänsel later described their friendship in a memoir, where he claimed that the task Wittgenstein turned down was a religious one: 'One night, while he was a teacher, he had the feeling that he had been called, but refused.'

This would fit with a diary entry Wittgenstein wrote after the start of his teaching career. In January 1922, he recalled a vivid dream where 'I felt totally annihilated and in the hands of God who could at every moment do with me as He wills . . . That he could at any moment force me to take the worst upon myself and that I am not prepared to take the worst upon myself. That I am not now prepared to renounce friendship and all earthly happiness.'

Many monks and nuns claim that joining a religious community requires some sign from the divine. They often tell stories about trying to flee their vocation, only for a nagging voice to keep repeating in their mind. For those with a calling to religious life, no other career will satisfy. For those without a calling, to live that way is a torment.

According to Dr Hänsel, Wittgenstein was wretched because he did not have the courage to follow his vocation. But it's equally possible that he was trying to become a monk without being meant for the role. This was the explanation of his sister Hermine, who wrote to Dr Hänsel that 'It is not easy to have a saint for a brother, and I would rather have a happy person for a brother than an unhappy saint.' Any calling that makes you miserable is probably not going to last, but rather than ask whether he had followed the wrong path, Wittgenstein blamed his own failings for the wretchedness he felt. There was no test so hard as living in humility, no ambition so daunting as giving up desire.

For me, the best explanation of Wittgenstein's misery is contained in one of Tolstoy's stories. 'Father Sergius' is the tale of a brilliant and handsome Guards officer called Prince Stepan Kasatsky. On the night before his wedding to a beautiful young heiress, the prince learns that his fiancée once had an affair with the Tsar. So, he breaks off his engagement, gives up his estate, retreats into a monastery and eventually becomes a solitary.

In the eyes of fashionable society, the prince is a perfect example of piety. But his sister recognises that behind the apparent humility lies a deeper pride: 'She understood that he had become a monk in order to be superior to those who wanted to demonstrate their superiority over him . . . And she understood him correctly. By becoming a monk he was showing scorn for all those things which seemed so important to others and which had seemed so important to him when an officer; he was placing himself on a new eminence from which he could look down on the people he had previously envied.'

Reading this story is painful to me, because the pride it describes is so familiar. The pride of one who tries for the things the world values, only to be humiliated in the attempt. Who renounces all worldly ambitions, not out of virtue or wisdom, but to hide his hurt behind a show of devotion. Who wants to make himself exceptional, even at the cost of his happiness. All this I knew from my own life, and I wonder whether Wittgenstein's decision to teach shared in the same confusion: attempting to surpass his peers through the path of humility.

Fr Sergius becomes famed for his holiness, but he remains troubled by doubt and desire. After bedding the daughter of a local merchant, he flees his hermitage to wander the Russian Empire. Years later he ends up in Siberia, where he finds some respite teaching the children of a local squire and working in his garden. The lesson of Tolstoy's story is a simple one: self-denial done for selfish reasons is another kind of vanity. If you really want to become a saint, you must not expect any reward.

Wittgenstein's teaching career lasted seven years, across three different mountain villages. Each time he arrived at a new school, he was filled with hope about the future. Each time he rented a modest room, containing little more than a bed, a desk and a chair. And each time he became frustrated with the slow-witted children and the interfering parents, until his hopes gave way to despair once more.

These years might be called a lesson in the limits of retreat. You can leave behind your name, your work and those you love, but you cannot make yourself into someone new. And the harder you try to force the change, the more likely you will buckle and break.

Nonetheless, Wittgenstein still believed this retreat was essential to mend his flaws. As he explained to John Maynard Keynes in 1925, 'I have resolved to remain a teacher as long as I feel that the difficulties I am experiencing might be doing me some good. When you have a toothache, the pain from the toothache is reduced by putting a hot-water bottle to your face. But that works only as long as the heat hurts your face. I will throw away the bottle as soon as I notice that it no longer provides that special pain that does my character good.' This letter suggests Wittgenstein's teaching career was a kind of penance, a painful operation to remove the worst parts of his character. But the moral medicine was proving less effective, and things came to a crisis the following spring, when a violent incident brought his exile to an end.

In April 1926, Wittgenstein was teaching at Otterthal, another mountain village close to Trattenbach. Among the pupils in his class was Josef Haidbauer, a slow and sickly eleven-year-old boy. One morning, midway through lessons, Wittgenstein hit Josef two or three times on the head. The boy collapsed unconscious.

Wittgenstein carried his pupil to the headmaster's office and then left the building. Within twenty-four hours he had left the village too, and later that month gave his resignation to the local school inspector. The inspector was sympathetic, suggesting he take a holiday to calm his nerves. However, the following month he had to attend a hearing at the district court, where the judge wondered whether he was mentally ill. In the end, the hearing was adjourned so that a psychiatric report could be prepared.

Again, Wittgenstein sought the comfort of a religious community. Shortly before coming to Klosterneuburg, he had visited a Franciscan friary to enquire about joining the brothers, only to be put off by a surly porter. This time he called at another monastery, but the father superior turned him down, suspecting he was there for the wrong reasons. Instead, he was hired as a gardener for the Barmherzige Brüder, or Brothers of Mercy.

This order was established in 1539 to care for the sick. Their founder was a Portuguese soldier, shepherd and book-seller named João Cidade, who gave away his belongings after an encounter with God. When Cidade's family took him to hospital – worried their son was insane – he was appalled by the treatment of the patients, so he vowed to create his own institution with new standards of care for the poor, the destitute and the mentally ill.

After Cidade's death, an order of priests was established to continue his work. In the priests' hospitals, patients were given their own beds and separated into different wards, while written records were used to keep track of their conditions. These innovations transformed medicine in early modern Europe, and the order soon spread through the colonies, too, building hospitals in Africa and the Americas. At the same time, their founder was canonised as John of God, patron saint of the sick and those who work in nursing care.

The Austrian branch of the Brothers of Mercy occupied a large hospital in the centre of Vienna. In 1875 they acquired a second site, at an old teaching institution in the suburbs to the west of the city. This neighbourhood was known as Hütteldorf and here they started a convalescent home.

A postcard from the early years of the twentieth century shows a horse and cart approaching the monastery over an unsurfaced road, with the Vienna woods rising up in the distance. The photograph gives the impression of a country retreat, with its track of beaten earth and its hillsides bare of buildings. This was where Wittgenstein began working towards the end of April, remaining for the next three months. Again, he watered the flowerbeds, pruned the orchards and tended to the vegetables in the allotments. He even spent his nights in the tool shed, just like at Klosterneuburg.

But the nursing home at Hütteldorf was no pilgrim site. The grounds were much smaller, the monastery too, and there would have been little distance between the gardener and the patients. This may explain the respect Wittgenstein developed for the medical profession, later encouraging a favourite student to become a doctor and working in the pharmacy at Guy's Hospital during the Second World War, as well as the laboratory at the Royal Victoria Infirmary in Newcastle upon Tyne. He even considered training as a psychiatrist, hoping that medicine might serve the same therapeutic purpose he sought in philosophy.

At some point Wittgenstein was cleared of any responsibility for the Haidbauer incident. Then, in early June, his mother died and he began repairing relations with his family. By late summer he was living in Vienna again, and by late autumn he was involved in a plan to build a new house for his sister – designed by his friend Paul Engelmann. Wittgenstein also renewed contact with his academic colleagues, and soon after the house was completed he went back to Cambridge. In the past he had withdrawn to flee from grief and shed his shame, to leave behind temptation and make himself perfect. But perfection alone cannot create; it is complete unto itself. Recognising the futility of his moral project marked the start of his return.

It's tempting to assume that Wittgenstein's teaching career was one long flight from his family, his sexuality and the trauma of war. However, Wittgenstein believed that he needed to transform his character, and that only by remaking himself could he resume philosophy. When later asked what was required for serious thinking, he answered, 'The edifice of your pride has to be dismantled. And that is terribly hard work.'

So his retreats were no evasion but a necessary step. To

have new ideas he must become someone new, which meant defeating his desires and overcoming his will. That project had taken him from the fjords of Norway to the Eastern Front, from a monastery garden to the mountains of Lower Austria. In the end he discovered that retreat was not an antidote to his failings and flaws, and that perfecting himself required more than simply withdrawing. But this was the discovery that dismantled his pride. This was the discovery that let him live again.

I once assumed Wittgenstein travelled through life with total certainty. In fact, his biography was a muddled thing, the result of accident as much as design. Relationships and careers, books and ideas – many of these choices were provisional, decided with little sense of the outcome. Genius cannot protect against making mistakes or the worry that you have wasted your life. Nonetheless, once Wittgenstein started along a course, he committed himself completely – like David Jones and Simone Weil. All three of them struggled with doubt, yet remained certain they were put on earth for some special purpose. Despite their many disappointments, they persevered in their solitary pursuits, and their greatness lies in their character as much as their talent, pushing on in the face of every failure.

Hütteldorf was the final place I had to visit. Leaving Klosterneuburg on Saturday morning, I travelled to the centre of Vienna and then caught a metro train to the north-west corner of the city. This neighbourhood consisted of small villas and widely spaced apartment buildings, my route passing through several residential streets before it joined a wide road leading west out of the city. Two or three restaurants were open for lunch, though their tables were deserted and their waiting staff gone, while the offices and shops were mostly closed. And everywhere I saw signs of autumn starting early, with shrivelled leaves on the paths through the parks and rusted brown foliage littering the boulevards.

After thirty minutes I reached the former hospice, its central block two storeys tall with cream-coloured wings of slabbed stone and weathered render. From a distance it resembled a military barracks, except for the tiled steeple above the entrance and the spire capped with a metal cross.

The hospice was now divided into flats, with a dozen names listed on the intercom. For a few minutes I knocked on the door and pressed the intercom buttons, hoping for a porter who might show me inside. But nobody answered the bell or opened the door, and the ground-floor windows were frosted and dark.

Eventually I gave up and tried walking round the back. The street was bordered with building façades, no passage or alleyway leading through. According to my map, a cemetery occupied the space behind the buildings, reached via a steep street at the far end of the block. So I began marching towards the entrance gate in the afternoon heat, my T-shirt clammy against my back, the fabric damp with sweat.

A few gardeners were working among the graves, one driving a tiny lawnmower, another tending to the flowerbeds along the border. Two more were sitting on a wooden bench, speaking to each other in Turkish, their voices slurred with heat. At the lower end of the cemetery, I noticed timber walls, a wire fence and banks of shrubbery in the gardens beyond. Then I circled round the edges of the graves, looking for a gap in the fencing.

After a while I spotted the cross-capped spire I had seen from the street. Next I parted the shrubbery and peered through the leaves, until I could make out a sloping lawn and several planted allotments. Standing on tiptoe, I counted half a dozen pieces of garden furniture on a sun-damaged patch of grass, and the peeling plaster walls of the hospice beyond.

That was it. That was all I could see. No avenues of trees, no open lawns, no footpaths bending between beds of flowers. I did not know how the grounds were laid out a century ago, but little evidence remained of the place where Wittgenstein worked. Instead there was the sprawling furniture, the cracked earth and the smell of spoiled cuttings from a compost heap rancid with heat. For a while I tried to picture the philosopher kneeling among the allotments, tending to the garden with infinite care, each movement patient and every gesture precise. But the branches obscured too much of my view, their leaves beginning to blister and brown as if they were diseased.

In that moment the whole journey seemed futile. Whatever I was searching for, this was not the place to find it. All the same, as I walked the hot half hour back to the station, and sat another half hour on the metro train, I felt a growing sense of achievement. At first I could not explain this feeling, because there was no insight I had gained from the bare façade of the building, nor any history I could summon from the parched remains of the garden. Instead, I had shed one final illusion about Wittgenstein's life.

I used to think the philosopher's retreats were romantic gestures. The months he spent in the Norwegian cabin, or the years he taught in those mountain schools, or the summer he worked in the gardens of Klosterneuburg – all this seemed a kind of performance. The majesty of these surroundings hid the loneliness of his existence, but at Hütteldorf there was nothing to disguise the isolation. In that abandoned garden it was absurd to think of retreat as some picturesque pause in the upward course of a life, because there was only the baked mud, the dying grass and the rows of graves with nobody to visit them. And, as I returned to the city centre, I realised how penitential a path the philosopher had followed, and how close he must have felt to failure.

When I came to Vienna, I wanted to colour an empty space in Wittgenstein's biography. Instead, I discovered an absence where that story should be. Perhaps this was true of every retreat: less an event in our lives than the moment when every event is suspended. The blankness, the anonymity, the mystery too — these things Wittgenstein was seeking when he stepped out of the world. In Hütteldorf he was no longer remaking himself, but simply trying to disappear for a while. He had come here to hide, and he was hidden still, and no trace remained in this absented place.

# The Hermit

*David Jones (1895–1974)*

The artist drew all he saw of war. Men stood upright in sandbagged trenches. The shattered shapes of bombed churches and shelled farms. Sleeping soldiers, abandoned weapons, the bodies of rats laid out like the dead. Then he closed his eyes and drew armoured knights, or angels with the smiling features of girls he used to know.

The artist's name was David Jones. In the first days of 1915, he enlisted as a private in the Royal Welch Fusiliers. By the end of the year he was serving in the trenches, and by next summer he was taking part in the Battle of the Somme. That July, Jones joined the battalions marching towards the German guns in Mametz Wood, until he was wounded in the leg during the fearful night fighting.

Mametz Wood was not the only time during the war that Jones came close to death. One day, he took off his clothes to find a series of holes left behind by a bullet. It had passed through his pocket, his cardigan, his waistcoat and shirt, even grazing the skin of his chest. Another day he watched a mine explode in front of him, the debris almost piercing the metal shell of his helmet. On coming to he made a sketch of himself, a black eye disfiguring his baby face, like a schoolboy injured in a scuffle.

In 1917 Jones joined the forces at Ypres shortly before the Battle of Passchendaele. During those months he was stationed at headquarters, tasked with drawing maps and touring the trenches. One Sunday morning he was searching for firewood between the reserve and support lines when he chanced upon a disused cowshed. So he placed his eye to a crack in the cladding, hoping it might hold some dry timber.

Once his sight had adjusted, Jones glimpsed the twin flicker of candle flames, caught in a gusting breeze. A priest stood between the candles, facing a pair of ammunition boxes stacked side-by-side to form a table. Soldiers knelt down behind the priest, their knees pressing into the straw-strewn floor. The soldiers were surrounded by shadow, and Jones could barely make out their uniforms in the dimness of the shed. But he recognised two men kneeling in the mud: a pair of bullies from his unit bowed down in poses of complete surrender. They could have been soldiers from any point in history, this mass taking place on the mired fields of France sometime during the Hundred Years War.

At first Jones heard nothing more than the patter of rain and the soft heave of a dozen men breathing in tandem. Then he heard a chiming bell and the murmur of words in an ancient language, *Nobis quoque peccatoribus.* The dancing flames from the candles and the whispered words of the service, the shining vestments of the priest and the soldiers bent down in prayer — all this was transporting to Jones, as if he had slipped free from the snare of time and entered the deep retreat of the past.

For a while, he watched the scene. Then he withdrew to resume his search, reluctant to spectate at something so intimate. But he would return to this memory again and again, as if what happened in that shed was more lasting than the violence taking place close by. Because this ceremony would endure when the fighting was done, the men in communion with countless soldiers before them.

Long after the war was over, the artist would retell this story. The mass he called 'a great marvel', as though there was something of the conjurer's trick in this moment of devotion, rescued from the desolation all around. Like he had left the war behind, or been given a glimpse of his own future.

The name of David Jones is little known. This is partly due to the nature of his work — the intricate complexity of the later paintings, the dense allusions of the longer poems — and partly the nature of his character. Though one of the most talented artists and writers of the interwar period, he was also one of the most elusive. A small and softly spoken man, who spent his life half-hidden from view.

This reclusive life was largely a result of the war. Jones was stationed at the front for over a hundred weeks, despite being injured several times. Like Wittgenstein, he turned towards faith in response to the fighting and retreated from society in the wake of the war. But, unlike the philosopher's punishing moral project, Jones withdrew to become an artist – to find his own subject, medium and style. In other words, he withdrew to discover himself.

To this day, he is less celebrated than the officer poets of the Great War: Wilfrid Owen, Rupert Brooke and Siegfried Sassoon. Less celebrated, too, than the landscape painters who became famous in the '20s and '30s, such as Eric Ravilious and Ben Nicholson, Paul Nash and John Piper. There is no single picture that proves his talent, no line of poetry every admirer could quote. Only when several pieces are seen together does his unique perspective emerge.

I first encountered the watercolours while at school, and then again at university. They were too idiosyncratic to make much sense to me – composed from faint lines and faded palettes, yet cluttered with symbolic detail – and it was not until my twenties that I began to read the poetry.

*In Parenthesis* is a long poem written in verse and prose. Over seven sections it describes the experiences of a Welsh private sent to the First World War. The poem captures all the muddy baseness of that conflict, mixed with passages of visionary beauty and experimental daring. As I read, I began to wonder what turned this painter of English and Welsh landscapes into one of the most ambitious poets of the twentieth century. Then I started learning about his biography and discovered the painful path Jones travelled to create the poem. Although recognised by the major critics of the day, he endured long years of sickness, poverty, solitude and silence. And the more I read about this fragile figure, the more I wondered whether exile was the price of his originality, and whether it was worth the cost.

Part of the answer might lie on Caldey. This was an island off the Pembrokeshire coast that Jones visited in the spring of 1925, when it was home to a community of Benedictine monks. The community had a shared emphasis on arts and crafts – from sewing vestments to making stained glass – and Jones would return almost annually for the next seven years. He was enchanted by the island's curious light and beautiful bays, and the latter he painted countless times, trying to capture the delicate dance between wave and rock, sea and sky.

It was during these retreats that Jones discovered his own style as a painter and began working on his great poem of the war. But it was also during these retreats that Jones committed to the solitary path he would follow for the rest of his life. He came to Caldey seeking a place to work, and the island made a hermit of him.

In the winter after visiting Klosterneuburg, I travelled to Caldey to experience that enchanted setting for myself. I hoped some trace would remain of the inspiration he found there: hoped the voices of the monks still echoed from the chapel and the rhythms of the sea still sounded in the distance; hoped the silence of the night still gathered all things together, holding them in perfect peace.

I arrived in Tenby on the slow Sunday coach that followed each curve of the coast. It was a dark evening in early December, and when the bus dropped me off in the centre of town, I felt the first nagging of doubt. Most of the hotels were closed for winter, as the wind blew bitter off the water and the salt seemed to bite inside my cheeks.

That night I was staying at a guest house on the edge of town. The light in my room was pallid and a four-poster bed took up most of the floor. Somewhere in the building I could hear another guest bumping between the furniture, but otherwise I was alone. Sitting by myself in that sallow space, the sense of uncertainty increased.

When Jones first came to Caldey, it housed a community of English Benedictines. A few years later they were replaced by Belgian Trappists, who remain on the island to this day. That word – Trappist – has always fascinated me, conjuring silence and penance and shadowed figures hidden beneath hooded cassocks. I did not know what I would find on Caldey, except that it would be much less comfortable than Klosterneuburg, but, after the extravagance of the Augustinian canons, I was eager to see monastic life in its more primitive form. Besides, there was something thrilling about the monks' austerity, taking the wager of faith to its farthest limit.

That said, I have never felt drawn towards islands. The safety others feel when separated from the mainland is for me a sense of confinement. For all that Caldey's setting appealed to my romantic notions about religious life, there was no phone reception, no Wi-Fi either, nothing to bridge the surrounding waters. Though my rucksack was filled with supplies − extra pairs of socks and several boxes of cereal bars − I expected to spend the week hungry and cold. And I worried that I would feel trapped in this refuge, impatient to end the retreat and return to the mainland.

Next morning, I went down to the beach on the town's southern shore, glimpsing Caldey across the water. The western edge of the island arced towards the mainland, as if I could have walked along the coast and reached the monastery without wetting my feet.

The postal boat departed the pier at high tide, its deck piled with deliveries. Among the orange shopping bags, I spotted a stack of Amazon parcels and several twelve-packs of Strongbow cider. A bearded sailor stood at the wheel, while the estate manager sat in the bow, wanting to know whether I was vaccinated and when I received my last test.

After we launched from the pier, I turned back to watch the town recede. Most of Tenby's hotels were pastel-painted houses set on the cliffs behind the beach, perched three storeys above the sea. To the east was the broad sweep of Carmarthen Bay, its wooded shores seeming to smudge the waves, while yellow light softened the western horizon where the bay broke into the Bristol Channel. Below the boat, the water was a dense grey very close to green, like the streaked surface of banded quartzite.

Caldey lay three miles from the shore, a 550-acre plateau balanced on limestone and sandstone cliffs. Soon I could see the dull white of the sand, the pale green of the gorse and the darker green of the pine trees clustering between the rock face. An old stone watchtower rose from the pines and a few wooden cottages teetered towards the water, while a concrete pier pushed out from the shore, where a small crowd of people stood waiting for the boat.

Once the mooring ropes were tied, the locals began lifting the parcels from the deck, dividing the deliveries among themselves. I helped unload the contents until I heard my name called, and when I looked up a slender man in his seventies was waving to catch my attention. He was wearing a white tunic, a black scapular and a putty-coloured puffer jacket, standing beside a battered van with crates of fruit piled in the boot. When we shook hands, he told me his name was Br Titus.

Br Titus was the guest-master at the monastery. He became a monk fifty years ago, having first worked in the Netherlands as a press photographer for Formula One. He still spoke with a slight Dutch accent, explaining how the storm last weekend meant this was the first boat since Thursday. The postal service was supposed to be daily, but in the winter months they could spend several weeks cut off, and the forecast for the next few days was unsettled, meaning they did not know when the next boat would arrive.

The guest-master said this with laughter in his voice, but in response I felt a faint sense of panic. My plan was to pass six days on the island, yet now there seemed a chance I would get stuck here for much longer. Still, Br Titus smiled at my anxious expression, adding that I could stay as long as needed.

An unsurfaced path led up from the shore, curving past a bank of cliff and cutting into the woodland. Next the track lifted through a screen of cedar and pine, until we reached the open lawns laid out beneath the monastery. To the left was a pavilion made from timber planks; to the right, three small buildings with tiled roofs: the gift shop, the post office and a shop selling lavender scents.

These shops were intended for tourists and closed during the winter months. According to Br Titus, in the spring and summer hundreds of visitors came to the island. Families sitting on the picnic tables, children playing on the grass, and a café serving cakes and ice cream all day.

'Pilgrims?' I asked.

'Pilgrims, tourists,' he replied. 'Sometimes it's hard to tell.'

'Do you find it distracting, all those families running round?'

'We did not come here to hide from the world. Besides, I wouldn't be the guest-master if I wanted to keep Caldey to myself.'

There were no children on the lawn that morning, practicing cartwheels or playing games of tag. There were no parents on the picnic tables either, surrounded by plastic glasses, polystyrene cups and paper plates smeared with icing sugar. Instead, a row of cottages lined the far side of the lawn, while the monastery sat above on a shelf of rock. It resembled a fortress from a fairy tale, all pointed towers and angled turrets, monumental arches and ornamental battlements. But the mock-antique style was ageing well, as if the whole island was a stage set and this eccentric architecture part of the performance.

We walked round to the western wing of the monastery, which was built as the abbot's private residence. Now it was used as a guest house, the walls whitewashed and the roofs tiled red. The exterior had been decorated with curious details – the drainpipe capped with a miniature model of a castle and a crow's-nest belltower rising above the chapel. One stained-glass window depicted a devil with an overlarge nose and an uncanny resemblance to Aubrey Beardsley.

Inside, the design suggested a country hotel. From the panelled entrance hall, a grand set of stairs rose to the first floor. My bedroom was lofty too, with a single bed placed in the middle and a wardrobe occupying one corner, shuddering each time I tried to open it. The desk offered a view of the monks' enclosure and an orchard of apple and pear trees, their fruit all fallen, their leaves gone too. Even though there was enough space for half a dozen guests, because nobody else was visiting, I had the whole place to myself.

Before leaving, Br Titus explained the routine to me. The monks woke in the early hours of the morning for the first office of the day, gathering in the chapel to pray. They would return to the chapel six more times before bed, with Vigils and Lauds in the morning, Terce, Sext and None during the day, and Vespers and Compline towards evening. Breakfast for guests took place in the kitchen, lunch and a light dinner were served in the refectory, and from nine o'clock the whole community retreated to their rooms. Then the great silence settled over the island, with no sound but the waves brushing back and forth in the bays and the distant bellowing of the wind as it rushed across the Atlantic.

The islands of northern Europe were once home to count-less religious communities. England, Scotland, Wales and Ireland all boasted their own holy isles, each containing the remains of some solitary saint. Meanwhile, the Scilly Isles beyond the western tip of Cornwall were known as a Celtic sanctuary, the archipelago entirely occupied by hermits and monks. And, according to one twelfth-century bishop, Bardsey, off the coast of Wales, was the island of twenty thousand saints: the best place to be buried if you wanted to reach heaven.

Augustine was not the only Christian inspired by the life of Anthony the Great. However, many of those admirers lived far from the deserts of North Africa and the Levant. As a result, they had to seek their own wildernesses in the mountains and forests, marshes and moors. Monks based close to the coast built their homes on islands, the open sea, like the desert sands, an empty expanse the mind could fill with the divine.

An island makes physical the concept of retreat. In some places islands are sanctuaries, protecting people who might be persecuted on the mainland. In others places they are prisons, removing those who are unwanted by society. By crossing the water to make their home on an island, a religious community sought both safety and separation.

Celtic Christianity had a special connection to islands. This was the penitential version of the faith found on the fringes of Europe during the Dark Ages. Celtic Christians were encouraged to seek 'exile for Christ': either becoming missionaries among pagan tribes, or else withdrawing to fast and pray.

Islands were the perfect place for Celtic saints to exile themselves, and their biographies are filled with improbable acts of endurance. In Northumberland, for example, St Cuthbert retreated to a tiny island off Lindisfarne, where he spent long nights standing up to his neck in seawater, or else cased in a cell without windows or roof, so that he could see nothing but the sky. Similarly, the community of Skellig Michael huddled on a steep cone of rock eight miles from the Irish coast, mortifying themselves daily with the wind, the rain, the beating waves.

In the Middle Ages, water was the fastest way to travel, meaning islands were also staging posts for people and ideas. Celtic Christianity soon spread through the British Isles via the community of Lindisfarne, as well as Iona in the Inner Hebrides. Then, as the Roman Empire collapsed and Christianity retreated, Celtic communities on island outposts kept the monastic tradition alive. Their monasteries also preserved European art, architecture, history and literature, long after the fall of Rome.

Caldey was another missionary centre, its monastery established in the sixth century. The founder was an abbot named Pyr, who drowned one night after drinking too much wine and falling into a well. Like the communities of Iona and Lindisfarne, the monastery played a major role in the conversion of tribes in the kingdoms of southern Wales. Several centuries later, a medieval priory was established on the same spot by monks from Normandy, which lasted until the Reformation. But the present priory was much more recent, built in 1910 to house a group of Benedictines.

This was the community Jones encountered in the spring of 1925. In establishing a new monastery on Caldey, the monks wanted to emulate the lonely piety of the Celtic saints. They also wanted to become self-sufficient, with some brothers responsible for the dairy farm, others looking after the poultry, and the rest in charge of cooking, cleaning and repairs. There were several cottage industries too, including a printing press, a medicinal herb garden, and a mixing room that made incense from frankincense blended with spices and oil. Meanwhile, the community's afternoons were spent on painting, pottery, metalwork and sculpture, with a scriptorium for illuminating manuscripts and a workshop for sewing vestments, its shelves filled with bolts of silk and damask, or lengths of velvet and lace.

Caldey owed this commitment to arts and crafts to the prior, Dom Wilfrid Upson. A cockney born to a strict nonconformist family, he had been an Anglican monk before joining the Catholic Church. As well as the priory's main manuscript illuminator, Dom Wilfrid was an amateur magician who put on shows for the locals and directed passion plays for the crowds at Tenby.

Unlike at Klosterneuburg, this was not a community of scholars. In fact, most of the monks at Caldey had worked as clerks or in manual trades, and preferred practical pastimes to academic pursuits. The prior encouraged their creative efforts; after all, the earliest Benedictine monasteries were also centres of culture, and Dom Wilfrid considered the arts a higher calling, bringing humans closer to their creator.

Jones was moved by the idea of islands as lonely outposts of faith, surrounded on all sides by doubt. He also saw a parallel between the small number of modern monasteries and the religious communities adrift in the Dark Ages. Despite the loss of belief separating contemporary life from the religious societies of the past – what Jones and his companions called 'The Break' – Caldey seemed a slender bridge across that divide.

Faith was threaded through the fabric of Jones's childhood. His Welsh father worked as a printer for the evangelical *Christian Herald,* attending mission meetings four evenings a week. He also preached to the crowds on Clapham Common and led services at the nonconformist chapel of St George, close to their home in Brockley. But Jones's English mother was more traditional in her tastes, preferring the ornate ceremonies of Anglo-Catholicism to the simplified services taking place in Protestant chapels.

By the time Jones turned eighteen, he felt uncomfortable in either space. The Low Church services lacked any ritual, while the High Church services appeared nothing more than the pageantry of the English establishment. Though curious about Catholicism, he avoided their services for fear of offending his father.

At this point Jones was a student at Camberwell College of Arts, but his education was interrupted by the First World War. Once sent to the trenches, he befriended a Jesuit chaplain called Daniel Hughes, who regularly risked his life to give the last sacraments. Jones was impressed by the priest's courage, and borrowed his copy of *The Introduction to a Devout Life* by Francis de Sales. Here Jones found an articulation of his own sense that, for all the inhumanity of war, the virtues shown by the combatants – patience, courage, compassion between soldiers – implied a moral system that could overcome this lack of meaning.

After the war Jones not only went back to art school, but also began worshipping at Westminster Cathedral. The cathedral had recently been decorated with a carved Stations of the Cross designed by Eric Gill, mixing Art Deco minimalism and Christian primitivism. Gill was a letter cutter and typeface designer, architectural sculptor and ecclesiastical artist, as well as lecturer, writer and pacifist. He was also a Catholic convert who had started a semi-religious community in Sussex devoted to teaching traditional crafts.

During the decades between the wars, the Catholic Church in Britain doubled in size, its number swollen by some twelve thousand converts a year. A surprising number were drawn from the arts: G. K. Chesterton converted in 1922, Graham Greene and Graham Sutherland in 1926, and Evelyn Waugh in 1930. Anglicans also turned towards the Catholic wing of their church, with Dorothy L. Sayers and John Betjeman, C. S. Lewis and Rose Macauley, W. H. Auden and T. S. Eliot, all finding a home in Anglo-Catholicism. But Jones worried about how to reconcile his religious faith and artistic ambitions, lacking the easy belief of a cradle Catholic, with its capacity for boredom and ridicule. Instead he had the earnest sincerity of a convert, anxious to follow every teaching as proof that he belonged. Eventually, his priest suggested leaving art school to spend some time with Gill's community.

The community was based at Ditchling, beneath the tender

slopes of the South Downs. It was inspired by a mix of cottage socialism and Catholic social teaching, as well as John Ruskin's belief that revived medieval guilds could counter the ugliness of the Industrial Revolution. Members would spend their days printing and carving, weaving and woodworking, farming the land and worshipping in a makeshift chapel.

Jones lived at Ditchling for the latter half of his twenties, learning to make engravings and even proposing to Gill's daughter, Petra. Unlike Wittgenstein, he did not join the community to reform his character, but to protect his nascent faith. However, he also wondered whether he might have a vocation, once telling Gill that he felt called towards religious life. He even went on retreat to test this theory, spending a fortnight at the Charterhouse in Sussex, eighteen hours a day alone in his cell, and a week at Campion Hall in Oxford, working in libraries, dining in halls, and praying in panelled chapels. But he felt out of place among the solitary Carthusians and the scholarly Jesuits – a humble engraver who never finished art school.

By contrast, Jones felt at home in Ditchling, surrounded by other soldiers. Unemployment was high throughout the '20s and the guild became a refuge for veterans learning some artisan craft. Perhaps there was a trace of their military experiences in the disciplined simplicity of communal life, as well as the brotherhood found among bands of strangers, brought together by a cause they shared.

Medieval monks were often compared to soldiers. After

all, both careers were marked by strict routine, singleness of purpose and total submission to an institution. Similarly, the deprivations of military life meant soldiers took their own temporary vows of poverty, chastity and obedience. Of course, a religious calling was far safer than a military one, but soldiers and monks both shared the belief that they were sacrificing themselves for the sake of others. At the same time, a monk risked everything on God's existence, spending each day in preparation for death, meaning he tasted something of war's intensity, too, each decision weighted with the heaviest consequences.

When Gill decided to establish a new community in the Welsh Marches, Jones soon followed him there. In December 1924 he arrived at Capel-y-ffin, a hamlet in a remote valley on the eastern edge of the Black Mountains. Gill's community was housed in a former Victorian monastery belonging to the monks on Caldey, which was how Jones learned about the holy island off the Pembrokeshire coast.

During winter months at Capel-y-ffin, the low sun never lit the building. At mealtimes the guests wore overcoats and gloves, their food losing its heat long before it was finished. When Jones could not endure the cold any more, he decided to visit Caldey Priory for Lent, never guessing that he would remain until summer and return almost annually for the next seven years. Nor guessing that he would find here the sanctuary he had searched for since the end of the war, the place where he could rebuild the broken parts of himself.

THE HERMIT

Jones travelled to Tenby in the first week of March 1925 in the company of Eric Gill. When I picture this scene, I imagine the boat driving south into the Bristol Channel and the bay opening out like an immense blue canvas. I imagine the spilled beauty, the bobbing light, the island seeming to sway in the current. And I wonder whether Jones felt a sense of discovery, as if the water was something he would paint one day.

The artist was nearing thirty now, but looked a few years younger, with the round cheeks, flat fringe and pebble glasses of a schoolboy. He wore a trilby with the brim turned down and tweed trousers that smelled damp even when it was not raining, belted round his waist with a length of rope. He also wore a dark shirt, dark tie, dark trench coat too, the kind of clothes that could be stained without becoming spoiled.

When the two men reached the priory, they spoke with Dom Wilfrid Upson. The prior knew that Jones was an artist, that he was unmarried and that he owned little else in this world. So then he invited the young man to stay, offering him a desk in the scriptorium and a cell in the cloister. He could remain with the community for as long as he needed: no money, no charge, please.

Soon after Jones arrived on Caldey, he wrote a letter reporting that, though the priory was 'pretty hit and miss', he thought the island 'a marvellous place'. He was drawn to the 'strange light' that spread from the sea, and the bays and coves surrounding the shore. Paul Jones Bay, named after the pirate who once hid in its waters; Drinkim Bay, with its 'tawny-red' coloured rocks; Chapel Point, where the Atlantic waves came surging in; and West Beacon Point, where you could watch the ships out on the horizon and hear the clatter of gulls overhead.

Most days Jones attended mass, followed by breakfast in the refectory. Then he moved to the scriptorium, where he worked alongside Theodore Baily, the monastery's stained-glass artist. Baily also loved the curious geography of Caldey and the two men started exploring together, until Jones could boast that he knew 'every inch' of the island.

Once the weather was warm enough to sketch outside, Jones neglected his work to paint a garden of small trees and winding paths in the island's north-east corner. The whole scene was 'very thrilling – like the Garden of Gethsemane & the Garden of the Tomb & the Garden of – well – the other sort of garden where Venus disports herself . . . I have been nearly demented trying to capture its beauty even vaguely.'

The work Jones neglected was a set of woodcuts, commissioned to illustrate a new edition of *Gulliver's Travels*. His engravings show something of the frustration he felt when stuck inside, with figures cramped against the edges of their frames. However, the best prints – like the giant Gulliver trapped in the tiny land of Lilliput, or the miniature Gulliver lost among the vast Brobdingnag – use dizzying shifts in scale to evoke the bewilderment of Swift's story. Here Gulliver steals a fleet of ships, dragging them behind him like a plough. There he stands upright before a massed rank of cavalry, his body no higher than the horses' hooves. Here he lies trapped in the arch of a gatehouse, and there he plays an immense keyboard with a pair of crutches – always struggling to fit into the world where he finds himself.

Over the next few years, Jones was commissioned to illustrate several books. Many of these engravings were made on Caldey and almost all of them featured the sea. For instance, in 1926 he completed thirteen engravings for *The Book of Jonah* and in 1927 made ten more for *The Chester Play of the Deluge*.

At Ditchling, Jones was taught to engrave with a linear simplicity and childlike clarity, but the scenes he made on Caldey were intricate. In *The Chester Play of the Deluge*, as the rain begins to fall, the elements became confused, solid and liquid blending together and turning the illustrations into a fluid pattern. The sense of proportion is also disrupted, with near and far starting to overlap, until it's difficult to tell what is wood and what is water, or feather and fur and human flesh, or fire and cloud and an angel in flight.

Jones was not the only artist drawn towards apocalyptic scenes. In the years after the First World War, several painters borrowed from the Bible to evoke the catastrophe they had seen. Stanley Spencer, Winifred Knights and Paul Nash all used the imagery of the flood or the rapture to create a sense of cataclysmic change. But, looking at Jones's engravings more closely, the impression they give is less the drama of the deluge than the oppressiveness of agoraphobia. This was a condition he had suffered ever since the war, the first attack coming in Artois, when stationed near a swampy region criss-crossed with duckboard tracks. One night, Jones had to make his way over a muddy ditch balanced on a wooden plank. In that instant he was seized with a fear so intense it felt like being smothered. The thick mud, the narrow plank, the darkness surrounding him on every side: he had a sense that he was no longer fixed to the earth, but might fall at any moment into the sky. Nothing else in three years of fighting – not the constant shelling, nor the night-time raids, nor the slow march into machine-gun fire – would ever cause such terror again.

Agoraphobia recurred throughout Jones's life, each time paralysing him with panic. What troubles the agoraphobic is the impossibility of escape – not the open field, but the crowded street; not the vaulted church, but the underground train – so it's interesting that he spent so much time on Caldey, where a rough sea or a winter storm could turn the island into a prison. In this case confinement may have been a comfort, because, like the strict routine of the monks, there was freedom found in constraint.

Jones evokes this safety in the final pages of *The Deluge*, which shows a floating ark on settled waters. At last the elements are restored, with the division between sea and sky made clear by a tree risen above the receding tide. The ark is often used as a metaphor for the Church – keeping safe the learning of the classical world through the storm of the Dark Ages – yet here it resembles an island. Perhaps it resembles Caldey Island glimpsed from the mainland, close enough for a dove to fly between the two, bringing back a sprig of hope in its beak.

Some trace of that artistic tradition remains to this day. At least, this was the claim of the community's poet, when he took me for a tour on my second morning at Caldey. The poet's name – confusingly – was Br David.

We started our tour in a prefabricated bungalow occupying the garden behind the main monastery. This was once a dormitory for postulants, but the rooms were so cold the would-be monks went home rather than remain here all winter. Now it was used to store the community's books: rows of theology, philosophy, church history too, lined up in cases of perforated metal, beneath the bleached glare of fluorescent lamps. Meanwhile, the crates of apples and pears my guide picked each autumn were stacked in a couple of cupboards.

Br David had studied law and practiced as a solicitor, before joining the monks on Caldey. Now he spent his time looking after the library, tending to the orchards, and writing poems inspired by the island. He was pleased to discover that we had been to the same university and eager to share his views on David Jones. The prose he liked, the fragments of poetry too, but he struggled with the longer texts.

'Bit over my head, if I'm honest. Not sure what he's trying to say.'

I replied that it was not the kind of verse you saw on posters decorating Tube trains. 'But part of him liked the difficulty. Probably the reason he's not very popular.'

'Try to write more plainly, myself,' David added. 'Something everyone can understand.'

Next we walked round a covered cloister with leaded windows set into wide arches. A few of the windows were decorated with stained glass, showing saints emaciated as Orthodox icons. More panes of stained glass decorated the old chapter room (martyred monks dressed in white robes) and yet more decorated the guest house chapel (Caldey's former abbots posing above an altar of pink alabaster). That morning the skies were overcast and the glass was colourless in the sodden light. What's more, there were bubbles and bulges in the laminate flooring and damp seeping in through the whitewashed walls, their surfaces turning the texture of porridge.

Overnight another storm had blown in from the sea. Now the rain sounded loud against the roof or poured down from the flooded gutters. A few of the windows were loose in their frames, causing water to bleed in from outside, while gusts of wind whined in the passageways and the wooden stairs had started to creak, like the monastery was a sailing ship lost on the ocean. As we toured round the ground floor, my guide would close each door with care, warning me about the squirrels that crept inside to search for food.

Br David was the novice-master at Caldey. Several of his stories seemed to involve young men visiting the island filled with romantic ideas about monastic life. Most abandoned their callings after a few months, not because they lacked the faith but because they could not cope with the discomfort. Other anecdotes involved the community's failed attempts to keep the building warm: the heat pump, the gravity boiler and the cast iron radiator that turned one room into an oven but sapped the temperature from all the rest.

'Not that I mind the cold any more,' Br David added. 'You get used to it after a while.'

Last night I had gone to bed in walking socks and a jumper, with a pair of rugs piled over the duvet and a beanie to keep my head warm. In spite of the portable heater plugged in beside the desk, I could not work for long before my hands became numb and my joints started to ache. The rest of the guest wing was too large to heat, let alone the rest of the monastery, meaning I had to wear a scarf and coat whenever I left my room. Perhaps over time the monks grew accustomed to the cold, but I sympathised with those postulants who gave up Trappist life rather than endure a whole winter here.

Of course, the hardship was half the point. As Br David explained, the Trappists were started in the seventeenth century by a dissolute French aristocrat named Armand Jean le Bouthillier de Rancé. After the death of his mistress, de Rancé retreated to a monastery and adopted the strictest version of the Benedictine Rule, which required monks to labour in the fields each day and sleep in their own coffins at night. These penitential lives were intended to lessen humanity's burden of sin, suffering to atone for the wickedness of the world.

Contemplative communities leave behind society to devote themselves to prayer. That is the work they perform for four, six, even eight hours a day. The rest of their lives are structured to support that work, with all the austerities of the religious calling – the poverty and confinement, the solitude and silence – designed to make space for prayer. Unlike the priests who become teachers or doctors, Trappists believe contemplation is their only calling.

Br David gave little impression of despising the world, let alone fleeing from disappointment or grief. I did not sense that he was misfitted for life on the mainland, nor sense some hunger to punish himself. When I asked whether he enjoyed the rigour, he replied, 'The monastic rule makes space for human frailty too. It's not an act of endurance.' However, when I talked about the discipline needed for this calling, he interrupted me: 'Trappists might look disciplined, but really we're the opposite. We could not make enough space for God in the secular world. That's why we came to Caldey.'

Most people retreat in order to return, seeking the strength to face the world. For a monk or a nun the retreat is the end of the journey, the place they will never leave. These losses are less a sacrifice than a way of freeing themselves to focus on what matters most. The result, Br David implied, should not be suffering but serenity.

Towards the end of the tour we visited the scriptorium, a square-shaped room in one of the towers. This was where my guide taught the occasional postulants, and where the brothers would work on their own creative projects. Windows on three sides caught the dregs of daylight, while the tables and chairs were laid out like a classroom. A few spidery phrases stained the whiteboard's surface, with words like *atonement* and *grace* left over from the last lesson.

Paints and coloured pages had been collected in the corner, as well as several sheets decorated with calligraphy. One of Br David's poems was written out in a flourishing hand, the letters green ink on a blue-washed background. My guide stood with head bowed as I scanned the text – *joyfully, prayerfully, golden days* – and struggled to come up with a compliment. But I was pleased by this little workshop all the same, like a souvenir from the community of artists and artisans that Jones encountered a century ago. And I was moved by the idea that only the monks would ever witness their efforts.

The thought of these unseen artists returned to me that evening, as I sat at my desk and heard piano music rising from the common room below. I assumed one of the brothers was visiting the room in the empty hour before Compline, working through a cautious collection of waltzes and mazurkas. The sound of a stranger practicing piano has always seemed mournful to me, and it was a shame he had no audience to hear him. Sometimes I pictured a crowd of people gathering on the sofas and armchairs, or else phantom figures waltzing back and forth over the parquet floor, dressed in loose lounge suits and cocktail dresses of crushed velvet, as if the guest house were hosting a recital. Of course, if I went downstairs I would find only an elderly man hunched over the keyboard. Like the poems and the paintings, and the prayers taking place in the chapel each night, this performance was offered to God alone.

Jones planned to stay on Caldey just two or three weeks, but ended up remaining until the middle of June. On leaving the island he spent a month with his parents in Brockley, before travelling back to Capel-y-ffin.

The name Capel-y-ffin means 'Chapel on the Boundary'. It referred to a small white chapel on the banks of the River Honddu, the fast-flowing stream running the length of the valley. A single road ran next to the stream, but in winter the way was often blocked by snow, or else occasional landslides. The hills on either side were steep: in places climbing towards heights of heather and bracken, elsewhere falling sheer as cliffs. Hay-on-Wye lay eight miles to the north, but it took several hours to reach the town on a horse and trap, rising over the bleak reaches of the Gospel Pass.

When Gill and his companions arrived, the Victorian monastery was in disrepair, with no hot water or electric light. The only occupants of the valley were a few isolated sheep farms and come nightfall the darkness was complete. Similarly, when mist settled on the hilltops and clouds blotted out the sky, it could feel like living at the bottom of a lake, with every settlement sunk beneath the water's surface. And a weighted quiet lingered over the valley, as if all the live-stock had been struck dumb. This was where Eric Gill came to escape England: retreating from the crowded counties that surround the capital and seeking a landscape unpolluted by the age.

Capel-y-ffin was one of many communities founded during the interwar years. Some were based on religious models, others shared a cultural or political purpose, but each one tried to live more simply and encourage social change. Most of these communities were based in remote corners of the country, where they practiced traditional farming techniques, alongside blacksmithing, carpentry and pottery. For instance, there were the Tolstoyans at Whiteway in Gloucestershire, hosting conscientious objectors and refugees from the Spanish Civil War; Dorothy and Leonard Elmhirst at Dartington Hall in Devon, sharing the progressive teaching of Rabindranath Tagore; and the Guild of Handicraft at Chipping Campden in the Cotsworlds, where the architect Charles Robert Ashbee brought silversmiths, cabinetmakers and bookbinders from the East End of London.

These communities were popular with the creative classes. Like Wittgenstein in his mountain school, they imagined there was something honest about a rural way of life. Retreating to the countryside meant leaving behind the busy cities, as well as the disconnection of modern society. Nonetheless, this draw towards peasant simplicity was also coloured with nostalgia. Nostalgia is as much about the future as the past: less a love of what is lost than a fear of too much change. Some were searching history for a solution to contemporary crises, while others were trying to recover the security destroyed by the First World War.

In Jones's case, that safety was found in Wales. He had visited the country several times as a child, but never stayed for long. Now he was living among its hills and valleys, he became fascinated by the local history, and the moment he arrived at Capel-y-ffin, he began to paint his surroundings.

The pictures Jones created during this period have a vivid sense of place: *Capel Landscape* (1924), *Melting Snow* (1925), *Hill Pastures* (1926), *Y Twmpa, Nant Honddu* (1926), *Capel-y-ffin* (1926–7), and *The Orchard* (1927). Some are more formal in their composition, with a stillness created by interlocking plains and colours. Others are more loosely arranged, outlines overlapping to convey how close the scenery, with visual rhymes in the sculpted shapes of the landscape, such as the folded slopes and encircling hills, or the coiled streams and knotted tracks, the whole valley appearing to dance.

Jones once explained that the conventional layout of a picture – with a clear background, foreground and sense of perspective – was impossible in Wales. The nearness of the hills meant his technique had to adapt: the summits reaching high overhead, the patchwork fields filling the page, and the sky a slender ribbon at the top of the frame. So, this isolated edge of the Black Mountains not only gave him a subject, but also forced him to paint in a more original fashion.

Retreat can play a vital role in the early stages of an artistic career. When a writer is learning their craft, or a painter is searching for material, there is value in creating work without any audience. To begin with commitment is a fragile thing, easy to discourage with criticism or displace with the urgent concerns of the wider world. This was something I knew from experience, and by isolating myself from other people I had strengthened my own sense of purpose, too. At the start that purpose mattered more than the work I produced, and the greater the distance, the fewer doubts I felt. But that distance also made it hard for me to return from retreat and enter the world once more.

In the years after the war, Jones sought a protected place to make mistakes. While staying at Capel and Caldey, he also discovered a subject equal to his abilities. For landscape painters, the places where they spend time often become their subjects, yet a single location can also inspire their subsequent work. Looking back on his career, Jones would call this period 'a new beginning', and one of the first paintings from Capel, *Tir-y-Blaenau*, still hung above his bed three decades later. From this image, he claimed, all his 'subsequent watercolour thing . . . developed'.

In *Tir-y-Blaenau* the trees and hills are coloured by an eerie light, like the exhausted glow of a winter sun. A group of Welsh cobs graze on a hillside, yet there are no paths or people, no hint of human presence. The subject viewing the scene seems raised off the ground, floating over the hills as if in a dream. But the experience of floating and falling are uncomfortably close, and this sense of being unmoored would soon prove prophetic, as the landscape of Jones's ancestors became the setting of his collapse.

When Jones returned to Wales in the summer of 1925, he was reunited with his fiancée, Petra. Gill's daughter was now living with the community, and Jones passed the days painting and engraving in her room, while she would spin and weave at her loom. Sometimes they went for strolls together, climbing from the valley into the surrounding hills or else hiking the ditches and earthworks of Offa's Dyke. These were the ancient fortifications dividing England from Wales; Jones walking quickly over the uneven ground and Petra struggling to keep up.

Petra's shoulders were fleshy, her hips broad, her breasts ample. Jones loved to hold her hand or kiss and cuddle with her. When living at Ditchling they sometimes climbed onto the South Downs together, removing their clothes to pleasure one another. But fear of pregnancy and their belief in the sanctity of marriage meant they never actually made love. Instead, Jones painted his fiancée in idealised scenes, and to Petra they seemed more like brother and sister than husband and wife.

Jones had little formal education, but he read relentlessly and discussed books with friends. Petra struggled to contribute to these discussions and worried that her fiancé found her boring. Growing up at Ditchling, Gill refused to send his daughters to school, teaching them only the domestic skills required to keep a home running. In one telling description, he referred to the ideal woman as 'mother, bed-companion, helpmate and comforter, housekeeper, baker and wine-maker, seamstress and embroidress, and very likely farm-manager and dairy-woman as well'.

But Gill's parenting was more than simply neglectful. While at Ditchling he had an incestuous relationship with his teenage daughter, Betty. He also attempted anal intercourse with Petra, giving up in self-disgust before the act of penetration. This was in addition to his long-term relationship with his sister, Gladys; numerous affairs with male and female friends; and relations with maids, prostitutes and even his pet dog.

It's hard to measure the damage growing up in such a household would have caused. In an interview given towards the end of her life, Petra claimed her father's 'endless curiosity about sex' was taken for granted by his family. Because the daughters never went to school, they were less likely to realise how unnatural the situation, and Jones seemed unaware of his mentor's behaviour. This may be evidence of his naivety; lack of experience was later cited by Petra as one of the problems in their relationship.

By the summer of 1925, the couple had been engaged for a year and a half, yet seemed no closer to marriage. Jones complained that he could not afford a family and worried the responsibility would distract from his work. These excuses may have hidden a deeper doubt over the intimacy a relationship required: devotion to art disguising uncertainty about life. Alone we are rarely forced to compromise, or overcome the selfish sides of our character, while a place like Caldey offered companionship without emotional or physical demands.

In the second week of July, Jones returned to the island, staying until the middle of August. While at the priory, he was able to balance his religious and artistic ambitions without having to decide between them, remaining in limbo for as long as possible. Whereas Wittgenstein retreated to confront his failings, Jones did so to avoid committing.

Though Jones was eleven years older than Petra, he seemed overwhelmed by the obligations of adult life. This mix of sexual diffidence and romantic immaturity was made worse by his lack of practical skills. At Capel he wanted to work without distraction, but offered little help with the household chores and refused to join Petra on trips to Abergavenny or Hay-on-Wye. He was often ill as well: complaining of a stomach ache or a sore throat, and then staying in his room and demanding his meals in bed.

At times Jones behaved like a helpless child, but it's unclear whether the issue was physical or mental. Throughout his life he showed a confusing combination of toughness and fragility: able to endure the trenches and the hand-to-mouth hardships of various religious communities, but often suffering from vague illnesses and withdrawing at the smallest disturbance. That said, Jones's psychological problems were real enough, and one year on from the first Caldey retreat they became so serious he was afraid to step outside.

That summer Jones was back at Capel-y-ffin. Out walking with Petra in the afternoon, he felt like he was floating several feet above the earth. This was not the weightless sensation of someone in love, but the experience of being tethered too lightly to this world. It recalled the panic he had experienced in the second year of the war, when trapped on that narrow plank over a darkened expanse of mud. And it was followed by a fortnight of anxiety, depression and insomnia so severe he could not leave his room.

In the middle of July, Jones was taken to a doctor in Bristol. He was given a prescription for stimulants and strychnine tonic, and assured that the feeling would pass. Two weeks later the symptoms faded, yet the fear of a relapse remained. By autumn it was clear his engagement to Petra was in trouble, and several members of the Capel community suggested they break their commitment. But their promise to marry seemed a solemn bind, carried out in a church and witnessed by all their friends.

Instead, Petra proposed another period apart to make up their minds. As she wanted to remain at Capel, Jones returned to Caldey.

Twice a day I joined the monks for meals: once at lunch and once more in the evening. The refectory was the biggest room in the priory, a great hall with oak-panelled walls and a timber truss supporting the roof. Its tables were long enough for fifty people, but each one was laid with just two or three place mats, and the carved stone fireplace resembling a medieval hearth was only lit on Christmas Day. Otherwise the hall was too large to heat, but given that meals lasted twenty minutes at most, it was barely worth warming the room. Instead, when the lid was taken from the tureen of soup on the central trolley, a pillar of steam would pour up towards the sky. Sometimes the sun broke out from behind the clouds and the vapour became vibrant in the sudden shafts of light, as if the monks were robed in incense or ringed with golden halos.

The community ate a vegetarian diet, the bowls of soup

followed by boiled vegetables. Thick slices of bread were served on the side, as well as apples and pears picked from the gardens. One of the brothers would read during the meals, mixing popular books with religious texts. But I did not listen to these readings, distracted by the sounds of eating: the slop of soup and the slap of spoons and the gulp of swallowed mouthfuls. In the absence of any conversation, these noises seemed much louder, though a single cough could interrupt the speaker and a shifting chair would disturb the entire room.

After the meal, the monks piled their plates on the trolley and pushed it through to the kitchen. This was an octagonal room inspired by the abbot's kitchen at Glastonbury, with great metal ranges lining the walls. Here the community gathered around a pair of sinks, one person cleaning the cutlery and crockery, another one drying, and a third tidying the items away.

Because I volunteered to help with the clean-up, the monks started speaking to me. It turned out the Trappist vow of silence was a myth and these men were eager to talk. At first, I tried asking about solitude, and sacrifice, and the long dark winters alone on the island, but they showed little interest in these subjects. Instead they wanted to discuss the guests who had visited Caldey and the occasional rumours that reached them from the mainland. One story involved a former Archbishop of Canterbury, who came on retreat a few years ago and insisted on doing all the washing up. Another concerned a postulant who had left the monastery to walk the whole way to Jerusalem.

The monks were quick to laugh and make fun of themselves. They would also repeat the same jokes several times in a row, until every member of the community was nodding along. Over the years these men had begun to share the same mannerisms: pinching their ears with a peeling motion, or resting their thumbs in the weathered grooves of their leather belts. During the long decades they passed together, they must have learned to recognise one brother's shuffling steps, or another brother's stuttering breaths, their familiarity a kind of fondness. At the same time, no amount of familiarity was a substitute for intimacy, and I wondered how much loneliness was hidden beneath these cheerful exteriors. Of course, monastic life channelled that loneliness towards the divine, yet the divine was often slow to respond, the answers so hushed you could barely hear them.

My favourite conversations took place with Br Gildas, who looked like a prophet from the Old Testament. He had long white hair and a long white beard, the latter often stained with food. Yet he spoke to me in the gentlest of voices, sharing the local history and Celtic folklore he had collected over the years.

Br Gildas grew up on another island, the Isle of Wight, and left school at the age of fourteen. Like Jones he wanted to become an artist, but made a career painting formal portraits. However, he soon grew bored with his clients –

mostly lord mayors and the members of City livery companies – and started designing windows for department stores instead. He also attended the early Glastonbury festivals and spent seven years as a Buddhist, but he would not say more about the curious route that brought him to this monastery. Instead, he wanted to speak about the pre-Christian pilgrims who visited Wales and the Celtic shipping routes that linked Caldey with northern Spain. He also wanted to talk about the smugglers' caves in the island cliffs and the German submarine once spotted off Pembroke Bay. And he had a theory about the covert Catholics living along the Bristol Channel, who may have helped with navigation for the Spanish Armada.

After we tidied each meal, Br Gildas waited for me by the kitchen door. When I tried to leave, he would present another piece of trivia from his storehouse of local history, speaking without a pause as if worried I might run away. Did I know that Beatrix Potter and Lewis Carroll both spent time in Tenby? And that Virginia Woolf and Dylan Thomas both came to the town as well? And surely I knew that Augustus and Gwen John were born in Tenby, and that J. M. W. Turner visited to paint the Pembrokeshire coast? And maybe I recalled that George Eliot began to write fiction during a summer holiday here?

David Jones was less interesting to him, though he thought some of the watercolours very pretty. But Lewis Carroll was a favourite author and *Alice in Wonderland* the one book he carried with him to Caldey. Br Gildas called it a work of philosophy, with more wisdom in its rhymes and riddles than any other novel. Like the Cheshire Cat, he went on, who tells Alice that she will be sure to get somewhere, if only she walks for long enough.

'You go this way, you end up here. You go that way, you end up there,' he said, now pulling his palms apart as if performing the final stages of a spell, hands open wide to reveal a secret.

Meals were not the only occasion when I encountered members of the community. Seven times a day a bell would chime and the monks would gather in the chapel on the far side of the cloister. No matter how early I arrived, half the brothers would already be sitting in their stalls or kneeling on the floor, as if they never left the place but stayed here chained to their prayer. Then one of them would switch on an overhead light, the community rising to their feet in a wave of white cassocks, before the abbot blew his harmonica to sound the first note of the chant.

A middle-aged couple came to most of the services, sitting side-by-side in the pew behind mine. I guessed they must live on the island, but we never spoke to one another, merely nodded back and forth at the start. Once the office was underway, I would hear them repeating the chants behind me, or else reading from a set of lever-arch files filled with laminated sheet music. I could also hear the strain of their silence in the heavy pauses between each prayer: now clearing their throats, now rubbing their hands, now rising to stand and causing the pews to creak.

Over the years, I have attended enough church services to know how to pass the time. Though I rarely recited the prayers, I still tried to follow the liturgy, and to stand, sit and kneel alongside the rest of the room. That said, the three and a half hours the monks spent in worship were too much for me, and I soon began skipping the shorter services, or else staying in bed for the earliest office. Besides, the liturgy was pared down to its simplest form, and the English psalms contained few of the haunting harmonies I associated with plainchant.

This church was also an ugly space: the nave naked, the chancel bare and the altar nothing more than a plain slab of stone. An aisle that once housed the side chapels was being used to store gardening equipment, with buckets of tools hoarded in the shadows. On the original designs for the priory, the church was a grand basilica at the centre of an Italianate complex, but this one suggested a village hall, crouched on the eastern edge of the cloister.

The monastery was designed by John Coates Carter, an English architect who made his name restoring churches in South Wales. Caldey was by far his most ambitious creation: an Arts and Crafts fantasy with stone arches at the base, tapered turrets at the summit, and a slender tower to one side. With its whitewashed battlements and bright red roof tiles, it resembled one of those cartoon castles built by King Ludwig in the Bavarian Alps, a bombastic style that did not imply confidence so much as its lack, as if the monks were worried they would not be taken seriously.

This makes sense when you consider the community's history. During the dissolution of the monasteries, religious life was banned in Britain. Abbeys and convents were looted for building materials and their ruins abandoned in lonely valleys or farmers' fields. Then, in the nineteenth century, a group of priests known as the Oxford Movement began encouraging the Anglican Church to rediscover its Roman roots. These priests started restoring elements of Catholic liturgy and theology, architecture and vestments, as well as forming dozens of religious orders.

A first community of Anglican Benedictines was founded in 1895. After several moves, they were given Caldey Island with funding to build a monastery from the politician Lord Halifax. Though religious orders were popular in the suburbs of industrial towns and the parishes of colonial cities, they were treated with snobbery by most members of the establishment. Their fondness for ritual and ornament was considered suspicious by religious authorities – the Church of England was still officially Protestant – and the monks at Caldey got in trouble for exposing the blessed sacrament, performing services of benediction and celebrating the Feast of the Immaculate Conception. They kept observing Catholic holy days, however, until the Bishop of Oxford intervened.

More than a century later, this may sound like a minor dispute, but at the time it caused a major scandal. In 1913, almost the entire community converted to Rome as an act of protest, remaining on the island and soon adopted by the Catholic Benedictines. So, when Jones came to stay a decade later, he was not visiting some historic centre of the faith, but a new community in a new set of buildings. Like him they were recent converts, and like him they wanted to prove themselves worthy of their adopted religion.

Though the monks ran out of money before building their basilica, there were enough donations left to furnish the smaller chapel in a lavish fashion. The altar screen was made of oak and the floor was tiled in slate, while the vaulted ceiling had gilded bosses set into each panelled square. More panels lined the sides of the nave, along with wooden choir stalls dating back to the fifteenth century, and a chancel housed the relics of St Samson, which had arrived on the island in a ceremonial barge fitted out with heraldic shields.

The altar was even older, constructed from slabs of stone rescued from the ruins of English abbeys. These remains were mortared together into a single block, forming an architectural reliquary to the religious houses destroyed during the Reformation. In the lower left corner was a stone from Selby dated 1069, and nearby a square from Rievaulx carved with the year 1132. In the upper right corner was a slab from Glastonbury dated AD 64, and in the centre a stone from Westminster, its Roman numerals reading 948. An ornate reredos rose up behind the altar, carved with statues of saints, while rich velvet hangings hid the back wall of the building.

Little trace of that church remains today. Neither the velvet hangings that flanked the reredos, nor the six golden candles that stood on the altar, nor the shining symbol of the cross itself. Some were taken away when the Benedictines left the abbey in 1928; the rest were destroyed in 1940 when a fire gutted the chapel. At the time, the community's members were mostly serving in the war, which meant the fire burned for eleven hours before it was extinguished. The screen was charred, the stalls were split, and the blackened roof was broken in two, yet the altar constructed from the masonry of ancient monasteries somehow survived. Sadly, its precious stones have since disappeared; Br Gildas suspected they were buried beneath the sanctuary.

The building was restored in 1951, following the plain tastes of the Trappists: bare walls and blank altars, but no garish paintings or statues of saints. Perhaps Jones would have preferred this simple space, since his own faith was something rescued from destruction, or put together from the splintered pieces of the past.

On Caldey the landscape was porous. Even when I could not see the sea, I was always aware of its presence. The vast expanse of air beyond the fields, and the open horizon behind the trees, and the distant washing of the waves, heard each time the wind dropped down. Meanwhile, the surrounding waters were a giant mirror, reflecting the sky to twice its proportions and reflecting the weather as well.

In the autumn of 1926, Jones was living on Caldey again. Before visiting the priory, he had never tried to paint the sea, but now it became the focus of his work. Away from his mentor, his parents and his peers, he could explore the subject with complete freedom. He was fascinated by the way the elements on Caldey were inverted, trying to convey this confusion in his watercolours. 'I had a thing,' he would remember, 'about the "solid" rocks against which the "liquid" sea washed being, because of its pounding, more substantial than the rocks.'

The longer Jones spent on Caldey, the stronger the effect on his style. Working outside, he had to paint quickly in case the weather changed, finishing each picture in less than a day. His paints were also thinned to make them last longer – the pigment faint and the surfaces insubstantial – adding to the sense of movement.

The first of these pictures, *Tenby from Caldy Island* (1925), was the most traditional in technique. It depicts the upright houses of Tenby seen from the island, with the sea a blank band of water between. The firm contours and cross-hatching are borrowed from Jones's engravings, but the water seems static despite the boats floating by. Later that year he painted *A Ship off Ynys Byr* (1925), where the sea has started to dominate the page. The land is now a frame fitting round the water, but the surface of the sea remains featureless as a pane of clouded glass.

In *Sandy Cove, Caldy* (1927), land and sea are woven together, while the pattern of the surf recurs in the crooked shape of the shore and the coiled fabric of the foliage. That same bay forms the subject of *Path by the Coast* (1927), its vegetation becoming more detailed with writhing tendrils and flailing ferns, their colours almost tropical. Finally, in a 1929 sketch called *Surf*, the water is yellow and green, blue and grey, each wash of colour threaded through with spindles of pencil lead. At the same time, the brushwork is dabbed, dragged, dotted across the page – conveying not only the rhythm of waves, but the drama of foam and spray, or the pounding pattern of the current.

Jones later explained to Jim Ede, a collector of art and assistant curator at the Tate, that he had done 'an immense amount of tearing up at Caldey'. But he kept coming back to the island, because the few pictures that remained were 'in a curious way the best things I have done so far'.

Long after Jones left Caldey, he continued to paint the sea. Even his landlocked pictures evoked the ebb and flow of the tide, or an occasional sense of seasickness. Many of these pictures were exhibited at the Beaux Arts Gallery in Mayfair, a centre for avant-garde work. Though watercolour is the most traditional of mediums, Jones's idiosyncratic style meant he was welcomed by his abstract peers. Towards the end of the '20s he was invited to join the Seven and Five Society, the leading group of abstract painters and sculptors in the country, which included Ben Nicholson, Henry Moore and Barbara Hepworth.

Several of these artists had also left London to search for new subjects. Ben Nicholson was already visiting Cornwall, and would make his home there with Barbara Hepworth at the start of the Second World War. Similarly, Virginia Woolf and Vanessa Bell were gathering in Sussex villages, where they hosted the intellectuals associated with the Bloomsbury Group. And plenty of the period's most talented painters were looking for inspiration among the ancient landmarks of the English countryside: the prehistoric stones turned into geometric shapes by Paul Nash, or the chalk figures on the slopes of the South Downs that became folksy icons in the paintings of Eric Ravilious. So, by retreating to the little-known borders of England and Wales, Jones not only discovered his own style, but also moved to the heart of Britain's artistic scene.

Of course, Jones was not seeking to innovate, so much as illustrate the bewitching beauty of his surroundings. Nonetheless, the unique relationship of earth, air and water that he encountered on Caldey required a new way of painting, the island a stepping stone towards abstraction. Once the geography was familiar, he could leave behind figurative principles and instead try to capture the impression of movement and light.

In the final years of his life, Jones's essays and poetry recalled this draw towards islands. For him, they were enchanted places, 'where lithosphere and watersphere and atmosphere merge with each other'. They also 'come and go in the changing light – now sharply defined, now lost in a diaphane of mist-drift'.

I was reminded of this line each time I walked the northern border of Caldey, over stretches of sand untouched by a single footprint. From here, the layers of sea, sky and cloud formed a great blur of grey, a curtain of thick fabric drawn across the entire bay. When the wind caused the curtain to tremble, I glimpsed the distant shoreline behind the folds of vapour, Tenby appearing and disappearing like a flickering image in an ancient film. And I wondered whether retreat was less a refuge from the world than a window onto it; less closing our eyes than learning to see our surroundings for the very first time.

Most afternoons I went walking. Sometimes I hiked to the Victorian lighthouse on the island's southern side; other times strolled through the wooded enclosure bordering the eastern bays. Once or twice I even completed a wide lap of the coast, tramping as far as Caldey's western shore, before turning back to the monastery.

My favourite place to walk was the gardens of the medieval priory. These gardens were once sown with exotic plants and filled with wild animals, so that, wandering among the stripped saplings and tattered shrubs, I was struck once more by the fantasy feel of the place. Here the black swans drifting across a pond; there the red squirrels scurrying between the trees, the last survivors of the island's Victorian menagerie. Otherwise, the foliage was sparse and the colours raw: flag-stones of burnished metal, branches bare as bones and the grasses a deadened shade of brown.

The ruins of the old priory stood on the southern side of the gardens, its ancient masonry forming three wings of a courtyard. Though the medieval structure was still intact, the windows were empty and the battlements cracked, with weeds pressing up through the paving stones. The lower levels consisted of crumbling archways and vaulted passages, as well as forgotten building materials piled on the earth. Meanwhile, the surface of the stonework was pitted, with blind eyes and gaping mouths set into the walls.

In one corner of the complex stood the church of St Illtyd, its spire of rough stone leaning to one side. Inside, the air smelled of old plaster and damp dust, the floor a mosaic of pebbles worn smooth with time, flashing like silver coins cast into the shadows. Close by the altar, I discovered a stone slab carved in Latin and Ogham script, which dated back to the fifth or sixth century and marked the first Christian presence on the island. The two languages were written side by side, their legend reading: AND BY THE SIGN OF THE CROSS, CARVED UPON THIS STONE, I ASK ALL WHO WALK THIS WAY, TO PRAY FOR THE SOUL OF CADWGAN.

Cadwgan's identity has long been lost, but St Illtyd was a popular Celtic saint and the founder of the first school in Britain. He was shown where to found his school by a friendly angel, and one of the windows in the church depicted this scene. These figures were pieced together from fragments of deep blue and rich red, bordered by a riot of yellow and green, like the frozen bursts of fireworks.

That window was the work of Theodore Baily, Jones's closest friend among the Caldey monks. A sensitive and temperamental figure, he did not live with the rest of the community, but alone in a two-room cottage above Paul Jones Bay. Jones admired Baily's love of mystical writers – Julian of Norwich, Walter Hinton and the anonymous author of *The Cloud of Unknowing* – as well as the ascetics of the Early Church. And, when remembering the stained-glass artist years later, he was reminded of an old Welsh proverb: 'The wise love places of retreat.'

Baily became a monk at the age of sixteen, first joining Downside Abbey in Somerset, and then moving to Caldey Island. He also spent a year in Paris, studying with the painters Georges Desvallières and Maurice Denis, the leading figures of the Ateliers d'Art Sacré. This was a movement that emerged after the First World War, its followers rejecting the artificiality of traditional religious artwork and instead attempting to decorate churches in modern styles. When Baily returned from Paris in 1923, he brought back the principles of the Ateliers, as well as the aesthetic ideals of the Russian refugees who gathered in the city after the revolution.

Both can be seen in the windows he made for the island's parish church: a fish, a tree and the figure of Mary holding the infant Christ. Each one relies on a simple design and a limited palette, flattening any sense of depth, while the expressions on his subjects' faces – their gazes set and smiles serene – show the influence of Byzantine art. This is a vision of faith as patient endurance or loving silence, yet they do not share the jewelled stillness of icons. Instead, their backgrounds are assembled from uneven cuts of glass, resisting any symmetry to create a colourful confusion.

The technique for making stained glass has changed little since the Middle Ages. A window was nothing like a painting, as Baily explained in an article for the community newsletter, *Pax*. Glass was closer to water, to light, than the blank white space of a canvas: 'of its nature crystalline and gemlike, it is ever associate with light; windows, mirrors, and make-believe jewels are all made of glass. One speaks of a sea of glass; is it not because at such times the sea is clear and transparent, shining inwardly with amazing colour? This lucency and gem-like quality should surely be preserved, so that the deep tones burn darkly, and the pale shine with soft brilliance.'

Baily's thinking about light can be seen in Jones's own work. The paintings from Capel and Caldey not only share this pale shine, this soft brilliance, but also turn the slope of a hill or stretch of water into a source of illumination.

It's a deliberate inversion of traditional perspective, which places the sun or bright sky at the back of a picture. Many of Jones's later paintings were viewed through a window, too, meaning every surface has the same transparent brightness, like sheets of gleaming gauze. Weather, glass, air – for Jones these substances acquire a tangible presence, and light becomes a living thing.

But the hermit's influence on Jones went beyond artistic technique. His vocation was also an example, with his days divided between art and prayer. Baily showed how the creative and contemplative callings could imitate one another, and how taken together they could occupy an entire life. Both practices involved long periods of time alone, enduring boredom, doubt and occasional despair. Yet the artist or monk persists in the belief that this practice is worthwhile, whether or not the world recognises its value. They share the hope that their sacrifice will make sense one day.

Some people believe because they have wishes the world will never answer. Speaking again with lost loved ones, or seeking the cure for a sickness no doctor can heal, or finding forgiveness for the hurt it's too late to mend. If the truth of this world is tragic – fate is blind, and random too – then faith promises a resolution in the world to come.

This is also the reason we turn towards art. In sounds and images, and above all in stories, we understand experience by giving it shape. The artist is the figure who transforms the raw material of this life into something beautiful, even meaningful. So, perhaps the impulse to believe and the impulse to create come from the same place: a wish to remake the world in our imagination.

By the middle of the week, there were still no boats to the mainland. Though I tried settling into the stilled rhythm of island life, it often felt like I was holding my breath. I kept waiting for the moment when I could open my mouth and gasp for air, but each day the news was the same: the weather was wild, the postal boat was stalled, there was nobody coming to rescue me. I even began worrying that I would have to stay on Caldey for another week.

Much of the island appeared neglected. Close to the medieval priory was a farm made up of ramshackle barns and sheds. A few of the pens housed rusted-looking tractors, but the rest of the buildings were empty, their walls and roofs overwhelmed with creepers. Two outhouses at the end of the yard had the words CHOCOLATE FACTORY printed above the door, while a farmhouse of grey render occupied the end of the lane, standing lonely and exposed.

In the village, most of the shops were shut for winter. Other buildings looked like they had been locked for much longer, their windows fogged with dust and blue paint flaking from their frames. I put my face to the window of one cottage, until I could make out the remains of a work-shop inside: the outlines of tables and chairs and a workbench littered with tools, emerging from the darkness like buried items dug from the earth.

But the post office was open for three hours each day. Its shop sold postcards of seals and puffins, while a miniature museum of black-and-white photographs narrated the history of the island. Another Dutchman – the brother of the abbot – was working behind the counter, and every afternoon I asked when the boat would come. But every afternoon he shook his head, replying that I must learn to adjust to island life.

'I've been to Bali, the Seychelles, the Caribbean too,' he claimed. 'Islands teach you patience. There's no now on an island, only waiting.'

As the week wore on, I stopped counting down until my return. In fact, I tried to suspend all thought of the future and keep my mind fixed on the present. On Caldey the days were no longer divided by hours, but by the regular routine of worship and prayer. Given the lack of other obligations, it was difficult to say what happened when, or how exactly the week was passed. Nonetheless, as the minutes slowed, my senses became sharper, and during those after-noon walks the island was loud with sounds I had not heard before.

Though the cloister was still during the daytime, the rest of Caldey could be busy: machinery clanking down by the docks, a tractor grinding along a pitted path, and the squealing of gulls as they circled the shore, not to mention the distant static of waves breaking somewhere in the background. Then I would return to the guest quarters and listen to the complicated patterns made by the rain – the drip and splash, the dapple and sing – playing on the roof of the building.

The quiet of the monastery muted most human noises, yet magnified every other sound. With fewer demands on my attention, I began to notice things I might have otherwise overlooked. Began wondering which word would catch the shining skeins of cloud, or which colour would conjure the puddles in the forecourt as they flushed with afternoon light. And wondering if this was the real reason artists and believers went on retreat: creating an absent space to concentrate their awareness.

This was most obvious during the Great Silence that filled the priory each evening. At the final service of the day, the brothers would leave their stalls to stand in the centre of the chapel, reciting the *Salve Regina*. By this point the lights had been switched off, but a single lamp glowed beneath an icon of the Virgin, an orange tear in the black shroud of evening. Then the community chanted in Latin, the antique language thickening the air of that darkened room, like the scented smoke from a smouldering ember.

When Compline was finished, the brothers marched from the church. Each one bowed his head as he stepped into the cloister, while the abbot sprinkled their crowns with holy water. From that point on, the members of the community made as little sound as possible until mass next morning. Returning to my cell, I tiptoed along the echoing corridors, anxious to preserve the stillness of the space. This was a silence I had never heard before, as if everything was motionless beyond the borders of the island and the wide world had ceased to turn.

On one of these evenings, I put on my boots and walked from the priory into the inked mystery of the night. Outside, the paths were dark, and the cottages dark, and the moon was clouded over. Nobody trod the curving track that led to the water, nor stood on the sand and listened to the sea. When I reached the beach, I saw the far lights of Tenby doubled up in the darkness, like the flares from a drowned city burning beneath the waves. I stared and stared until my eyes began to sting, and then shut my lids and the city was extinguished.

Jones was a guest on the island when the crisis came. It was early 1927, and he was still trying to decide what he wanted for his future: a life with Petra and the responsibilities of a family, or a life alone devoted to his art. He did not think he had the courage for either course, writing to Jim Ede about his confusion. 'We *all* know that God alone can satisfy our affections,' he explained, but religious celibacy 'is *only the vocation of the few*'. And, Jones claimed, 'I can't imagine anyone more bound up in terrestrial comforts than I — it revolts me to think of it.'

Petra stayed at Capel, where she was joined by a young man called Denis Tegetmeier. Like Jones, Tegetmeier was born in 1895, attending art school before the war and then serving on the Western Front. He had also become a member of the guild at Ditchling, where he shared a house with Jones and learned to make lettering from Gill. Later he lived with a community of Trappists, but his attraction to religious life was due in large part to his unspoken love for Petra. And, when he discovered that Jones had spent the whole winter hiding on Caldey, he hurried to Capel to take his chance.

Charles McHardy, the bailiff of Caldey farm, lived on the island with his wife and daughters. One of them ran the village shop, while her husband was in charge of a drinking room round the back. Jones often passed his evenings here, making pictures for the younger daughters and trying to charm the older ones.

In the first days of February 1927, he received a letter from Petra. He read the letter while sitting with the McHardy family, his mouth falling open and his face becoming pale. Then he cried out in an anguished voice, 'Oh no!'

The letter asked Jones to 'release' Petra from her engagement, so that she could marry Tegetmeier. It was clear to her that their relationship could not work and she did not want him to take any old job to support a family. According to one account, on finishing the letter Jones smashed his fist against the wall; according to another, he beat his head back and forth on the plaster. Given that he was the gentlest of men, these outbursts are hard to picture, unless the violence was born not of anger but despair, realising how much he once had in the moment it was lost.

To begin with, Jones was determined to leave Caldey. He must travel straight to Capel and try to change Petra's mind. But the boat for the day had already left, meaning he was stuck on the island for another night. That evening he went back to the McHardy family, drinking glass after glass of whisky until he was dreadfully sick. The next day the sea was so rough that he remained in bed, resigned to her decision.

Petra had also written to her parents, telling them the news. Gill responded with congratulations, reassuring his daughter that Jones would feel relieved. 'I think he would have broken off the engagement himself long ago had he not felt that loyalty to you,' he wrote. 'His love for you is real enough, but it is not "married love".'

Gill was surely right that Jones would have never made Petra happy, but he did not realise how distraught his former protégé. According to a postulant living on the island, Jones was so depressed that he seemed close to suicide, with the special sadness of one let down by the thing he loved most in the world. He was convinced that he had spoiled his only chance at love and blamed himself for the tortured ambivalence that drove his fiancée away. Eventually he would conclude 'What you do in religion as in love is a sign of what you are.'

Jones stayed on Caldey throughout the spring, celebrating Easter with the monks. Perhaps the monastic timetable was reassuring, now that his future had been cast adrift. When to sleep, when to eat, when to pray – these decisions were made for him, meaning he could enter into a passive state, surrendering any choice about how his time was spent. But, even if this perpetual present was a comfort, I doubt it offered much respite from his anger and hurt, and I can imagine Jones resenting the numbed routines and distanced impotence of island life, wanting to leave behind the confines of Caldey and be close to his beloved again – to hear her voice, to stroke her hair, to hold her in his arms one final time.

However, Jones could not return to Capel-y-ffin, nor the companions from the guild who might have shared his anguish. Philip Hagreen, a friend from Ditchling who worked as a woodcutter, was the one person who recognised that he 'was sore wounded and alone in the wilderness. All that was meant by home – warmth, trust, privacy, a fixed point on the map – all this was not for David.'

The following summer Jones spent six weeks with Hagreen in France. His friend would recall how the failed engagement changed his character forever. 'He had taken the solemn betrothal as a vow. A German bullet had gone through his leg but the news that came to him on Caldey went through his heart.'

★

So, war was not the only wound Jones hoped the island would heal. During his later visits to Caldey, he also hoped to overcome the hurt of losing Petra. By the end of these retreats, Jones had decided to dedicate himself to a creative career – in the same way that a monk dedicated himself to God. As a result, he would never again get engaged, let alone marry, his relationships sacrificed for the sake of his art.

Even before the engagement ended, Jones had been thinking about the link between religious and artistic life. This was due to friends like Theodore Baily and to the writings of the Catholic thinker Jacques Maritain. Jones was introduced to Maritain's work while living at Ditchling, where a translation of his long essay, *Art et scolastique* (1920), was being printed by the in-house press. More than any other work, this essay shaped his understanding of beauty and belief.

Maritain rejected the romantic image of the artist as a lonely figure cast out from society. Art was something physical, made at a specific time in a specific place, and any broader message came from embracing rather than rejecting this sense of rootedness. 'By its human subject and its human roots, art belongs to a time and a country. This is why the most universal and most human works are those which bear most openly the mark of their country.'

Jones returned to *Art et scolastique* throughout his career. He even developed these ideas in an essay of his own, 'Art and Sacrament' (1955), where he argued that the making of signs was basic to all human beings. By this, he meant the gestures and patterns behind every ceremony and tradition, every performance and picture, that reveal an impulse towards sign-making Christianity recognises in the sacraments. In fact, the sacraments could be considered the most meaningful sign, because during the mass a priest is not simply imitating the Last Supper, but also recreating the event for the faithful.

For Maritain art was something sacramental, yet Jones went further by suggesting that the eucharist offered a blueprint for all subsequent creative acts. Art not only shared in the creative instinct of the Father, but in the sacrifice of the Son. As a monk or nun surrenders their life to move closer to the divine, so the artist gives up some part of themselves to realise their creative ambitions.

Maritain argued that the artist and the contemplative share the same project. As he explained in *Art et scholastique*, 'The Contemplative, who looks at the highest cause on which every being and activity depend, knows the place and the value of Art, and understands the Artist. The Artist as such cannot judge the Contemplative, but he can divine his grandeur. If he truly loves beauty and if a moral vice does not hold his heart in a dazed condition, when his path crosses the Contemplative's he will recognise love and beauty.'

These ideas may seem abstract, but they influenced Jones's life in a lasting way. For him, the artistic and religious impulses expressed the same longing, even shared the same source. After reading Maritain, he came to believe in a hierarchy of experience, with sensual pleasures at the bottom, aesthetic ones above that and contemplative ones at the top.

Jones discussed this theory during one of his final visits to Caldey. By this point the Benedictine community, weighed down with debts from building the priory, had sold their island to a group of Belgian Trappists. In 1928 they acquired a former hunting lodge in the Cotswolds as their new home, dismantling the chapel, packing up the library and floating their furniture across the bay. The refectory tables were tied to a boat, bobbing back and forth in the current.

Because of the Trappist emphasis on working the land, the new community had little time for arts and crafts. And because the monks spent most of their days in silence, Jones made few friends among their members. But he still enjoyed painting Caldey, returning once in 1929, once more in 1931 and a final time in 1932. Afterwards he ceased these regular retreats, as if he had found whatever he was looking for, or else given up the search.

During the 1931 visit, Jones stayed for a fortnight at a cottage on Caldey with two friends named Harman Grisewood and Tom Burns. Their mornings were spent painting and their evenings passed with reading or working on poetry. In the afternoons they would explore the island together, and on one of their walks Jones told his two friends about the mixed relief and regret he felt over his failed engagement. He had recently renewed his friendship with Petra, after Gill's community at Capel-y-ffin relocated to a hilltop farm in the Chilterns. He had even proposed for a second time, and later fell platonically in love with another member of the guild named Prudence Pelham. However, Jones told his friends that he was uneasy with the idea of constant companionship, his fastidiousness sounding bitter at times. 'I don't want to wake up with a girl beside me,' he said. 'That would be revolting to me in some way.'

Of course, Jones was not the first artist to worry about the conflict between a family life and a creative one. All the same, his comment suggests a wounded pride in this stubborn desire to remain alone. When heartbroken there's a curious satisfaction that comes from refusing pleasure, proving your misery but making it much worse. However, if Jones hoped a life without love meant a life without pain, he was surely mistaken, because isolation was its own kind of pain, less sharp than betrayal or bereavement, but deeper and more destructive in the end. Sheltering from the world offered little protection, and rejecting new relationships meant his loss would never fully heal.

Jones was once asked about the biographical events that shaped his work most deeply. He replied to this question with two negatives: never attending university and never marrying Petra. These were the decisions that separated him from his peers — whether the domestic lives of the craftsmen at Ditchling, or the academic achievements of literary London. But this outsider status was also a source of pride, and when Jones started therapy with a psychologist years later, he announced: 'You're not going to make me normal, are you, because I don't want to be.'

Freud wrote that the artist was one who 'turns away from reality because he cannot come to terms with the renunciation which it at first demands, and who allows his erotic and ambitious wishes full play in the life of phantasy'. In other words, the compromises of this world were unbearable for the artist, so they created a new version in the limitless landscapes of the imagination. Again, this was familiar from my own experience, which made writing into the place where I could escape everyday existence, somewhere to remake disappointments and perhaps even redeem them. Yet the risk of denying reality is that the artist remains always a child.

In the case of Wittgenstein, Jones and Weil, all three of them could be naive, self-righteous, and earnest to the point of insufferable. All three showed the special selfishness of one who fixes their gaze on some lofty goal but lets others clear the path. It's much easier to hold yourself to an exceptional standard when you don't care about the inconvenience it might cause – but this is true of many men and women we call geniuses, and many we call saints as well.

★

On Friday the wind stilled and the weather calmed. Over breakfast I learned that the postal boat was leaving Tenby in the mid-afternoon, arriving at Caldey by teatime. Come half past three I had packed my bags and tidied my room, so Br Titus suggested we watch the sunset together. Then we sat in his van again, driving towards the lighthouse that looked out over the Bristol Channel, a lone spire on Caldey's southern border.

That afternoon, the guest-master might have been a schoolboy. His body was small, his frame slight, and his cheeks would colour each time he smiled. As the van rose up the track towards the lighthouse, we passed a field of unkempt ponies and he waved his arm, pressing the horn until the animals danced in circles.

'The animals know me by now,' he explained. 'They always respond the same way.'

For all my relief that I would not be trapped here another week, I worried there was some lesson from Caldey I might have missed. Perhaps Br Titus would leave me with a final piece of wisdom, but he did not seem interested in talking about retreat. Instead, as we drove from the monastery, he discussed a famous racing driver who had recently died.

When Br Titus worked in Formula One, he had known several drivers who were killed in car accidents. These men were still in their early twenties, and their deaths were the reason he became a monk. 'I wanted to make sense of the tragedies. I wanted to find a better way to live.'

GUY STAGG

We parked close to the cliffs and walked towards the headland. The waters were placid and the waves appeared motionless, marbled slabs of stone spreading out on every side. 'That's the Somerset coast,' said Br Titus, pointing towards the thin strip of land on our left. 'And that's Lundy Island,' he added, pointing at a shallow plateau breaching the horizon some fifty miles away. 'And there's the Atlantic,' he concluded, now gesturing towards the sweep of the sea, pouring unbroken into the sky.

Since lunchtime the weather had been clear, but now a few clouds clustered at the edges of the afternoon. The wind was also beginning to rise, drawing the clouds across the sun and causing them to burn with colour. At the same time, fragments of light crested the waves like precious treasure spilling from the sky.

In all the time I spent on Caldey, Br Titus had never asked about my beliefs. I still felt obliged to say something, so I told him that coming here had shown me the gap between the romantic version of religious life and the reality. In the romantic version, sacrifice was the only thing needed for salvation, and contentment just a question of giving things up. But I understood now that withdrawing was no guarantee of happiness, and that simply leaving the world behind would not save anyone.

Br Titus replied that many people were attracted to religious life for the wrong reasons. A few of them even became monks and nuns, only to find that they were miserable.

'This is the big mistake people make: living a life that's meant for someone else. If this is the right place, you will be happy here. If it's the wrong place, you will be sad. But to me it's not a sacrifice. I feel lucky to have found it.'

Besides, for Br Titus there was plenty to enjoy about life on Caldey. The sea, the seasons and the time spent outdoors. He had grown up near the coast and missed little from his former life, except the chance to visit art exhibitions. But he did not spend his days thinking about God and heaven and whether he was saved.

'It's what's down here that matters,' he added. 'It's what happens in this life that counts.'

The sun had almost set, no more now than a gleaming wound on the distant waters. When we turned back towards the island, I could see the pointed towers of the monastery breaking through the bundled pines, as well as the painted houses of Tenby on the far side of the bay. The first street-lamps lit the road above the harbour and car headlights climbed the hill like sparks cast from a bonfire.

'During the lockdown,' Br Titus explained, 'all the lights were turned off. The whole town looked like it was empty, like we were back in the Dark Ages again.' He pointed one last time to a tiny craft crossing the bay, leaving a trail of white wake behind. 'That's the boat which will take you home. No need to stay here another week.'

Soon we were driving down to the pier, past the old stone shell of the medieval priory and the weathered white walls of the new one. Again, a few locals had gathered at the water's edge, some of them collecting deliveries, others exchanging bottles and cans to recycle. After the boat arrived, I helped with the unloading, before lifting my bag from the pier and stepping onto the deck. As the captain loosened the boat's moorings, I waved to Br Titus one final time, before turning my back on the island.

When we left Caldey there was still light in the sky, but night had fallen by the time we reached Tenby. In the half hour between, the waters of the sea were streaked with orange, and purple foam patterned the current. The farther we travelled, the darker the island became: the beach a band of blue shadow floating on the water and the woodland black against the sinking sky. Meanwhile the clouds formed endless dunes of grey, mapping a great desert above the boat, and for a moment I experienced the wonder that comes in the presence of immensity, as if the landscape were being crafted by some unseen artist. But then the dunes were blown to the blank edges of the map and the evening chased the last light from the sky.

Sitting in the boat, it seemed as if there were two different kinds of retreat: the flight from one world and the journey towards another. Those who withdrew to leave their lives behind, and those who went in search of somewhere new. Br Titus suggested only the latter could last, yet I suspected most retreats were a muddle of both motives. And I wondered which motives were behind my own decision to withdraw: a flight away or a journey towards?

After the glittering riches of Klosterneuburg, I had been hungry for the hardships of the Trappist calling. On Caldey I sought the dramatic splendour of solitude, only to realise that monastic life was more about the quiet compromises of living in community. I also realised that my own attraction to austerity had been born from fear: the seeming safety of giving up wishes, rather than wanting things beyond my reach. Instead of trying to confront this fear, I decided that solitude was a virtue and self-denial an end in itself. I even convinced myself that wealth meant abandoning all desire and freedom came from cutting emotional ties. In consequence, I became brittle, and timid, and lonely too, trapped in a cage of my own making.

As the boat approached the mainland, this confusion was clear to me. Discipline, isolation, self-denial even – they had most value when the writer or artist needed to learn their craft. Yet they should not be mistaken for something sacred. They were not enough to create art that lasted.

If Caldey was a studio where Jones could experiment with painting, it was also a sanctuary where he could confront his past. He continued making retreats throughout his thirties, and from 1928 onwards he was working on a long poem about the First World War. That poem was *In Parenthesis*.

The war makes little appearance in Jones's painting, his weightless landscapes detached from any historical period. But the fighting was never far from his mind, and each summer he would relive his experiences of the Somme. Later he compared this memory to a disease, saying, 'I still think about it more than anything else.'

On one of his first retreats to Caldey, those memories were waiting to emerge. The habits of the community recalled Jones's time in the trenches: plain food, pressed uniforms, and conversations mixed from cockney, Welsh and military jargon. The damp weather and exposed setting also reminded him of war, and when a member of the community began cracking a set of wooden clappers at Vespers one afternoon, Jones heard the rattles used to warn of gas attacks. The unlit space, the echoing sound, the bodies standing motionless in the shadows – in that instant he was carried back to the front, pierced by the sharp splinters of the past.

During the later retreats, Jones had already started writing the poem. It began in a seaside village called Portslade on the outskirts of Brighton, which he visited in 1927. That summer his parents had borrowed a holiday property and Jones spent a month there painting the sea, before moving on to Caldey. He returned in the spring of 1928, again planning to paint the sea, but instead fell ill and passed the whole holiday in bed.

While in bed, Jones began sketching infantry soldiers from memory. Alongside these images he wrote fragments of prose, describing the morning before the soldiers were due to embark. His diary was lost during the war, but his recollections were clear despite the decade in between. Soon he started composing small scenes of military life, as well as snatches of slang and speech. These scenes were never meant for publication, which was why he called them *In Parenthesis*, as if bracketed off from the rest of his work.

When Jones recovered he returned to painting, yet he kept on writing in the evenings. The description of soldiers embarking became the opening of an epic text narrating the months leading up to the Somme. The protagonist – John Ball – shared many of Jones's experiences between the late winter of 1915 and the high summer of 1916, culminating in the Battle of Mametz Wood. Though the writing was mostly prose, in places it was arranged like poetry, with seven sections narrating how the soldiers trained, travelled through France, lived in the trenches and prepared for an assault.

*In Parenthesis* marked the start of another chapter in Jones's life. That said, he began work on the poem during this period of regular retreats and the presence of Caldey Island can be traced in the text. The sergeant who guides the soldiers to the front is said to be 'long professed', while the company are 'serving their harsh novitiate'. Assembling on parade, they share a 'silence peculiar to . . . refectories', and being woken for the stand-to has the 'quality of the monastic *Benedicamus Domino*'. These assemblies occur at the hours of Lauds and Vespers, overseen by officers instead of abbots, with the choirs of men facing each other like monks 'in stalls'. And after dark another kind of chanting begins, when the shelling is exchanged from one side to another to form 'the uneven pulse of the night-antiphonal'.

*In Parenthesis* is doing more than simply borrowing the language of religious life. Instead, Jones is turning the men's sacrifice into something sacred. Throughout the poem, the soldiers are both present at the most urgent moment of their lives and taking part in a timeless ceremony. That's why his descriptions of army life were overlaid with elements from Celtic mythology, Arthurian literature and the language of the liturgy, as Jones explains in the Preface to the poem: 'I suppose at no time did one so much live with a consciousness of the past, the very remote, and the more immediate and trivial past.' That's also why the service he witnessed in the trenches had such a lasting impact, the one moment of continuity among all that disruption. For Jones, the Catholic Church had a unique connection to the past – as the ancient faith of England, Wales, and the Roman Empire too. This was most obvious during the mass, because, if Christ was present in the bread and wine, nineteen centuries collapsed into a single moment – the sacrifice in Judea taking place today.

The Preface to *In Parenthesis* explains how the poem helps make sense of the conflict. If we want to find meaning in war, Jones argues, we must not look to the Christian promise of redemption, but rather to the virtues glimpsed

among the violence. Patience, courage, kindness: to main-
tain these qualities in the face of suffering is a redemption
that requires no religion, beyond a belief in the possibility
of goodness.

If painting for Jones was the medium of the living moment,
writing was the medium of memory, history and the mythic
past. Once he started composing *In Parenthesis*, he could not
only place these recollections on the page, but also begin
shaping them too. Rather than keep the world at a distance,
poetry became a way for Jones to make sense of his experiences, as well as the memories he had smothered all this
time. This did not heal the trauma of war, so much as open
new wounds; the true works of art are no fantasy, but a
confrontation with the deepest parts of ourselves.

In the past I believed that art, like faith, was a form of
therapy. And believed that history might offer a refuge for
those overwhelmed by the modern world. But Jones's story
shows how a work of art can embed the grief it's trying to
console, eventually causing the crisis that brought these
retreats to an end.

Jones's final visit to Caldey took place in 1932, staying on
the island during Lent. This was the most prolific year of
his career, because as well as painting dozens of pictures he
also finished the first draft of *In Parenthesis*. However, when
an editor at Faber approached Jones about the poem, he
replied that it required too much revision. A few weeks

later all work was interrupted, and it was many months before he could return to the manuscript.

The first signs of trouble started in August of that year, when Jones began feeling anxious and losing sleep. But he kept on painting, producing some sixty pictures over the summer and autumn. By September he had ceased to talk, his bouts of depression now mixed with periods of panic, where his heart beat faster and his breath became short. At the same time, nausea swelled his stomach and his sight would dizzy and blur: similar to the fear he experienced on the duckboard tracks during the war. The sweat on his palms, the sandpaper in his mouth, the twitching of his heart and the twisting of his intestines, severe enough now to overwhelm him completely.

During this period, Jones was staying with Gill and his family at their Chilterns farm. In October, he had to be driven back to his parents' home, where he remained for much of the next year, unable to read, to write, to talk, let alone step outside. It was the most complete retreat of his entire life, withdrawing from company, creativity, and even communication. All night he lay in bed, listening to his father's clock chime the quarter hours without missing a single note. 'I did not sleep for nine months,' he later claimed, 'no one I've told has believed me.'

Jones spent 1933 in a state of deep depression, his anguished mood mixed with anxiety and fear. When alone he felt a sense of impending disaster; when outdoors he would break into a run as if trying to bolt. The idea of being seized by such terror at any moment made him even more frightened of leaving the house.

That autumn Jones went to a doctor and was diagnosed with neurasthenia owing to shell shock. When he explained that working on pictures only made his mood worse, the doctor asked him to cultivate a 'masterly inactivity'. For the next decade and a half he painted little, reading and writing poetry between bouts of debilitating depression. During this period, he lived with his parents and with friends, or else in the coastal town of Sidmouth, walking along the beaches in a hat and two mufflers as if wearing a disguise. Increasingly people had to visit him, because he struggled with parties and public places and could not bear to travel.

Jones later described how the nervous collapse caused him to doubt most of the comforting claims religion made about suffering. That prayer might bring the Christian closer to God, or that faith might spare someone from depression – none of these arguments seemed credible now. Rather, he tried holding tight to the idea that, even in the moment of darkest despair, God was somehow sharing his anguish. Nonetheless, it tested his belief more than any other experience, and from that point on his sense of vocation was shaken. This was the paradox of faith Simone Weil would confront – the anguish that strips any sense of the divine – yet Jones was left unconsoled.

It was not clear what triggered the collapse, but Jones

believed writing *In Parenthesis* was to blame. 'I sometimes wonder if doing it didn't partly bring on this breakdown,' he said in 1939. And his therapist would agree, eventually concluding that the fear he had repressed during the war was released once the poem was completed.

Three decades later, he still remembered the breakdown, writing that its effects had endured ever since. He was never restored to the cheerful, childlike state of before, his enthusiasm giving way to a strain of lasting melancholy. Now there was a whispered quality to his voice and a hesitant manner to his movements, his expression weighted with sadness.

Even though Jones ceased making retreats, Caldey influenced his life for much longer. He did not leave the priory for a settled routine, let alone domestic responsibility. As well as never marrying, he never owned his own home and acquired only a small number of possessions. In other words, he remained committed to the monastic model of creativity: a vocation that cost all he had to give.

When I first learned about Wittgenstein, Jones and Weil, I was bewitched by their self-destructive devotion. And I was convinced there must be some link between original work and an original life. I had fallen for the myth of the artist as outsider, or the idea that great art requires an equal dose of misery. In truth, misery is no guarantee of genius, and, in the case of these three, their achievements came in spite rather than because of their suffering.

But even if suffering was not essential, solitude might

have been. After all, an exceptional life is a lonely thing, as it means following a path nobody else has taken. This was also true for making original work, which will resemble little else in the world. Those who break the rules in one form are less likely to follow them in others, so isolation was often the price of creating something new. This idea had once seemed inspiring to me, yet the more I understood about Wittgenstein, Jones and Weil, the more I wished to avoid the same solitude for myself.

Jones experienced a second breakdown in 1947, which caused a lasting change in his life. In the years after the disaster, he became much more cloistered, living with the habits of an invalid or recluse. From this point on he settled in North London, moving between a psychiatric clinic, a boarding house and a nursing home, reluctant even to leave his room. Retreat may have been a comfort but it was not a cure, and instead he looked for solace in the last calling that was left to him: the struggle to make a living sign upon the page.

In his final years, Jones was visited by the composer Igor Stravinsky. At the time he was living in a residential hotel in Harrow, where the other guests assumed he was an ageing vagrant who liked to paint. In a letter to a friend, the composer described entering the cramped bedsit Jones occupied, with his possessions kept close to the mattress like a wartime bunk. To Stravinsky, he resembled a hermit withdrawn into his cell.

The walls of the room were covered in paintings. When Stravinsky asked to buy one, Jones replied that none were for sale. After the visit the composer told his friends: 'I have been in the presence of a holy man.'

# The Martyr

*Simone Weil (1909–1943)*

She begged to be taken across the river. Though her eyesight was poor and her shooting erratic. Though her body was frail and her movements clumsy. Though she would rather be killed than end the life of a stranger. Still she begged to be taken across, to join the fight against the fascists.

This was Spain, the summer of 1936. A unit of Republican soldiers wanted to demolish a railway track on the far side of the River Ebro, some forty kilometres south-east of Zaragoza. Its eastern bank belonged to the Republican forces, its western bank to the Nationalist army; the soldiers were crossing into enemy territory. And their new recruit – a young teacher from Paris – kept pleading to come with them, until eventually they let her join the raid.

The unit made their way to Prato long before dawn, reaching the enemy shore under cover of darkness. Then they sheltered among the bushes and trees lining the water, watching the sun draw the darkness from the sky and flush the river with colour. Finally, they stepped from their hiding place, holding their breath to listen for the whine of reconnaissance planes passing by overhead.

Two members of the group were left waiting by the river. The first was a German man employed as a cook; the second was the French woman who had begged to come. The German was the nervous one, and the longer they waited, the more anxious he became. *The raiding party had forgotten them . . . the reconnaissance planes had spotted them . . . the Nationalist soldiers were coming for them . . .* But the teacher from Paris felt a curious sense of calm, as if nothing could harm her now.

The woman's name was Simone Weil. She had arrived in Spain soon after war was declared, posing as a journalist until she reached Barcelona. Then she travelled to the front line and joined one of the volunteer forces that later became the International Brigades. Though she was dressed in the mechanics' overalls of the workers' militia, she did not look like a soldier, with her dark eyes magnified by a thick pair of glasses. Then there was the nasal voice, the staccato speech, the constant smoking, too.

Eventually the demolition team returned to the bank, having failed to blow up the railway. But they had managed to capture a farm worker and two teenage boys, intending to rescue all three by taking them back across the river. However, their discussion was interrupted by the distant droning of an engine, as an enemy plane scored the edges of the sky.

The unit scattered for cover among the bushes and trees. Weil lay down on the ground and looked up at the sky, watching the plane flicker between the branches. If their unit was spotted, the route across the river could be cut off, and any fighter who was caught would surely be killed. Yet this thought caused little concern: the morning so beautiful that she could not feel afraid.

'I stretched out on my back,' she later wrote, 'looked up at the leaves, the blue sky. A very beautiful day. If they capture me, they will kill me. But it's what we deserve. Our side has shed a lot of blood, morally I am an accomplice.'

In that instant when death seemed closest, the world was vivid as never before, every outline sharp and every colour burning. Weil noticed the flat bed of the valley, the overgrown banks of the river, the cornfields humming with heat. She noticed the burned earth, the immaculate sky and the broken backs of the ridgelines fracturing the far horizon. This was more than the shining brightness of the morning light or the dazed delight of a summer's day: it was a sense of sudden perfection, as if the world had been made for wonder. So she rose to her feet, brushed the dust from her clothes and stepped out into the open.

Seconds later, the spell was broken. Another plane flew overhead, this one releasing a volley of small bombs. Then came the stuttering thud of impact, the splintered crack of an explosion, and the whole valley appeared to tremble and quake. Finally, she heard her companions calling out, shouting for her to take cover.

Weil did not remain much longer in Spain, injured the very next day. But she never forgot the weeks she spent at the front, alongside the soldiers of the International Brigades. What's more, she was haunted by the thought of that morning raid, asking how such beauty and such violence could exist side-by-side. Her writing became an attempt to answer this question, finding a reason for belief among the wreckage of war.

Anyone who knows about Simone Weil's life knows about her death as well. At the age of thirty-four, lying in a hospital bed in Kent, her heart ceased to beat. Afterwards, a coroner concluded that she had taken her own life by refusing food, starving herself to the point of suicide.

This was halfway through the Second World War, when Weil was working for the Free French in London. She was trying to get herself sent into occupied France, where those living under Nazi rule were hungry and malnourished. According to one account, she stopped eating in a misguided attempt to support the French cause.

Weil died as she lived, committed to absolute solutions and denying any compromise. The same approach can be seen in her writing: the essays and letters and journal entries she composed up until her final sickness. In the course of her brief biography, she wrote about philosophy, literature, politics and faith, but few of these pieces were ever printed. Then, four years after her death, her first book was published and she was recognised as one of the most original thinkers of the century.

That book, *Gravity and Grace*, is a collection of brief essays consisting of single sentences and short paragraphs. They were taken from Weil's journals and given titles like 'Detachment and Idolatry', 'Beauty and Chance'. Her journals were never written for public consumption and the selection was made by someone else, but they kept returning to the same set of questions: Is solitude our essential condition? Does love lead towards or away from truth? In times of violence, what responsibility do we have for the suffering of others? There was no reassurance in Weil's answers, just a relentless attempt to clear away the comforting lies most people tell themselves. 'The only way into truth is through one's own annihilation,' she argued, 'through dwelling a long time in a state of extreme and total humiliation.'

I can still remember the astonishment I felt the first time I read *Gravity and Grace*. The language was simple and the style direct – yet the ideas defied easy summary. Rather than a series of logical steps, the author constructed a sequence of arresting contradictions and asked how both claims could be true at the same time. 'Desire is impossible, it destroys its object . . . Society is a cave. The way out is solitude . . . You could not be born at a better period than the present, when we have lost everything.' Even though these arguments were baffling, I was convinced of the intelligence behind them.

Much of Weil's writing discussed political subjects, yet her best essays were the moral and metaphysical ones, as well as her explorations of belief. In fact, she was the first writer who made belief seem credible to me, because she did not promise salvation, let alone an afterlife of endless praise. Instead, she stared at the world's pain without flinching, yet still sought some cause for faith.

There were several reasons for Weil's interest in suffering. Her early life was scarred by migraines, while her later life was disrupted by war. Though raised in privilege near the colleges and universities of Paris's Latin Quarter, she spent time with workers' unions and on factory floors, deliberately seeking discomfort. Some deep instinct drove her towards danger, with no space between the way she thought and the way she lived, and each insight paid for in punishing experience.

All the same, there was a mystery at the centre of this life. Weil grew up in a non-practicing Jewish family, committed to pacifism and radical politics. However, after a series of encounters with Christianity, she produced the religious writing on which her reputation rests. The most important of these encounters took place at a retreat she made in the spring of 1938, passing almost a fortnight at the Abbey of Solesmes, in the Sarthe department of north-west France.

Wittgenstein and Jones began their retreats as believers, but Weil came to Solesmes as a secular pilgrim. During the Easter weeks she spent at the abbey, she had an encounter that changed her understanding of faith, even altered the course of her life. Here she experienced not only relief from her migraines, but a sense of how you might suffer while still having hope. So, midway through Lent, I made my own way to Solesmes, searching for some trace of the truth she encountered.

I reached Paris around midday. Lunchtime crowds were sitting on the terraces and the buildings were bright in the sun. But the newspapers were busy with stories of war and the Gare du Nord was full of signs written in Ukrainian, welcoming refugees to the city.

My train went south-west from the capital, heading towards Le Mans. Before long the suburban sprawl became flat fields of grain, and then rolling hills and wooded marshes. A second train carried me to Sablé-sur-Sarthe and from there it was a forty-minute walk to Solesmes.

Soon I had joined a narrow road leading out of town. It was early spring, the middle of March, and the late afternoon was warm. Hazel and hawthorn lined one side of the road, their branches trimmed in pale green, and the air felt powdered and pure. The River Sarthe lay a field's width away, but occasionally I spotted the water turning slowly beneath the bank, its surface a polluted shade of grey. Otherwise, I passed a pair of warehouses and the fenced lots of single-storey farm buildings, and I was reminded of the emptiness that haunts the French countryside. Roads with no cars, fields with no farmers, villages without pavements or pedestrians to use them. War and work and the busy streets of the city – all these seemed far away.

After half an hour, the road entered the village of Solesmes.

I expected to see spires massing above the treetops or a grand set of entrance gates. Instead, a long wall enclosed a park on my left, while a succession of townhouses lined up on my right.

Eventually I reached a paved square bordered with slate-topped benches. On one side was a parish church, on the other a townhouse turned into a three-star hotel. Beyond the church stood an archway of dressed stone, framing a pair of double-height doors painted petrol blue. A smaller door was propped open nearby, with a sign giving the name of the abbey in white letters on a navy background.

Inside, I found a gift shop selling postcards and carved medals of silver and bronze. An ageing monk sat at the register, offering each visitor a crumpled smile. But it was another monk who showed me around, an American called Fr Bozell. He was the guest-master at the abbey and the calm of the place had settled deep inside him. He moved slowly and spoke softly, his eyes pale, his eyebrows too, the features faint across his face.

Fr Bozell came to Solesmes in his early twenties, and had lived here for much of the last five decades. When he first arrived, there were still one or two monks who joined the abbey between the wars, around the same time as Simone Weil's visit. 'Oh, much more basic back then,' he said. 'Less heating, less plumbing and a single telephone for the entire community.'

I mentioned that I had recently stayed at a Trappist monastery in the first week of winter. 'Little island off the Welsh coast,' I added. 'None of the radiators worked.'

'I don't suppose anybody is colder than the Trappists,' he replied. 'They have a reputation to uphold.'

We left the giftshop and entered a private enclosure. A gravel path ran between the stone flanks of the chapel and the mismatched buildings backing onto the high street. Beyond the chapel rose a pair of massive cellblocks, five or six storeys tall, surrounding a cloister reserved for members of the community.

As we paced past these buildings, Fr Bozell outlined their history to me. 'Eleventh century . . . fifteenth century . . . late nineteenth century . . .' he explained, his voice deep and subdued at the same time. Then we reached the far side of the enclosure, entering a modern building with rendered walls painted yellow.

This was the hostel where I would be staying for the week. My cell was on the second floor at the end of a long lino corridor. It contained a sink, a desk, a single bed, and a window looking out on the garden. When I pulled open the window and leaned against the frame, my view was blurred by the cherry trees below, their branches flocked with blossom and more petals littering the lawn. The scent of new leaves was fresh in the air, and the garden messy with growth.

The rest of the room was familiar by now. The printed timetable left on the desk; the wooden crucifix pinned to the wall; the single bed pushed into the corner, its mattress thin and its blankets rough. But there was something tacky about this cell, squares of orange carpet coming loose from the floor and a flimsy grey curtain letting in the light. If Klosterneuburg had too much extravagance and Caldey too much austerity, the guest house at Solesmes was a functional space, with the anonymous composure of an executive hotel.

Before leaving, Fr Bozell asked why I had come. I told him that I was trying to understand what Weil experienced at Solesmes. 'To understand it,' he continued, 'or experience it yourself?'

I was not sure how to answer his question. Up to this point, I had been skirting round the subject of faith, hoping to find a secular version of religious life in these retreats. I had learned how withdrawing might bring moral guidance or aesthetic inspiration, but avoided the idea that retreat might give the believer some access to the divine. Yet in the case of Weil, neither her writing nor her life could be understood in secular terms, and if I wanted to make sense of what happened at Solesmes, I would have to reckon with spiritual experience. This was not simply a substitute for artistic practice or ethical teaching, but the centre of the contemplative life. And, more than that, I would have to reckon with Weil's call towards martyrdom.

*Martyr* means 'witness' in Greek. The first martyrs were the men and women who witnessed the coming of Christ. In most cases, this meant the apostles, carrying the message of the Gospels across the Roman Empire. One after another those witnesses were killed, until the word martyr came to mean someone who has died for their faith.

When Christianity was an underground religion, believers were often persecuted. The martyrs of the Early Church were stoned and burned and sawn in two, as well as being crucified like Christ. Artists would later celebrate these deaths in frescoes and icons, finding evidence of Christianity's truth in the believers willing to lose their lives. Though their limbs were twisted and their bodies wracked, their painted faces remained tranquil throughout these tortures, with a palm frond balanced between finger and thumb to symbolise the triumph of the spirit over the flesh.

Once the Roman Empire adopted Christianity, it became much harder to die for your beliefs. But there was another kind of martyrdom available to believers: the life of the monk or nun. They could go without sleep, without food, without drink; they could mortify their flesh and discipline their minds; they could torture themselves for the sake of their faith, proving their devotion by leaving this life behind. Now the red martyrdom of death was beyond reach, Christians began seeking the white martyrdom of self-sacrifice.

In the Middle Ages, this substitute martyrdom drew many men and women to religious callings. They became missionaries who risked their lives spreading the Gospel, and knights who fought to keep the Holy Land in Christian hands. And they joined communities who retreated into the cloister for a life of penance and prayer.

To begin with, Saint-Pierre de Solesmes was a minor priory, the offshoot of a larger monastery based at Le Mans. During the Hundred Years War, it was sacked by English soldiers, but by the sixteenth century the chapter-house had been rebuilt and the church restored. At first, few pilgrims knew the name of Solesmes, because it housed no precious relics and raised no famous saints. Then the French Revolution transformed its reputation.

The Revolution pitted the people against monarchy, aristocracy and clergy. To the National Constituent Assembly, which came to power in the early stages of the uprising, monasteries were no less symbols of corruption than palaces or châteaux. By 1790, all religious communities in France were banned, their buildings claimed by the state and their property dispersed at public auctions. In addition, hundreds of monks and nuns were tried for separatism before being executed – many of them drowned in the waters of the Loire.

The next year, most of the monks left Solesmes. Those who stayed behind were imprisoned or deported. In 1794, the priory's archive was set on fire and over the next few decades its land and farms were sold off. By 1832, the decision had been made to demolish the remaining buildings, until a priest called Prosper Guéranger intervened.

Guéranger was a local boy. Growing up, he was inspired by the romance of religious life. At seminary he became an expert in medieval monasticism, fascinated by the great Benedictine abbeys that turned France into the monastic capital of Europe. During the High Middle Ages, French religious houses had reached a peak of prosperity and influence never again matched.

By the ninth century, the Rule of St Benedict was the standard model for monastic life in much of Catholic Europe. Benedictine communities were semi-independent, with monasteries endowed by noble families and overseen by a local bishop. However, from the second half of the tenth century, many French monasteries went from autonomous institutions to centrally governed congregations, under the leadership of Cluny Abbey. This was a powerful Burgundian foundation, free from the influence of any feudal lord and loyal only to the pope. Thanks to the growing wealth of these congregations – the kings of England, Spain and Italy competed to give money to Cluny – monks could abandon manual work, living in greater comfort and devoting them-selves to prayer. They could even spend entire days in worship, imitating the choirs of heavenly angels.

Though the aim was poverty and humility, the result was wealth and power. Between the eleventh and sixteenth cen-turies, Cluny Abbey boasted the largest church in the world. In addition, four of its monks became popes, six of its abbots became saints, and dozens of its members were made into bishops and cardinals. By the time of the Revolution, Cluny was a symbol of the *Ancien Régime*, the abbots treated like kings and the church filled with priceless treasures. Nonetheless, on 25 October 1791, after the monks had celebrated a final mass, the abbey's library was burned, its church plundered and its cellblocks quarried for building stone.

This was the world Prosper Guéranger wanted to restore.

He dreamed of bringing back that former glory and rebuilding the country's abbeys from the wreckage of the Revolution. So, at the age of twenty-seven, he embarked on an improbable project. First, he acquired the priory buildings at Solesmes. Then, he assembled a small band of priests. Finally, on 11 July 1833 – the feast day of St Benedict – the priests moved into their new home.

In just four years Solesmes was raised to the status of an abbey. It was the first religious community to be restored in France, and the first abbey established after the Revolution. Furthermore, because major monasteries like Cluny were still in ruins, it was now the leading religious foundation in France.

Over the next half-century, Solesmes grew in size and influence. When the original buildings became too small, its monks established communities in other abandoned monasteries, creating a network of religious houses that might one day rival Cluny. However, the Third Republic brought a second generation of anticlerical politicians to power, who campaigned for the separation of church and state – no Catholic schools, nor hospitals, nor any other institutions. By 1880, religious orders in France were banned again, and over the next two decades the monks at Solesmes were expelled three more times. Eventually they left for the Isle of Wight, where they would remain until after the First World War.

For much of this period, the abbey buildings lay empty and abandoned. During the war, they were requisitioned by

the health ministry and turned into a sanatorium for tuberculosis patients. The great cellblock was filled with hospital
beds and doctors occupied the surrounding houses.

Once the war was over, the departmental authorities hoped
to acquire the site as a permanent sanatorium. But the buildings belonged to a local landowner, who wished to restore
them to the original community. Though it was another four
years before the monks' exile ended, eventually they were
allowed to return home.

Trials can build belief as much as break it. In the case of
Solesmes, persecution gave them a purpose and suffering a
kind of strength. All these obstacles were tests of faith, the
community growing more committed each time it faced
destruction. When they were bullied or banned, threatened
with arrest or sent into exile, they could take courage from
the way the first Christians welcomed death. Because the
longing for martyrdom was the shadow side of their faith:
the wish to make that absolute sacrifice.

Suffering was the reason Weil came to Solesmes. The reason
she left her family's flat in Paris, caught the morning train
from Gare Montparnasse and travelled to the station at
Sablé-sur-Sarthe. On Palm Sunday she arrived in the village,
remaining there for the next eight days.

During Holy Week the place was busy with pilgrims: the
men staying with the monks in the abbey and the women
with the nuns at the nearby convent of St Cecilia. But Weil

was visiting with her mother, so they chose one of the hotels in the village where the meals were more generous and the timetable less strict. Most of these hotels were full as well, with queues forming at the door of the boulangerie and the counter of the café.

Mother and daughter made a curious couple. Selma was fifty-nine, a dumpy woman given to wearing navy Basque berets. Simone was in her late twenties, pale and delicate and dressed in shapeless sets of clothes – baggy skirts, loose capes – that barely disguised her slender figure. Where Selma was lively and a little dominating, with a taste for holidays and lavish treats, her daughter was much more frugal. As a result, when Selma wanted to feed asparagus to the family, she would claim the vegetables were being given away in the market or unearthed from a rubbish bin. She also nicknamed her daughter *la trollesse* and worried she was unsuitable for marriage.

If Wittgenstein was born into wealth and Jones into the petite bourgeoisie, Weil was raised among the prosperous professionals of the Sixth arrondissement. Selma belonged to a well-off family of Russian Jews who had emigrated to Antwerp from Rostov-on-Don, but kept little attachment to religious tradition. Her husband Bernard's family were strictly Orthodox – Jewish merchants who had lived for several generations in Strasbourg – but he became a doctor and a committed atheist. According to one account, Weil did not know she was Jewish until her older brother, André, was told by their parents at the age of fourteen. André grew up an atheist just like his father, not to mention a brilliant mathematician, while his sister decided when young that the question of God's existence was too difficult to solve. For all it seemed important, reaching the wrong answer was such a grave mistake that it was better to leave well alone.

Pain was what changed her perspective. The headaches began in her last year at university, when studying philosophy at the École Normale Supérieure. This was the most competitive of France's *grandes écoles*, and even though women had been allowed to attend since 1910, Weil was the only one in her class. She was revising for her final exams – feverishly attempting to read through much of classical, medieval and modern philosophy – when she began to feel a compressing sensation in her forehead. At times the pain was so intense she had to lie on the floor, helpless even to open her eyes.

Once the migraine had passed, Weil was forced to rest in bed for several days, refusing food in case it made her vomit. Yet this did not damage her final performance, and, in the exam required to teach philosophy, she was ranked seventh out of 107 candidates. But the headaches recurred throughout her adult life, and by her late twenties Weil had no choice except taking a sabbatical from her teaching career and spending six weeks at a Swiss clinic in the spring of 1936.

Midway through the stay, Weil accompanied her father to Zurich to consult an ophthalmologist. Because their trip was made during Easter, they stopped at the Abbey of

Einsiedeln to hear the community's famous choir. The abbey's main church was a monument to the Baroque, its ceilings overflowing with angels and painted saints cluttering the sky. Meanwhile, its Lady chapel housed a Madonna and Child in a tomb of dark stone, the statue's skin blackened by smoke from centuries of votive candles.

Weil sat in her pew for one service after another, mesmerised by the voices of the monks as they recited the Easter liturgy. Neither the clinic nor the ophthalmologist could cure her migraines, but when she listened to the chant with complete concentration, she experienced a brief release from pain.

A year later, the migraines were worse than ever. Weil applied for a second period of medical leave and visited a surgeon in case she had a brain tumour. The doctor could discover no tumour, nor any other cause for her headaches, but she never returned to the classroom. As she eventually wrote, from 1938 her 'whole existence was blotted out by physical pain', and in despair she even considered suicide. 'A time came, when I thought my soul menaced, through exhaustion and an aggravation of the pain, by such a hideous and total breakdown that I spent several weeks of anguished uncertainty whether death was not my imperative duty – although it seemed to me appalling that my life should end in horror.'

Rather than end her life, Weil went in search of the singing again. She did not return to Switzerland, but travelled to the Abbey Solesmes, where the monks were said to perform the purest chant in Europe. If Wittgenstein's retreat was a moral project and Jones's a creative one, for Weil the purpose was therapeutic. She came to the abbey to find a cure in the soothing sound of the chant.

Healing was once the main reason for retreat. People would withdraw to hospital wards run by monks and nuns, or holy shrines said to cure the sick. Medieval Europe was filled with pilgrim sites that promised the lame would walk and the blind would see and the dying be restored to life. This practice remained strong into the twentieth century, and during the decades between the wars hundreds of thousands visited places like Lourdes to bathe in the waters that poured from the grotto.

Solesmes was no healing shrine, but it still attracted pilgrims. By this point, it was the largest Benedictine foundation in France, responsible for a dozen other religious houses, in England and Canada, Luxembourg and Spain. It was also an important member of the Liturgical Movement, the late-nineteenth-century attempt to revive traditional practices in sacred art, architecture and worship, while updating them for modern tastes. In the year before Weil's visit, Solesmes had celebrated its anniversary – 100 years since the community was raised to the status of an abbey – building a new cloister to mark the occasion.

The abbey was also famous for the quality of its music, which the monks had revived after centuries of neglect.

During Holy Week, crowds of people would assemble outside the church, before funnelling through the double doors and taking their places in the crowded pews. Then they would sit in silence as the service began, the monks' voices echoing down the nave and round the ancient chapels.

That Holy Week of 1938, it was forbidden to reserve seats in the church. However, thanks to a local contact, Bernard Weil had booked places for his wife and daughter. Though Selma soon grew bored with the chant, Simone kept returning to the dim solitude of the church, attending every service until the guests at the hotel began remarking on her piety. How devoted. How disciplined. How curious she's not a Christian.


Next morning I decided to explore the abbey. Yesterday's brightness had given way to rain, leaving a crystal gleam on the gravel of the enclosure and the grass in the gardens glossy with damp. The air was bitter like the flavour of frost, mixed with the foulness of wet earth and wet paving stones, too. The birdsong stilled, the spring colours stalled, the season doubting whether to turn.

In the last few days, a great cloud of dust had blown in from the Sahara and spread through the skies of Europe, the air in Madrid turning orange while the snow in the Alps was sprinkled with sand. Overnight, the cloud had moved over Solesmes, tainting the atmosphere with a reddish brown, like the sepia stain of an antique photograph.

The abbey occupied a sloping space between the village and the river, hemmed in on one side by water, and by the high street on the other side. As a result, the layout was cramped, with buildings positioned wherever space could be made and different styles fitted together over several centuries, giving an accidental feel to the design. In places, the architecture pressed close enough to confuse any sense of scale, like one of those houses with too many angles designed by M.C. Escher.

At the far end of the garden, a dozen steps led down to the bank. Footpaths bordered the abbey's base, with orchards and meadows separating the main cellblock from the water. That building rose above the river like a cliff, its façade honeycombed with buttresses and arches, vaulted chambers and balustraded balconies, and flanked by a pair of blockish towers ten storeys tall.

The morning was overcast and the river appeared settled. As I walked along the bank, the dim mass of the cellblock doubled up in the water, its walls descending deep beneath the surface. In that sodden light, the place looked ancient to me, a patina of lichen patching the building's skin, which was elsewhere blotted by pollution. This was not the regal grandeur of Klosterneuburg, nor the eccentric solitude of Caldey; the abbey was not trying to impress, nor was it attempting to charm. Instead there was something monstrous about the place, as if the monks were entombed in a mausoleum.

Beside the main building stood a smaller courtyard of

cream-coloured stone. Their two designs had little in common, like a neoclassical château next door to a medieval fortress. That courtyard housed the original priory, built with all the symmetry and restraint of the eighteenth century. At a glance you might guess the gothic cellblock was the older one, a relic left behind from the Middle Ages, constructed on a scale even history could not humble. In fact, the cellblock was completed in 1896, a few months after the Lumière brothers gave their first public screening in Paris. So this was a modern building meant to look ancient, its endurance an elaborate conjuring trick. But there was something uncanny about the reconstruction, and rather than giving a stamp of authenticity, it added to the sense of illusion. As if the community had not stepped back into history, but retreated into a dream of the past.

After walking along the river's edge, I returned to the enclosure and the abbey church. This was the oldest part of Solesmes, built in the eleventh century, rebuilt in the fifteenth and expanded in the nineteenth. The newer section of the church lay at the far end, where the altar occupied a hall of pale stone. The near end was a gaunt medieval nave lined with side chapels, each one containing a tiny window fitted with dark panes of glass, making their shrines look murky.

During the daytime services, the bays at the back of the nave were submerged in shadow. The level of light increased as you approached the sanctuary, pouring down from the plain glass windows on either side of the choir. A wooden crucifix was fixed above the altar, slender as a split in the plaster, and a trace of incense lingered in the air, like the scent of smoke from a blackened hearth where a fire once burned.

There was nobody else in the church that morning and my breath began to cloud before my face. Passing from the nave to the transept, I found myself surrounded by dozens of sculpted figures. On the south side, Christ was laid into a tomb; on the north side, Mary was placed in her own sepulchre. Circling them were more sculpted figures, crowding together to create a busy stage of saints, all sharing the utter stillness.

Another statue stood midway down the nave, this one depicting St Peter. The body was almost life-size, its limbs and robes dense as the grey slabs from which the church was built. An inscription was carved on the base in Latin, Greek and French. CONTEMPLATE THE GOD WHO IS WORD, it said, THE ROCK DIVINELY HEWN IN GOLD. FOUNDED ON IT, I AM UNSHAKEABLE.

Weil's pew was opposite this statue. Here she sat through one service after another, her headaches so excruciating that her body became contorted with pain. Years later, in a letter to a priest, she described listening to the music of the monks as it swelled from the choir to fill the church. Even though she was hunched over at the far end of the bench, the sound drew Weil outside herself.

I was suffering from splitting headaches; each sound hurt me like a blow; by an extreme effort of concentration I was able to rise above this wretched flesh, to leave it to suffer by itself, heaped up in a corner, and to find a pure and perfect joy in the unimaginable beauty of the chanting and the words. This experience enabled me by analogy to get a better understanding of the possibility of loving divine love in the midst of affliction. It goes without saying that in the course of these services the thought of the Passion of Christ entered into my being once and for all.

Simone Weil was a socialist, an anarchist and an activist for workers' rights. So what was she doing in a Catholic abbey, listening to plainchant and talking about the Passion of Christ? The truth was that, after a decade of campaigning for the far Left, she had begun to doubt her own doubt.

At the age of ten, Weil became a Bolshevik, taking part in protests throughout her teenage years. By her early twenties she had attended the meetings of trade unions, taught evening classes to miners, and attempted to find a job on a farm or fishing boat. Then, starting in 1934, she spent a year working on a factory floor.

In fact, it was closer to half a year: two months on the assembly line at Alsthom; a month at the Carnaud factory making gas masks and oil cans; and then another two months at one of the Renault factories. From the start, Weil was a poor fit for factory work, wearing a white blouse on her very first day, which was filthy and torn by the end of her shift. Over the next few weeks she lacerated her hand with metal shavings and flattened the end of her thumb, while also coming down with fever, burns and an ear infection. Even when she was not injured, she was overwhelmed by the heat, the noise and the suffocating odours – as well as the constant fear of missing her quotas or being fired for some other reason.

Eventually Weil realised that the easiest way to endure factory work was to adopt a state of passive submission. However, the fact that she entered this state of willing bondage made it harder for her to believe the labouring classes would one day unite to claim their political rights. After all, the best way to cope was complete surrender, turning yourself into a machine.

Writing about the year she spent working in factories, Weil would later report that: 'The contact with affliction killed my youth . . . There I received the mark of slavery.' This mark was the loss of individual dignity, smothered by the relentless rhythms of industrial machinery. She still hoped to restore that dignity via political means, yet she now questioned the practicality of her dream.

In early autumn of 1935, Bernard and Selma took their daughter on a tour of Portugal's northern shore. The coast between Porto and Viana do Castelo was lined with fishing villages that still followed a strict caste system, preserving many of the traditions that had disappeared in the rest of the country. Men dressed in coloured waistcoats and women in patterned headscarves, while their boats were powered by sails and oars.

One evening Weil left her parents behind to walk along a coastal path. As she eventually wrote: 'In this state of mind then, and in a wretched condition physically, I entered the little Portuguese village, which, alas, was very wretched too, on the very day of the festival of its patron saint. I was alone. It was the evening and there was a full moon over the sea. The wives of the fishermen were, in procession, making a tour of all the ships, carrying candles and singing what must certainly be very ancient hymns of a heart-rending sadness.'

Weil told nobody what she had seen that night, only describing the encounter some five or six years later. This gap may explain the vagueness of her story: the unnamed village, the moonlit scene, the timeless rite carried out for a solitary witness. Still, there are enough clues from the account to work out what she observed.

The holiday took place in the middle of September, meaning the ceremony probably marked the feast of Our Lady of Sorrows. This is the moment when the Church commemorates Mary as a grieving mother, and the hymns Weil heard were most likely lamenting the loss of her child. Some of the participants would have been praying for their husbands, brothers and sons to remain safe at sea; others would have been mourning the family members taken by the waves. Here, on the western edge of Europe, where the modern world left little trace, she might have recalled that Christ sought his first followers among fishermen. And recalled that Christ preached his message to the lowliest members of society: the lepers and prostitutes, the outcasts and thieves. And recalled Christ's teaching that those who had fallen farthest in this world would be raised highest in the kingdom to come. Even if Weil did not remember these details, it would have been clear that the fishing communities were not hoping for revolution in this life, but for restitution in the next one, when every wound will be healed and every loss restored. Because the happy have less need for hope; it's those who are suffering who seek salvation.

After this encounter, Weil came to see religion less as an intellectual proposition than a social force, binding together the dispossessed. 'There the conviction was suddenly borne in upon me that Christianity is pre-eminently the religion of slaves, that slaves cannot help belonging to it, and I among others.' She even began asking herself if there was another way justice might be achieved: not by setting the slave free, but by sharing in his or her suffering.

If factory work was the first reason for Weil's political disenchantment, her experience in Spain was the second. In the twelve months before the visit to Solesmes, Japan and China went to war and Italy left the League of Nations. Four weeks before the Easter retreat, German troops marched into Austria and annexed the entire country. Then, during Holy Week, the newspapers were filled with stories from Spain, as the Nationalist armies reached the Mediterranean and split the Republican forces in two.

Weil's own visit to Spain in the summer of 1936 had been a farce. She hoped to fight for the Republican cause, but her war ended before firing a single shot. A few days after joining her unit on the River Ebro, she stepped into a cooking pot filled with boiling oil. Though she was wearing a hiking boot that protected her foot, her lower leg was badly burned, the cotton socks and khaki trousers scalding onto the skin.

Travelling back to Barcelona, Weil chanced upon her parents sitting in a café, having crossed the border to search for their daughter. When her father saw how seriously she was injured, he took her straight to hospital. At first, Weil was placed in the military hospital at Sitgès, where she was visited by two members of her unit. These soldiers related how, during the recent fighting, they chanced upon a fifteen-year old member of the Phalangists playing dead. The teenage boy was taken to Durruti, the leader of the campaign, who offered to spare his life if he joined the anarchist cause. When the boy refused, he was shot.

This story marked the start of Weil's break with party politics. She explained why in a letter, written around the time of her visit to Solesmes and sent to the author Georges

Bernanos. 'Although I only heard it afterward, the death of this little hero never ceased to weigh on my conscience. Such an atmosphere immediately wipes out the very goal of the struggle.'

Weil had recently finished reading Bernanos's book about the war in Spain, *Les Grands Cimetières sous la lune* (1938). The author was a Catholic and a conservative who lived in Majorca, yet his writing denounced the ruthless tactics of the Nationalist army. Though their political views had little in common, Weil admired the honest criticism of his own side, writing to share her experience of fighting for the Republicans. 'One sets out as a volunteer with the idea of sacrifice,' her letter concluded, 'and finds oneself in a war which resembles a war of mercenaries, only with much more cruelty and with less human respect for the enemy.'

The idea of sacrifice. She would have been glad to give up her life, so long as she believed in the cause. But the ruthlessness of war, and the internal politics of the Republican factions, made such idealism impossible to sustain. Though Weil kept supporting the fight against Franco, she had lost faith in any political solution. And, soon after she left Spain, her unit was wiped out by the Nationalist forces, with every single woman killed.

At this point Weil still called herself a pacifist. In the face of fascist aggression, however, she started to question her commitment. A few months before coming to Solesmes, she read T. E. Lawrence's *Seven Pillars of Wisdom* and was seduced by his account of the Arab Revolt. She started showing Lawrence's picture to friends, comparing his appearance to 'an angel' and referring to him as 'an artist, a scholar, and with all this a kind of saint . . . I don't know of any historical figure in any age who expressed so fully what I admire.'

Lawrence reminded Weil of Leo Tolstoy and Francis of Assisi. Both were wealthy men who turned their back on privilege; both were former soldiers who spread the message of peace. All three had forfeited their status in the eyes of society, sacrificing themselves rather than surrender their principles. Weil even hoped that Lawrence had faked his death to be free of his fame, meaning she could meet him one day.

Shortly before coming to Solesmes, Weil wrote to David Garnett – the author who edited Lawrence's letters – repeating her claim that the Englishman was the first historical figure she could completely love and admire. Even though he was a natural leader, he remained committed to living on equal terms with those around him. This, Weil believed, was the reason he later entered the air force at the lowest possible rank: 'Who knows the whole extent of the empire of might and at the same time despises it?' she asked Garnett. 'T. E. Lawrence, the liberator of Arabia, was one.' The greatest act of heroism was not gaining power, but giving it up.

Lawrence thought of himself as a writer pulled into the world of action. When confronted by celebrity, he withdrew into solitude and anonymity. In fact, the modesty of his later military career resembled the severe routines of monasticism, living in the simplest conditions and performing only the most basic work. His final home at Clouds Hill was a kind of hermitage too – a whitewashed cottage in the Dorset woods with no kitchen or working loo – while his sudden death in a motorbike accident turned him into a secular martyr. And the more Weil learned about Lawrence's life, the more she dreamed of achieving her own martyrdom too.

In Portugal Weil had seen how religion could console the lowest classes of society. In Spain she had seen how war could corrupt any political cause. But one final lesson was required for her conversion: an encounter with the beauty of belief. That lesson came in Italy, a year before the Holy Week retreat.

Six months after joining the International Brigades, Weil travelled to the clinic in Switzerland seeking a cure for her migraines. Once her stay at the clinic was complete, she crossed the Alps and spent the spring of 1937 travelling round Italy. Over the next few weeks she visited Milan, Bologna, Ferrara, Ravenna, Florence and Rome, before journeying north towards Perugia.

Weil adored the gentle folds and gorgeous greens of Tuscany, as well as the carved classical majesty of Rome. But it was the mountainous region of Umbria that made the deepest impression, especially the landscape around Assisi. The town was spread over the western flank of Mount

Subasio, a great limestone boulder breaking out from the forested slopes of the Apennine Range. To the west was the Basilica of St Francis – a fortress of whitewashed brick set on immense arcades of stone – but Weil spent most of her time in a second basilica at the base of the mountain.

Santa Maria degli Angeli was another mass of marble, housing the tiny chapel where Francis founded his first convent. This was a simple space built from rough squares of rock, with bare walls and whitewashed ceilings. Frescoes covered the apse on the north-east side, painted on wooden panels and backed with beaten gold: here Francis walked in the company of angels; there he knelt before Pope Innocent III; and there he stood naked and wrapped in brambles, his halo bright as a crown.

In Rome, Weil had passed an entire Sunday at St Peter's. The music and voices, the sculptures and paintings, the crowds of believers filling the basilica – all this seemed a total aesthetic experience. However, it was not the triumphant pageant of St Peter's that moved her most, but the touching scenes in this tiny chapel, its frescoes vivid as Byzantine icons, its miracles garish with gilded light.

'There, alone in the little twelfth-century Romanesque chapel of Santa Maria degli Angeli, an incomparable marvel of purity where St Francis often used to pray, something stronger than I was compelled me for the first time in my life to go down on my knees.'

Up to this point, Weil was troubled most by the suffering

214

of the poor. This was a political impulse rather than a religious one, but now she wondered whether faith offered a more profound form of justice. The figure of St Francis was one answer to that question: the spoiled young man who left behind the wanton privilege of his youth to live in poverty and simplicity. Francis's life was one long act of penance, abasing himself for the sake of belief, but these humiliations inspired thousands to lives of charity.

Of course, none of this explains why a non-believer would bow down in prayer. But, during this trip Weil wrote a letter to a friend, arguing that, 'Nothing is more beautiful than the Catholic liturgy.' Later, in her wartime journals, she claimed, 'Through joy, the beauty of the world penetrates into our souls. Through sorrow, it enters us through the body.' Weil felt the splendour of beauty as acutely as the sharpness of pain. Both seemed a tangible presence that could render the body insensate, and both became a route out of the self towards the everlasting. Her response was less an intellectual assent than a physical surrender, so astounded by the interior of the chapel that she dropped down to her knees in prayer.

A few years later, in an essay titled 'Forms of the Implicit Love of God', Weil wrote that 'beauty is eternity here below'. In other words, beauty is the closest we can come to the everlasting, not because it shares in some flawless order found outside time, but because it displaces the finite self with a feeling of infinite awe. However, it was not until

Weil heard the chant at Solesmes that she realised how suffering and beauty might be experienced at the same time, the one making sense of the other.

Weil attended every service, so I tried to do the same. Matins was the least popular, drawing maybe half the guests from the hostel. More guests came to mid-morning mass, or else the lunchtime prayers of Sext and None. Afternoon Vespers had the largest congregation, a mixture of locals, tourists and a handful of nuns from the nearby convent who sat very close to the front. Then the crowds thinned for evening Compline, until the few worshippers were outnumbered by monks.

Each service followed a similar pattern. The community would enter from a door in the transept, lining up in the stalls on either side of the choir. Then the congregation would rise from their pews, feet stamping, furniture scraping, waiting for the chant to begin. Next, one of the monks would sing a single note or phrase, the rest of the choir joining in a moment later, their murmured voices amplified by the speakers mounted on the walls and sounding round the stone chambers of the church.

The community recited psalms in regular succession, while the congregation listened in a kind of dutiful silence. It was a simpler sound than I had expected, closer to speech than to song, and the delivery was much more functional, like reading a list or reciting the terms of a contract.

Or perhaps I was not trying hard enough. Occasionally

I would close my eyes and wait for the sound to carry me from the room. I would listen as the deep beating of the bass blended with the baritone's throb and the gentle purring of the tenor. But after a few minutes I became bored with the sound, scanning the faces of the congregation and wondering what they could hear. I assumed the music must be painting gorgeous pictures in their minds, but for some reason I lacked the imagination to conjure these images myself.

Nonetheless, I kept coming to the services and kept listening to the chant. The community contained some forty or fifty monks, gathering here six times a day. Their shortest services were fifteen minutes, the longest more than an hour, and most of the time was spent singing. Sometimes the singing was a call and response, the voice of the cantor posing a question that was answered by the rest of the choir. Other times the two stalls would sing at intervals, swapping lines back and forth to create an antiphon. Even though the music was repetitive, the iterations contained slight variations, so that sitting through a service I might have been watching a candle burn, each line similar yet never quite the same. Like the pulse and flicker of a flame, or the breathing of a body in sleep.

The music was meant to sound as if it had survived uncorrupted from the past. The choir's technique added to this effect: the first syllables firm but the final syllables faint; the phrases soaring but the peaks soft. Then, as the chant drew to a close, the voices would ebb and slow, until the whole church seemed to settle like the rippled surface of a lake becoming placid once more.

Sitting in the chapel one afternoon, I tried to recall Weil's account of the services – the splitting headaches, the beautiful chant, the love that was located in the midst of affliction. Though I struggled to understand how the music turned her into a believer, I remembered that between the singing she also listened to the Gospel accounts of the Passion. She would have learned how Christ was stripped and beaten, spat upon and mocked. How he was tied to a column and scourged with whips; how he was dressed in a crown of thorns and the purple robes of a king. How he was nailed hand and foot to the cross, hanging until the breath left his body.

The Easter story is so familiar, it can be easy to forget the horror it describes: a man rejected and humiliated and tortured to death. Whether or not that man was the Son of God, this story of suffering has been placed at the centre of the religion and turned into a symbol of overcoming death. That story could not cure her pain, but it might be able to make it meaningful.

'The Passion of Christ entered my being once and for all,' Weil wrote, referring to the arrest and trial, the crucifixion and death. Yet the modern meaning of the word can also be found in that phrase: passion as love, as adoration, as overwhelming emotion. In Weil's version of events these two meanings come together: passion as agony and passion as ecstasy. On hearing the chant at Solesmes, the one was transformed into the other.

But what exactly did Weil hear? That question is hard to answer without some understanding of Gregorian chant. When Dom Guéranger refounded Solesmes in 1833, the monks owned no manuscripts or songbooks. So he sent members of the community to visit the great libraries of Europe and copy the oldest manuscripts they could find. Then they would return to the abbey's scriptorium and transcribe them into modern texts.

Gregorian chant consists of prayers and psalms recited in Latin, used for the mass and other daily services. It's monophonic music, with a single melody designed around modes that set the pitch, the mood, the tone. It also relies on a technique called *melisma*, where several notes are sung to one syllable, so that words cascade across musical phrases.

The chant was attributed to a sixth-century pope, Gregory I, patron saint of musicians, singers and students. It actually dates from a few centuries later, when the relative stability of Carolingian rule allowed for the rhythms of religious practice in Western Europe to standardise. The music itself was assembled from Roman and Galician traditions, creating a sound that was collective but also anonymous, beautiful but also simple. This meant it could be sung by choirs of every level, from the smallest convent to the grandest cathedral.

Gregorian chant was used in the daily worship of religious

communities throughout the Middle Ages. However, towards the end of this period, composers began bringing together multiple melodic lines to be sung at the same time. The result was polyphonic chant – different voices reciting different melodies – which transformed the possibilities for a piece of music. During the Renaissance, the technical skill of the composer and the vocal range of the choir overtook the plain recitation of the text. By the time of the Reformation, local languages and musical traditions were increasingly incorporated into worship, meaning Gregorian chant became even less important.

For Dom Guéranger, these variations were a corruption. He attempted to recover the original sound through close study of medieval manuscripts. The first choirmaster at the abbey, Dom Joseph Pothier, based his chant on the stresses of the syllables in the Latin texts, resulting in a non-metred rhythm using notes of equal value. He also revised the scores, adapting the neumes found in these texts – the tiny marks above each word, indicating the tone and duration of the syllables – to a fixed form of square notation.

In the latter decades of the nineteenth century, Solesmes began to publish choir books based on their manuscript research. These were both works of scholarship and historical fantasies, featuring the kind of gothic script and medieval ornament made popular by the workshops of William Morris. Thanks to the spread of photographic technology, the monks could also create microforms of the original manuscripts, which were collected and compared in the workshops at Solesmes. Later editions of the books even contained facsimiles of the medieval sources to prove the purity of their chant.

But scholars soon started to question these methods. After all, the neumes used in medieval music served as mnemonic aids rather than melodic guides. Liturgical manuscripts were ambiguous and a degree of guesswork was required alongside any palaeographic analysis. According to critics, the monks at Solesmes inserted notation in some places, and in other places ignored the existing marks – imposing their own rhythms on the music while claiming to have discovered its authentic sound. What's more, in presenting Gregorian chant as something fixed, they ignored the rich variety of the tradition by replacing it with an imagined ideal.

Nonetheless, the chants developed at Solesmes were simple to understand and beautiful to sing. They soon spread to other religious communities, as well as smaller congregations. Even when the monks were exiled to the Isle of Wight in 1901, they continued producing definitive versions of each chant. By 1907, their work was endorsed by the Vatican.

A few years after the exile ended, the community released their first vinyl recording. It contained the *Sanctus* and *Agnus Dei*, the antiphon *Salve Regina* and the introit *Spiritus Domini*, the offertories and communions, and the final *Kyrie*. That recording had since been uploaded onto YouTube and most evenings in the guest house I would listen to the album again. The sound was much closer to the rough chanting of a crowd than the elegant harmonies of a choir, softened by the hiss of the needle and the cracks in the vinyl.

Each time I played the album, my mind travelled back to the dim corners of the church. Then the chant ended and the voices lapsed into crackling silence, the record lasting a few moments longer to capture the heavy hush after the singing stopped. It was the silence of the choir and the congregation too, their lips no longer moving, their breath becoming still. The silence Weil would have heard when she sat through the Easter services.

Every day new pilgrims came to stay. A handsome young lawyer with an aristocratic surname, who wore a leather biker jacket and a pair of perfectly fitted chinos. A student from Paris with the beginnings of a beard, who rolled cigarettes in the library before slipping outside to smoke. A middle-aged man who dressed all in black: loose trousers of black linen, a ribbed turtleneck of black cotton and Birkenstocks made from black rubber.

At lunchtime we gathered in the monks' refectory. This was a great stone hall with a vaulted roof and a row of granite columns running down the middle. It formed the centrepiece of the nineteenth-century cellblock, with a double hearth at the far end the size of a small cave. Our tables were placed between the columns, while the members of the community sat along the walls, bowing over their trays of food and eating as quickly as possible.

I often found myself sitting with three priests from northern Italy. They were staying at Solesmes for much of Lent, studying medieval manuscripts in the palaeographic workshop. One resembled a priest from a period drama, with a fur-trimmed overcoat and a felt fedora that he wore every time he stepped outside. Another had the bald head and chubby cheeks of a child, his eyes small and squashing smaller when he laughed, his temples creased with dozens of crinkles.

The midday meal was generous: wine on the tables, trays of fish and meat, as well as several servings of cheese. Often, the baby-faced priest piled my plate with extra food, whether or not I had asked for more. Meanwhile, one of the monks stood at a pulpit, reading from works of religious history. A few times I tried to listen, but soon lost my way among the lists of popes: Boniface and Honorius, Callixtus and Clement, Innocent the Second, the Fifth, the Seventh. Nobody else was allowed to talk, and the rest of the guests used a silent language of gesture and mime as they exchanged the trays of food, the earthenware jugs. But the baby-faced priest often whispered at me, until another guest motioned for him to keep quiet and his lip folded into a fleshy pout.

As we left the dining hall, my companion would start complaining, telling me that he regretted coming to the abbey for Lent. The food was too plain, the weather too cold, the guest quarters too crowded with pilgrims. He also complained that, since the Second Vatican Council, the revival of Gregorian Chant had gone into reverse and even Solesmes had few scholars now. When I asked about his faith more generally, he claimed that the pope was a prostitute, the Church was corrupt, and nobody cared about the liturgy these days.

After lunch we assembled in the guests' dining hall. This was a modern space big enough to seat sixty, with long glass windows looking out on the gardens and an abstract work of art covering one wall. Breakfast and dinner were served here in Lent, and a stubborn set of machines provided coffee during the day. The evening meals were always modest by comparison, and each time that same priest tried the bland soup, the boiled vegetables, the yellow stodge of the risotto, his mouth puckered up in a show of disgust, or else turned down in a pantomime frown.

At one of the lunchtime coffee breaks, I began speaking with the Knights of Malta. I had already spotted them attending mass, where they dressed in dark robes with bands of white at the collars and cuff, as well as Maltese crosses appliquéd to the chest. Even when they stripped their robes, they still seemed to be wearing a uniform: tweed jackets and corduroy trousers, woollen waistcoats and cravats of coloured silk. And they still moved about in a stately manner, pacing from the guest quarters to the dining hall as if braced in suits of armour.

There were sixteen knights in total, most in their late sixties. They came from prosperous cities and suburbs like Orléans and Fontainebleau, Versailles and Saint-Cloud. Some had worked as lawyers and accountants, others were civil servants or the owners of family businesses. Their tweed jackets were buttoned tight, and their signet rings flashed on plump little fingers, and they snorted as they they struggled to work the coffee machine.

When I spoke with these men after lunch, they talked to me about history. How de Gaulle shaped the Fifth Republic in his image; how Napoleon fell out with the Papal States. But, when I asked why they had come on retreat, the conversation stalled.

'It's tradition,' said one. 'Every Lent we visit an abbey,' added another. 'We've been doing it for decades now,' a third chipped in. 'Otherwise, we never see each other.'

I tried asking more questions – Why Solesmes? Why the Knights of Malta? – but their answers became vague, repeating words like *honneur* and *respect*. 'These words are not in fashion any more,' one of them explained, before turning to speak with a priest who had entered the room, bringing our conversation to an end.

Watching the knights that week, their religion seemed a social distinction, like reading the right newspaper or belonging to the right club. Whatever their reason for coming on retreat, it had little to do with rejecting the things the public seemed to prize. Instead, their faith meant a sense of order and stability, the one constant in a changing world. Most afternoons they would gather in the guesthouse chapel for lectures or prayers, and even though I had no wish to join them, I was left feeling out of place.

Loneliness is not an absence of company, but connection; though I was surrounded by pilgrims in Solesmes, I did not feel like I belonged.

However, on Wednesday evening I was invited to dinner. My host was a local landowner, living in a large house on the far side of the Sarthe. It was his family that had acquired the abbey buildings when the monks went into exile, returning them to the community in 1922. His name – surprise, surprise – was Guy.

I was picked up at seven o'clock outside the abbey gates. Guy arrived in an aging jeep with a French pointer propped on the passenger seat. The dog had a charcoal coat and a beseeching gaze, while my host had a loud voice and a cheerful expression. Parking opposite the slate-topped benches, he waved for me to step inside, before driving fast down the high street.

The family home stood on a low hill across the valley. We arrived in the early evening, winding through the wooded grounds before coming to a stop on the gravel drive. Guy explained how the first house dated back to the seventeenth century, but the whole place was rebuilt between the wars – around the same time Weil came to Solesmes. Now it was a neoclassical château of dull yellow stone, three storeys high with steep mansard roofs and windows dressed in white stone.

My host's study lay at the end of a long corridor, its walls papered with floral patterns and its wainscoting painted a mossy green. Thick carpet cushioned the floor, while the sofa sagged so deep that sitting down felt like being swallowed. Books had been piled on the side tables or laid out on the coffee table; Guy enthused about one history of the writers who came to Solesmes, and another on the musicians and composers who visited the abbey as well.

When I asked about about some of the pilgrims to Solesmes, my host started discussing the Empress Zita, wife of the exiled Habsburg emperor. He also mentioned one of the Bourbon-Parma princes, a claimant to the throne of Spain who was buried in the abbey grounds. Three more members of the royal family became nuns in the next-door convent. But Simone Weil was the pilgrim who interested him most. He had read all her works and most of the biographies. 'A genius,' he told me, 'but too clever, too extreme. That's why she never felt at home in the Church.'

When I asked him to explain, Guy said that the Church was not meant for saints. 'Saints are not an example the rest of us should follow: they're a symbol of what might be possible. The Church is reserved for sinners.'

Half an hour later we left the study, passing through a modern kitchen and into the dining room. Here the walls were hung with hunting scenes and crushed velvet curtains were drawn across the windows. The two of us sat at one end of the table, eating roast pheasant on a bed of Brussels sprouts. Then Guy offered me yoghurt or cheese, and when

I asked for both he joked about the Lenten regime at Solesmes.

'No meat, no dessert – it's like visiting a health spa.'

After several days of whispered politeness and tiptoed formality, it was a relief to leave behind the earnest quiet of the guest house. My host wore trousers of brown moleskin and an olive-coloured waistcoat with a herringbone pattern, yet he had none of the self-important seriousness of the Knights of Malta. As a young man he had dreams of becoming a writer, but now he worked in the hospitality industry, turning Paris apartment buildings into grand hotels. Though he lived in the capital during the week, he would often return to this house at weekends and host the monks from Solesmes.

At one point Guy told a story about a friend from his early life who attempted to become a monk. He joined a monastery for several years, only to realise he had no calling. 'My friend felt a failure because he never stayed, but I told him that being a monk was like being an astronaut: you've gone higher than most of us will ever reach. Even if he did not make it to the moon, it's a privilege to spend a little time in the stratosphere.' Guy stood from the table and gathered our plates, moving back into the kitchen. 'Like writing a book,' he went on. 'Most of us give up by the time we turn twenty.'

Once the meal was over, Guy showed me the rest of the house. During the winter months, the family lived in the northern wing and left the state rooms on the south side unoccupied. Now he turned the lock on a heavy door leading through to a suite of chambers with panelled walls and patterned moulding. One room was hung with Belgian tapestries, another lined with antique books, the third was cluttered with scroll-backed armchairs and a brocaded chaise longue.

Guy said little as we toured the house, reluctant to play the part of a guide. These traditional interiors recalled the careful copy of history I had found at Solesmes: the perfected past that exists only in the present. But the air in these rooms was bitter, with a smell like damp coins in the shuttered stillness, while the furniture looked brittle and stiff, as if the cabinets were never opened and the chairs never occupied.

Before I had left the abbey, Fr Bozell warned me that the gates to the enclosure were locked at ten o'clock, remaining shut until the following morning. When I reminded Guy of the curfew, his easy expression became alarmed, as if worried I would have to spend the night. Then he marched the length of the corridor, fetched our coats from the study and bustled me back into the jeep. As we accelerated through the pools of darkness drowning the park, I turned round to glimpse the château's mansard roofs like pyramids rising above the trees. Moments later the building disappeared from view, its lights a smear of stars against the sky and its enchanted proportions lost to the night.

Heading downhill towards the village, I asked Guy whether he had grown up in the house. He began talking about his grandparents, who owned the place when he was a child, filling it with family and friends, as well as nannies and house-keepers, gardeners and maids. Of course, nobody could afford so many staff these days, but it made the property feel much emptier, all those echoing rooms with nobody to use them, all those precious antiques shut up in the shadows. There was no trace of melancholy in his voice, let alone a nostalgic wish to bring back the past, only a confession that nothing could stay the same. Though I waited for him to keep speaking, from that point on he remained quiet, driving fast through the streets of Solesmes to reach the gates before curfew.

The next day, in the guesthouse library, I found a copy of the book Guy had shown me. Then I sat among the shelves for several hours, reading about the other pilgrims to Solesmes. Between regular periods of exile, the abbey welcomed journalists and writers, musicians and historians, come to witness this ancient way of life recreated in modern-day France.

Many of those who stayed at Solesmes were seeking a refuge from the dissipations of Paris. Surrounded by the routines of medieval monasticism, they glimpsed a deeper meaning their lives seemed to lack. The most well-known was Joris-Karl Huysmans, who became famous for his stories of aristocratic decadence and modern-day Satanism, inspiring Oscar Wilde and other fin-de-siècle dandies. Towards the end of the nineteenth century, Huysmans converted to Catholicism before building a house beside the Benedictine abbey in Ligugé and joining the order as a lay member.

He described this process in a series of semi-autobiographical novels: *En route* (1895), *La Cathédrale* (1898) and *L'Oblat* (1903). In the last of these three, the protagonist goes on retreat to Solesmes, attracted by the reputation of the chant and the spectacle of the ceremony. He even considers joining the monks, but is put off by the lack of solitude at the abbey and the sense of having entered a barracks. He also doubts whether he could write much in such a setting: living in that sombre village and surrounded by that dreary landscape. However, the beauty of the monks' life makes a deep impression on him: 'Solesmes stands alone; there is no place like it in the whole of France; religion there has an artistic splendour to be met with nowhere else.'

Huysmans' journey from disbelief to devotion was the most dramatic example of a wider trend. The poet Paul Claudel stayed at Solesmes in 1900 to test his vocation, wondering whether to abandon his diplomatic career and devote himself to God. The novelist Léon Bloy and the poet Charles Péguy both came here as well, journeying from unhappy agnosticism to committed Catholicism. So, too, Jacques Maritain and his wife Raïssa, who visited the monks in exile soon after their own conversion, while another doubting pilgrim – Antoine de Saint-Exupéry – wrote during the Second World War that, once the fighting was over, the only future he could endure was at the Abbey of Solesmes.

Seen in this light, the abbey becomes a refuge for writers

wearied by too many worldly pleasures, with salvation just another aesthetic experience, perhaps the most refined of all. However, they were not the only figures drawn towards monastic life, as the decades after the First World War saw a religious revival across much of France. The persecution that marked the first years of the Third Republic gave way to a renewal of popular piety: Catholic journals and societies, youth groups and political parties were started, while a new generation of Catholic craftsmen began restoring the churches damaged during the fighting. Solesmes took advantage of this movement by inviting Maurice Denis and Henri Charlier — two leading craftsmen of the revival — to decorate the abbey with sculpture and stained glass.

At first glance, the Catholic emphasis on tradition and dogma might seem a poor fit for twentieth-century France. But this strictness offered a set of fixed values that contrasted with the confusion of post-war Europe and the collapse of established hierarchies. Like the public intellectuals in Britain, who rejected secular society by converting to Rome, numerous French thinkers found security in the familiar rituals of the Catholic Church. Then, as the hedonism of the '20s gave way to the activism of the '30s and faith promised something more than security, the traditionalists were joined by idealists like Simone Weil, seeking a way for society to move beyond material values.

Some of the artists who retreated to Solesmes ended up staying. In fact, a pair of writers were living in the village during Weil's visit. The first was a poet called Pierre Reverdy, who once belonged to the artistic circles in Montmartre. As a young man he was friends with poets like Max Jacob and Guillaume Apollinaire, collaborated with artists like Picasso and Braque, had his portrait painted by Modigliani and started a relationship with Coco Chanel. However, at the end of this relationship he burned his manuscripts, before leaving Paris in 1926 for a cottage beside the abbey.

Reverdy remained in Solesmes all the rest of his life, visited now and then by his famous friends. But he kept away from the dissolute scenes of his youth and published almost nothing. His few poems from this period are filled with fugitive figures, lonely landscapes and gestures of farewell – a long goodbye to the bohemian society he had known. His letters echoed this message, as when he explained his retreat to Jacques Maritain: 'I need to die. That's right – to disappear, to become nothing [. . .] completely leaving behind the loneliness and the existent world and senseless whirlwind of men who still believe in other things than God and the life beyond this envelope of nothingness.'

Even before Reverdy's retreat, friends would comment on his apparent purity, yet there was something showy about this total separation from the past. Perhaps these writers and artists were trying to prove their dissolution by how devoted they had become, or substitute one kind of abandonment for another. If retreat can be a place of healing, the strict routines of religious life can also imitate the careful habits of the invalid. This we have seen already in the lives of Wittgenstein, Jones, and Weil: no cure but a new kind of sickness.

The spiritual tourists at the abbey were satirised in a short book published in 1925 called *Le Triptyque de Solesmes*. Its author, Marguerite Aron, identified the three types of pilgrim who visited Solesmes: the Aesthete, the Curious and the Well-Meaning Man. One is drawn for the architecture and liturgy, another out of a traveller's interest, while the third comes to the monastery to share in the monks' way of life. Unlike the anonymity Wittgenstein sought at Klosterneuburg, or the creative community Jones joined at Caldey, *Le Triptyque de Solesmes* suggests that Weil's trip was a highbrow holiday, the abbey an essential destination for any aspiring writer.

Aron was an author and teacher a generation older than Weil. She too was born in Paris and grew up in a secular Jewish family, converting to Catholicism at the start of the First World War, before retiring to a small house in Solesmes. That house was barely a hundred paces from the abbey entrance, and Weil would have passed by several times during her stay. There's no record of their ever meeting, but in Aron's later life we see a shadow of the fate that the younger woman was fortunate to escape.

Weil had an uneasy relationship with Judaism. Her writings often contrasted the lofty rationality of the Ancient Greeks with what she believed the base materiality of the Hebrews. But her attacks on Jewish religion came closer to bigotry, more vicious than any critique she made of the

Catholic Church. At the same time, she showed little concern for the contemporary suffering of Jews in Germany, and critics have wondered whether she simply absorbed the prejudices of the period, or whether this antisemitism was another example of her self-loathing.

André Weil believed that, had his sister survived, she would have eventually returned to the family faith. That said, during her life she identified little with Judaism, and when denied a teaching position in Vichy France because of her Jewish heritage, she wrote a sarcastic letter to the minister of education, claiming, 'The Hebrew tradition is foreign to me; no text of a law can change that for me.' Of course, for many of the Jews living in France, their ethnic and religious identity was something optional, and only the strict racial rules imposed by the Third Reich made assimilation impossible – conversion, too, as seen in the fate of Marguerite Aron.

Aron remained in the village for most of the war, until, leaving mass one morning, she was arrested by the Gestapo. Despite becoming a Catholic several decades ago, she was transferred to Drancy and then deported to Auschwitz. She died on 14 February 1944.

Weil encountered all three types of pilgrim at Solesmes. The Curious was an American named Charles Greenleaf Bell, who was studying for a degree at Oxford and hoped to become a writer. He spent several hours discussing Shakespeare with Weil, and even showed her some of his poetry. At the time she was reading Marlowe's *Doctor Faustus*, so she nicknamed him the 'devil boy'.

Bell was born in Mississippi in the year 1910 and earned a physics degree from the University of Virginia. He then won a Rhodes Scholarship to spend two years in England, bringing him to Europe shortly before the war. In the spring of 1938 he visited Solesmes, only to learn that every cell in the abbey was booked for Holy Week. However, an American friend found him an attic room in a hotel, which was how he came to meet his fellow pilgrim.

After the war, Bell taught at a number of colleges in America and began to publish poems. By the '60s he had produced a pair of novels, the second containing a loosely fictionalised autobiography. In *The Half Gods*, the protagonist Darren Leflore recalls the major encounters of his life, as well as the social, moral and political crises of his time. Ominously, the blurb to the first edition called the book 'a subjective *War and Peace*'.

During one of the novel's central chapters, Leflore looks back on his meeting with a young mystic named Heloïse Frank. In the acknowledgements to the novel, Bell was careful to distinguish fiction from fact: 'As for Simone Weil, I met her at Solesmes when I was a student abroad, and (as in the novel) it was long after that I discovered the fact; but my relation had none of the significance I have given to the relation of Daren Leflore to Heloïse Frank . . . It would be wrong to search here for any kind of portrait of Simone

Weil, or for any insights into her writing, which happily speak for themselves.'

In truth, the novel offers no portrait at all. Frank shares some of Weil's habits of appearance: the mannish clothes, the slender physique, the oversized spectacles and the penetrating gaze. Otherwise she remains an insubstantial character, the audience for Leflore's poetry and the witness to his intelligence.

As with most accounts of a spiritual quest, *The Half Gods* often sinks into solipsism. But the value of Bell's novel lies not in the hazy pages of New Age clichés, nor even the fictionalised description of meeting Weil. Instead, the book gives us a picture of Solesmes in the spring of 1938, with young people, brought together under the distant supervision of adults, having earnest conversations in atmospheric locations. Bell recalls reading poetry in 'a candle-lighted storeroom' filled with discarded furniture; listening to 'the hypnotic pulse of the responses' in the vaulted darkness of the chapel; and taking windswept walks along the banks of the Sarthe, 'grass rippling and cat's-paws running over the water'. In other words, the village resembled a sacred spa town, where fashionable visitors came to meet and flirt and sample the spiritual delights.

Weil befriended a second pilgrim during Holy Week, a Well-Meaning Man named John Vernon. He was an English Catholic, who she called 'angel boy' due to 'the truly angelic radiance with which he seemed to be clothed after going to communion'.

Based on this sketch, Vernon probably looked like T. E. Lawrence, the other blond Englishman Weil admired. But, despite her schoolgirl crush on Lawrence, it's unlikely that she spent much time with the angel boy, because ever since adolescence she had sworn off romance and all forms of physical affection.

At six months, Weil had struggled to wean properly. At eleven months she stopped eating food, losing so much weight that the doctor feared she would die. Selma refused to let anyone except close family members kiss her, and, by the time she was four, both parents avoided embracing their daughter. Then, when she was still a teenager, a stranger exposed himself in front of her at the Jardin du Luxembourg, which left Weil with a sense of 'revulsion and a fortunately invincible feeling of humiliation at being the object of desire'. As an adult, she could not bear to be touched and rarely ate enough – blaming the difficulties she had digesting food. She also vowed never to fall in love.

Neither Wittgenstein, nor Jones, nor Weil started families, too dedicated to their solitary calling. But, whereas the first two attempted relationships, Weil rejected the idea from the start. For her, love meant a willingness to give up everything, and she would only make that sacrifice for the absolute.

For those who feel conflicted about sex, celibacy can look like freedom, sparing them the confusions of desire, as well as the frustrations of domestic responsibility. Religious life makes celibacy into something sacred, channelling all our longing towards the divine. In this context, erotic love is a compromised approximation of divine ecstasy: better to lust after perfection than the base equivalents found in the fallen world.

When young, Weil signed letters to her parents, 'Your loving son, Simon'. At university, classmates called her the Red Virgin, in part because she refused to wear make-up or high heels. It's simplistic to say that Weil was afraid of physical intimacy, given the reckless courage she showed in other parts of life. But the deliberate way she faced danger and refused affection might have been born of the same source: a contempt for her own body.

Nonetheless, it was Vernon who gave Weil her most lasting souvenir from Solesmes, when he introduced her to the Metaphysical poets. Up to this point, she had little interest in prayer, let alone in mystical experience. However, once the retreat was over, Weil began reading George Herbert's religious poetry collected in *The Temple*.

The final poem in the collection, 'Love (III)', tells the story of a believer reluctant to accept the sacrament because of a shameful sense of his own sin. For Weil it was 'the most beautiful poem in the world' – one that she learned by heart, copied out for friends, and referred to several times in her notebooks. She also began reciting 'Love' each time she had a headache, and later described how, 'Often, at the culminating point of a violent headache, I make myself say it over and over, concentrating all my attention upon it and clinging with all my soul to the tenderness it enshrines.'

Weil continued to experience migraines, but 'Love' offered a kind of cure. The beauty of the poetry, like the beauty of chant, provided a point of focus beyond her suffering. Again and again she repeated these lines, until the remote concept of the divine became something personal, even intimate. 'Guilty of dust and sin . . . I cannot look on thee . . . Let my shame go where it doth deserve . . . So I did sit and eat . . .'

A few months after the retreat to Solesmes, Weil was reciting Herbert's words: 'At a moment of intense physical pain, while I was making the effort to love, although believing I had no right to give any name to the love I felt . . . a presence more personal, more certain, and more real than that of a human being; it was inaccessible both to sense and to imagination, and resembled the love that irradiates the tenderest smile of somebody one loves.'

Before coming to Solesmes, Weil's understanding of religion had started to change. All the same, God was still a philosophical proposition she could neither prove nor refute. She was put off by the idea of the supernatural, or a deity who intervened in human affairs, performing miracles like so many magic tricks. But, 'in my arguments about the insolubility of the problem of God I had never foreseen the possibility of that, of a real contact, person to person, here below, between a human being and God.'

From now on, Weil was convinced that the divine was

synonymous with love. This belief did not mean she gave up her concern for the suffering of society. Instead, her writing became a desperate attempt to reconcile the two.

Weil and her mother left Solesmes on Easter Monday – one year, four months, two weeks before the war. On returning to Paris, she reread *King Lear*, before drafting a letter to the devil boy Charles Bell. Here she described for the first time her theory of affliction, which became the abiding theme of *Gravity and Grace*.

For Weil, affliction was not just pain, but the suffering that strips away our humanity. It had a physical and a metaphysical element: the greatest works of tragedy captured both. 'Lear is broken by the external world,' she wrote, 'and his suffering has something great in it inasmuch as he is broken but not crushed.'

Her letter used the French word *malheur* for 'affliction'. This includes not only a sense of anguish, but also inevitability, suggesting misfortune or even tragedy. Pain could be explained by human nature and the mechanics of physical matter, but affliction was much harder to reconcile with the divine. This is the paradox of a loving creator and a suffering creation, which theologians call the problem of evil. For me, the problem of evil was the main barrier to belief, because I could find no hint of divine love in all the world's hurt. However, this paradox was the foundation of Weil's faith.

Previously, her writing had argued that suffering was

structural, caused by the injustices of capitalist and colonial societies. After visiting Solesmes, suffering became something fundamental, closer to the texture or cost of experience. Now, as Europe descended into conflict once more, she tried to find the divine in a place without relief from pain.

Weil's most sustained attempt to resolve the problem of evil was an essay titled 'The Love of God in Affliction'. Writing after the start of the war, she argued that creation was the result of God renouncing himself, the absolute and infinite giving way to the finite and flawed. Human suffering was caused by the distance between the perfection of God and the imperfection of mankind: affliction was the sting of His absence. This sting was what allowed us to know the divine.

To illustrate the idea, Weil turned towards the metaphor of music. Her essay described how certain types of music can also shape the silence that surrounds them. As a result, we can hear both the beauty of the song and the quiet that it frames.

This tearing apart, over which supreme love places the bond of supreme union, echoes perpetually across the universe in the midst of silence, like two notes, separate yet melting into one, like pure and heart-rending harmony. This is the word of God. The whole of creation is nothing but its vibration. When human music in its greatest purity pierces our soul, this is what we hear through it. When we have learnt to hear the silence, this is what we grasp more distinctly through it.

Weil was surely talking about Gregorian chant. After all, this was the music that gave her a glimpse of how divine love might exist in the midst of affliction. Her language even evokes the description of that first mystical encounter at Solesmes: tearing apart, piercing the soul. The absence of God becomes the silence between two notes, the empty space that gave resonance to the music.

This argument recalls the idea of *metaxu*, which Weil encountered among the Neoplatonist philosophers. She used the word in her notebooks to describe those 'intermediaries' through which God was known to humanity: beauty, justice, love. Pain became another intermediary, the paradoxical proof of the divine presence, as she later summarised in *Gravity and Grace*: 'Every separation is a link.'

Her argument also recalls the concept of *tzimtzum* from the mystical Jewish tradition of Kabbalah. According to the sixteenth-century rabbi Isaac Luria, God made the world by withdrawing. As a result, we discover the divine in the gap left behind after His departure. So retreat was a necessary condition of creation, opening the space to make something new.

Weil had read few of the Christian mystics, let alone any Jewish ones, but she shared the mystical impulse to value a direct encounter with the divine over the dogmas of religion. Rather than passively accept any teaching, she kept wrestling with Christian doctrine, and when compared with the beliefs of Wittgenstein and Jones, Weil was surely the least orthodox of these three, arguing that other faiths offered their own paths towards truth.

Plato, Kabbalah, piercing the soul – all this can sound bewildering at times. What's more, Weil wrote with a bracing certainty, expressing each argument in absolute terms and rarely attempting to consider other perspectives. Of course, she was trying to describe something that lies beyond the limits of language – the kind of effort the *Tractatus* warned was futile – so it's little wonder that her writing can confuse. Perhaps sounding reasonable is a kind of deceit, at least on the improbable subject of belief.

Weil's certainty was also a pose, wanting most of all to convince herself. Soon after she completed her essay on affliction, she wrote to an old schoolfriend named Maurice Schumann, confessing that: 'I feel an ever-increasing sense of devastation, both in my intellect and in the centre of my heart, at my inability to think with truth at the same time about the affliction of men, the perfection of God, and the link between the two.'

So Weil was not simply confronting the boundaries of rhetoric, but trying to twist her mind around a logical impossibility. That desperate effort is heartbreaking to me: striving after a truth that can never be known for sure. Here is courage, here is hope, and here is self-destructive determination, torturing her thoughts in an effort to understand. Yet this futile striving is one of the things I admire most about her.

★

If Klosterneuburg was a mirror to the riches of Vienna, and Caldey to the remote edges of Wales, Solesmes seemed only to reflect itself. Roaming round the gardens, or wandering through the village, or crossing the river to walk on the far bank: still the gothic cellblock loomed above the tiled roofs and the budding trees. Several buildings in the village echoed the architecture of the abbey – stone structures decorated with towers and turrets, or modern properties topped with metal crosses – and always I could hear the tolling of the bells, calling the community to prayer.

But the monks remained distant figures. Many of them were slight and smiling strangers whom I passed on the gravel pathways of the enclosure. Ageing men with their hair all gone from their crowns, their chins, their eyebrows too, as if their features had been rubbed away, leaving indistinct but benign expressions.

That said, I was often aware of their presence, not only in the chapel and the refectory. Each evening, walking back to the guest quarters, I would look up at the great cellblock to see a dozen lighted windows in the façade of dark stone, and imagine the monks bent over desks or kneeling at prie-dieus, busy with their whispered work.

I had always assumed prayer was a quiet indulgence that might bring some inner peace. The word contemplation meant even less to me: if prayer was muttered voices and a furrowed brow, contemplation was closer to dreaming. At Solesmes, contemplation became a regimented task, the monks filling their days with the regular routines of worship. Yet the longer I spent at the abbey, the more I felt confused about the purpose of all this prayer. So many muffled voices and murmured words, taking place in darkness and leaving little trace.

When I arrived at Solesmes, Fr Bozell explained that the chants were at the heart of this worship, praying for those who could not pray for themselves. But it was hard for me to believe in a God who answered prayers, provided you ask enough times. Conversely, if prayer made nothing happen, why place it at the centre of your life?

On my last afternoon at the abbey, I visited the guest-master's office to ask. Outside, rain leaded the sky and wind blew the blossom loose, pouring past the window like the wreckage of a storm. Inside, the room was dim, the two of us sitting on opposite armchairs and sharing the light from a single lamp.

To begin with Fr Bozell talked about his childhood. His parents ran a Catholic magazine, and growing up he spent several years in Switzerland and Spain. After college in America he came back to Europe, reading the works of Herman Hesse as he travelled around. Hesse used medieval monasteries in several novels, and at some point a priest recommended the young man visit Solesmes to see that way of life for himself.

Fr Bozell was in his early twenties when he came to Solesmes, staying a few weeks before going home to America. Something kept calling him back to the abbey, however, and two years later he decided to return. 'At the beginning, I never imagined that I was committing to Solesmes for my entire life. To tell the truth, the idea would have scared me. I was just trying the place for a few months, seeing what it felt like to live here. There's five years between joining the community and taking your final vows – by the time you make the decision, you know it's what you want.'

I was impressed by the way the guest-master spoke. He never made any grand claims for his calling, let alone tried to persuade me of his faith. Instead he compared it to a job or a marriage, with the person and the institution growing side by side.

'But you must have had moments of doubt?' I asked. 'Your calling can't remain the same the whole time?'

'What helps you keep the course is the community: making this commitment in the company of other men. You arrive when you're young and vow to attempt this remarkable thing together. As the years go by, you hold each other to account, make sure your brothers stay the distance. Of course, it's possible to live this life without a community, but it's much harder that way. Even the earliest monks formed groups of hermits in the desert rather than trying alone.'

I explained that, in the beginning, I was drawn towards religious life because it seemed to offer a certainty I had encountered nowhere else. The monks and nuns I met in monasteries and convents wagered everything on God's existence, giving up the world for the sake of their beliefs.

At the time, I doubted my own artistic ambitions and their conviction was something I wanted for myself.

Certainty has a special seduction at the start of life. There's a relief that comes from setting our existence in a single direction, because it means we no longer need to weigh our options or debate which course would be best. In the first years of adulthood, when those questions take up most space in the mind, even false certainty offers a welcome alternative to confusion. What's more, sacrifices seem smaller at that stage, when the ties that link us to people or places feel like binds we want to shake off.

However, certainty that has never been tested is a fragile thing. It's like holding your breath and diving into the water, hoping you will have enough air to rise again. Similarly, the conviction that never questions itself can become brittle, breaking rather than making space for doubt. And a life without doubt is also a life without reflection.

'But joining a religious community is not a single decision,' Fr Bozell replied. 'It's a commitment you renew each single day. Besides, the Church does not teach that everyone should become a monk or nun. People need to make a living, provide for their families. But it matters that there are communities somewhere devoting their whole lives to prayer.'

When I asked about the value of all this prayer, Fr Bozell replied: 'The Church teaches that prayer makes a difference. Just not one that can be measured easily.'

'So,' I went on, 'what about the mystical experiences Simone Weil had when she came to Solesmes? What difference did they make?'

Now the guest-master's voice became slow, choosing each word with care: 'Simone Weil had experiences that most monks here will never share. Mystical experiences don't mean that someone is closer to God, and maybe the monks don't need them. But those encounters had a deep effect on her writing, on her life – even her death. The important thing was what she did with her experiences.'

'Does that mean her death was an act of devotion?'

Fr Bozell fell silent, his features soft in the lamplight. 'That's probably above my paygrade,' he replied after a while. 'What matters to me is whether the story helps others believe. Her writing has brought people comfort, even brought them to faith, and her death is part of what makes that writing powerful. So, if something was lost, something was gained as well.'

He turned to the window, the glass now stained with rain. 'But the thing that interests me about a calling is: where does it come from? An idea enters your mind from somewhere outside, but it's also from somewhere inside, an inner compulsion that feels like it was there all along. What's the cause of that compulsion? Who put it there in the first place?'

Weil kept searching for ways to recreate her retreat. First, by looking for a place to withdraw from company. Then, once the war was underway, by seeking a chance to sacrifice herself.

The German army occupied Paris on 14 June 1940. Weil escaped with her parents on the last train south, heading into the *zone libre*. Arriving at Marseille in the first half of September, they hoped to sail to North Africa and then reach America. But they ended up staying here for the next twenty months, living among refugees and struggling to obtain exit visas.

While living in Marseille, Weil moved in the Catholic circles of the city and also distributed a Catholic journal in support of the Resistance. Then, in the summer of 1941, she began asking friends to help her find farm work. Soon she was put in touch with Gustave Thibon.

Thibon was a traditional Catholic and a self-taught philosopher, living with his wife Yvette on a family farm in the Rhône valley. The farm was set among orchards and vines on the edge of a village called Saint-Marcel-d'Ardèche, looking east towards the snow-capped cone of Mont Ventoux. Weil travelled to the village in early August, but, when offered a room in Thibon's house, she asked to sleep outside instead. So, she was given a half-ruined cottage on the banks of the Rhône: the floor beaten earth, the bed wooden boards, the mattress stuffed with pine needles and the nearest stream one hundred and fifty paces away.

Weil called the cottage her 'fairy-tale house'. The month she spent there was among the happiest of her life, with the freedom that came from a life pared back to its most basic demands. She was alone for much of that month:

cleaning the cottage, preparing food, reading and writing in her journals. The rest of the time she worked on the farm and in the evenings taught Greek to Thibon, so that they could discuss Plato's *Phaedo* together. In between, she spent long hours staring at the Rhône valley – a landscape of red clay, of rocky slopes, of high hills bordering the horizon – gazing at the view in a state of total absorption.

In a letter written earlier that summer, Weil stated: 'I don't know whether silence is not more beautiful than all the songs. When the sun sets or rises in a vast landscape, there is no more complete harmony than silence. Even if men talk and make noise around them, one can hear the silence that glides above and that extends as far as the sky.'

During their classes, Weil and Thibon promised one another to learn the Lord's Prayer in Greek. Up to this point, she had worried that prayer was a form of self-hypnosis, but once she began reciting the text in its original language, her mystical encounters returned with newfound intensity.

At times the very first words tear my thoughts from my body and transport it to a place outside space where there is neither perspective nor point of view. The infinity of ordinary expanses of perception is replaced by an infinite to the second and sometimes the third degree. At the same time, filling every part of this infinity of infinity, there is silence, a silence which is not an absence of sound but which is the object of a positive sensation, more positive than that of sound. Noises, if there are any, only reach me across this silence. Sometimes, also, during this recitation or at other moments, Christ is present with me in person, but His presence is infinitely more real, more moving, more clear than on that first occasion when He took possession of me.

Weil's first mystical encounters were inspired by the chant at Solesmes, while her later encounters came when reciting the poetry of George Herbert. Now, it was the words of the Lord's Prayer that carried her mind beyond its body, sinking into a silence as profound as the pressureless depths of space. It was the same silence she perceived when staring at the wide expanse of the Rhône valley – larger than any human noise, deeper than any social bond.

For all the wonder of these encounters, Weil might have been describing the shallow dazzle of a drug trip. But, elsewhere, her writings argue that prayer is a way of training the attention, the patient process of moving one's thoughts towards virtue. At its highest, this becomes a moral act, because by giving our whole focus to someone else, we can experience their trials as our own. Which was why Weil called attention 'the rarest and purest form of generosity': we are what we focus on. Seen in this light, prayer is not a journey inwards, but out.

Fr Bozell claimed that the best measure of retreat was the

way it shaped someone's life after they returned. In the case of Weil, she grew determined to sacrifice herself for the war effort. While staying at Thibon's farm, she began telling friends about her plan to lead a cadre of nurses who would be parachuted onto the battlefield with the Allied army. Their purpose was symbolic as much as practical: some might care for the wounded soldiers, but most would be killed alongside them. Nonetheless, their willing martyrdom would puncture the enemy morale by proving the Allies' commitment to freedom.

The rest of Weil's life was a futile attempt to realise her plan. How you feel about that life may depend on whether you think symbols have any value. Certainly, there was little medical or military benefit to this proposal, and her niece Sylvie came closest to the truth when she argued: 'Simone's true plan is to feel the pain of poor people, not to provide them with bread or clothing. Her personal brand of charity is to become the beggar and then refuse any help.' A symbol, but no solution.

In late September, Weil began helping with the grape harvest in a nearby village. She hoped to spend all winter as a farm worker, but could not find a long-term job. So she went back to her parents in Marseille, and by the following spring the family had received exit visas.

Before leaving France, Weil had one final retreat to make. In the spring of 1942, she wanted to hear the Easter liturgy again. So, nearing the end of March, she travelled to St

Benoit d'En Calcat, another Benedictine abbey famed for its chant. The abbey stood on the wooded western spur of the Massif Central, some two hundred miles from Marseille, with cellblocks built from grey slabs of stone like the gothic range at Solesmes.

Whereas the fortnight in Solesmes marked the start of Weil's journey towards faith, the stay at d'En Calcat began her break with the Church. She arrived in time for Maundy Thursday and again attended all the services. In between, she spoke about baptism with a composer and Catholic convert called Dom Clément Jacob.

Earlier in the year, Weil had discussed this subject with Fr Joseph-Marie Perrin, a Dominican priest in Marseille who became her spiritual mentor. He hoped the young woman would enter the Church, and yet, despite her love of 'the Catholic liturgy, hymns, architecture, rites and cere-monies', she felt more deeply drawn towards isolation, resisting any institution, congregation or creed. 'I feel that it is necessary and ordained that I should be alone,' she wrote to Perrin, 'a stranger and exile in relation to every human circle without exception.'

During the first discussion with Dom Clément, Weil presented a list of her beliefs which departed from Catholic doctrine. These included her view that the God of the Old Testament was a tyrant, that figures like Krishna or Osiris were earlier manifestations of Christ and that the Catholic Church was an oppressive force for much of its history.

After several days of fraught discussion, it became clear that Weil would not give up a single one of these views, and in response Dom Clément explained that her opinions were heretical. As he later wrote, 'There was in her moral and intellectual demands a rigour that left no escape route.'

Though Weil remained a believer, she resolved never to enter the Church. This was not simply the pride of the solitary, but also the fear of losing her intellectual freedom. Like Wittgenstein before her, Weil was too committed to the principle of honesty to submit to anyone else's scheme of thought. And she rejected the obligations that came from community, seeking the seeming liberty of unbounded independence instead.

On her way to the abbey, Weil spent a night at Carcassonne, where she had been put in touch with a poet named Joë Bousquet. In the final months of the First World War, Bousquet was paralysed by a bullet in the spine and forced to spend the rest of his life in bed. From there he corresponded with André Gide and Louis Aragon, as well as writing collections of poetry and taking opium to soothe his pain. Another of those artistic lives aborted by the war, his creativity was expressed in the compassed confines of retreat.

Weil reached his house late at night and the two them talked until dawn. We do not know what they discussed, though their later correspondence offers some hint. Bousquet was no believer, but he was impressed by the purity of Weil's spiritual life and asked for an account of her mystical experiences. In response, she wrote her first description of the visit to Solesmes and the discovery of Herbert's poetry.

Up to this point, Weil's mystical experiences had been a secret. Now, she began telling the story of her journey towards faith, from her early sense that the divine was an insoluble problem, to the later encounters with a living God. In Weil's account, these encounters gave some respite after years of painful migraines, where her suffering was so acute it transformed into self-loathing. Alongside this letter she shared three works that inspired her above all others: Herbert's 'Love', Lawrence's *Seven Pillars of Wisdom* and a copy of the New Testament in Greek.

It was during this spring that Weil wrote 'The Love of God in Affliction' and many of the journal entries that formed *Gravity and Grace*. Her entries returned again and again to the question of suffering, rejecting the idea that pain was part of some divine plan. This was simply a comforting delusion that takes us away from the truth: 'We must leave on one side the beliefs which fill up voids and sweeten what is bitter. The belief in immortality. The belief in the utility of sin: *etiam peccata*. The belief in the providential ordering of events – in short the consolations which are ordinarily sought in religion.'

Some people think that belief offers comfort in the dark days of our lives, but for Weil it did the opposite, upsetting all her certainties. There was nothing therapeutic about this view of religion; real faith was believing without the hope of salvation. After all, God's perfection meant he could exist nowhere else in creation, so knowing God required knowing an absence.

For Weil, pain was the deepest encounter with this absence. Trials should be treated as a path towards the divine; any attempt to console moved us away from His love. 'Relentless necessity, wretchedness, distress, the crushing burden of poverty and of labour which wears us out, cruelty, torture, violent death, constant distress – all these constitute divine love. It is God who withdraws from us so that we can love him.'

When I read a line like this, I am helpless to explain it in secular terms. Weil's longing to starve, to suffer, to crucify herself: there is no rational justification for these ideas. But she measured her life against a different standard now. That standard was expressed by Cardinal Suhard, another member of the Benedictine order who conducted mass at Solesmes for their anniversary celebrations, one year prior to Weil's retreat. 'To be a witness,' he claimed, 'means to live in such a way that one's life would make no sense if God did not exist.'

That word – witness – was the original meaning of *martyr*. And it comes closest to explaining the tragedy of Weil's life after Solesmes. In her last letter to Fr Perrin, shortly before leaving Marseille, she wrote: 'Every time I think of the crucifixion of Christ, I commit the sin of envy.' Most Christians understand the cross as a symbol of eternal life, but Weil had little interest in what lay beyond death. Her attention was fixed on martyrdom now, sacrificing herself so that others might be saved.

In May 1942, the family finally left for Morocco and then travelled on to America. Weil joined her parents on the journey, but only because it would allow her to reach Britain. By November she was catching a boat to Liverpool and by January 1943 she was employed by the Free French in London.

The letters to Bousquet and Perrin were among the last she wrote in France. She also sent her notebooks to Thibon for safekeeping, adding that, in the case of her death, 'I would be very happy to have one or two of the masses – especially from Solesmes with Gregorian chant – said for me.'

For my final service at Solesmes, I sat in the same place Weil occupied when she came here in 1938, midway down the nave, too far from the altar to watch the mass. This was where she listened to the divine office taking place, her eyes tight with anguish and her fingers knotted in pain.

The next day was the Feast of St Joseph, which meant the service was accompanied by an organ. The singing was softer that evening, resembling the noises of the natural world. Like the pouring of water, or the sloughing of wind, or the branches of trees brushing together in the breeze. At times the voices resembled no natural noise but something more mysterious, as if the building were exhaling or the shadows had started to speak. Once or twice, it sounded like nothing of this earth, but the music the dead might make, if only we could hear them.

Of course, I did not expect a mystical experience from occupying the same seat as Weil. Instead, I tried again to imagine what the services were like almost a century ago, with no electric light casting an even gleam across the chapel, nor any speaker system relaying the chant to each corner. In this sheltered position, Weil would not have noticed the front door creaking open and shut, nor seen the busy movements near the altar. Yet she might have heard some trace of the choir's voices echoing round the room after the chanting ceased, as if their singing was still carried on the currents of air that circled the church. And she might have wondered about the communities repeating these chants across the earth, forming an unbroken chain of prayer that had started long before she came here and would continue long after she was gone. A ritual with no beginning or end. Some tremoring trace of the infinite.

A few days earlier, one of the Knights of Malta had told me that the monks' lives were a drawn-out preparation for death. Certainly, death seemed much closer that week: the great tomb of the cellblock, the emptied streets of the village, the weighted silence of the chapel. Perhaps death also explained the peace of retreat: giving up hunger and lust, ambition and pride; giving up all the appetites of existence and letting go the ties that bind us to this life. Surrendering our deepest desires so that neither hope nor disappointment can hurt us any longer. What was this but a taste of mortality?

I used to think ritual had value whether or not you believed. Pilgrimage, retreat, even prayer – there were lessons here for non-believers too. However, the more time I spent at monasteries, the more I glimpsed the harshness at the heart of the religious calling: in order to be saved, you must die to the world. Which may explain why over time my subjects' lives began resembling the sicknesses they were supposed to cure. As Guy had explained to me, symbols were not meant to be imitated, only prove what might be possible.

So I felt no regret to be leaving Solesmes, nor did I feel any relief. Instead, the feeling was closer to gratitude, knowing that nothing I loved was left in the abbey and that the confusion beyond its walls was where I belonged. It's easy to picture some perfect place where we can escape the frustrations of everyday existence, yet that sanctuary exists nowhere except in the mind. Wishing to withdraw was the price of remaining in society, and the retreat that left you longing to return was a success rather than a failure, learning to value what you had once more. Besides, the world was not the enemy of creative and intellectual work, but its one sustaining source.

At least, that was the conclusion I reached when I left the abbey after breakfast next day. At the start of my journey, this would have seemed a disappointment, yet now I felt the relief that comes from shedding a long-held illusion, or letting go of those what-ifs that shadow our path through life. The relief that comes from surrendering a false sense of self, from finally telling the truth.

That morning the sky was frigid and the sun formed a bright mark behind the haze, struggling to burn off the cloud. My fingers were cold without any gloves, my knuckles numb as they gripped the canvas rucksack straps. So I marched along the path as quickly as possible, heading back to the station at Sablé-sur-Sarthe. The route followed the river for half an hour or more, and soon I was moving through open fields, with plots of settled water resting calm beside the bank.

Sometimes the path was a line of earth worn into dewed grass. Other times it was a stony track skirting a strip of woodland. Though the daylight was hazed, each detail appeared vivid, outlines sharp in the pale air and colours shining beneath the cloud. Bursts of birdsong splashed across the route, while the fields gave off a damp, green odour of orchards and nettles and mud. Yellow blossom had fallen along the track, like sprinkled breadcrumbs or scattered coins, and the treetops were sugared where the first buds began to show.

For a while I walked in silence – not the weighted quiet of the chapel, but the calm composure of a Saturday morning. I imagined that I could hear the steady flowing of the river and the slow turning of the sky, until the silence was broken by the chiming of a bell: the churches of Solesmes ringing ten o'clock.

Once the bells had counted the hour, they kept on

chiming. At first the sound seemed a gentle trembling, as if the clouds were hung with silver sheets, each one quaking in the breeze. Then the chiming became heavier, no longer consisting of a single note, but instead made up of half a dozen different bells playing all at once. One produced a high clanging much sharper than the rest, while another produced a deep drumming, the bass notes beating in time to my footsteps. As I marched towards the town, other bells began to toll, the churches in each village joining the chorus, and before long the whole valley was vibrant with ringing, the music of their chimes flooding downstream and resounding into a choir of sorts. Now the overcast weather was beginning to clear and the ashen clouds were withdrawing from the skies. Now the grass was ragged in the paddocks and the petals were blushing on the orchard trees; now the morning was brimming with light and the air was bright with promise. Now the retreat had ended and the spring had started and the landscape was reborn at last.

But then I left the path and joined the pavement, crossing the crowded roads and rushing to make the station. By the time I reached the platform, the chorus of chiming had fallen silent, or else been smothered by the busy sounds of the street, the square, the city of man. Soon I was sitting on a train back to Paris, the bells still playing in my thoughts like the trace of a dream, sounding farewell from the world within.

# Conclusion

After these retreats, I had pierced some of my illusions about religious life. I had also pierced the romantic image of the writer I found in the figures of Ludwig Wittgenstein, David Jones and Simone Weil. I realised that retreat was not only a religious experience, and that there were other ways of working beyond the self-destructive devotion shown by these three. All the same, I was uncertain what lessons to learn from their biographies, let alone from the weeks I spent staying with monks. So I decided to withdraw one final time, but rather than visit a monastery, I tried a secular setting instead.

Next spring, I travelled to Norway and the village where Wittgenstein left the world behind. The road from Bergen went west, then north, skirting a series of fjords. There was little traffic that weekday in May and my gaze kept straying from the road – to the ridgelines scoring each side of a valley and the pine forests pouring down from the slopes. Five hours of driving ended up lasting seven: stopping to rest, waiting for a ferry, and then parking outside Skjolden for forty-five minutes as a crew of workmen repaired the coastal road. But I did not mind taking my time, because the day was warm and the skies were clear and the water by the roadside a brilliant blue.

Skjolden occupies the northern end of the Sognefjorden, the innermost point of the country's longest fjord. A lake stretches out to the east of the village, fed by torrents from the surrounding summits. The two bodies of water are linked by a stream, the village bridging the stream and rising up the grassy foothills of the valley. Wittgenstein's cabin occupied the lake's farthest shore, looking back towards the houses of Skjolden.

I reached the village in the early evening. The place had changed little over the years, though the quay was restored and the lemonade factory replaced, with the main hotel now a modern building containing a swimming pool and spa. Otherwise, there were maybe a hundred wooden houses, their gardens bordered by picket fences, their porches turned towards the fjord.

That evening the café was closed, the tourist centre too, and no cars were parked outside the Co-op. The battery on my phone was exhausted, so I had to drive down unsurfaced tracks, asking for directions to Eide Gard. Eventually I spotted the name of the place written on a sign, the house set back from the road and flanked by farm buildings, its clapboard whitewashed and its window frames green. Inside, fabrics hung from the walls and the floors were covered with Persian rugs, making the hallway appear cushioned and warm. The lamps cast a peach-coloured glow onto a map of the nearby mountains and a guestbook lay open on the table beneath the stairs, yet nobody stood waiting for me at the reception desk.

For a while I roamed round the ground floor, knocking on doors and calling hello. The house had little of the spotless sameness you might find in a hotel: the front room looked like it was furnished a century ago with a cabriole sofa of velvet upholstery and a chandelier made from pendants of pointed glass. The rest of the downstairs rooms were filled with dining tables, while the terrace on the western side of the property gave a view over the fjord. And strings of lights had been suspended above the terrace, like a necklace of beads hung from the summits of the hills.

After fifteen minutes of waiting, an elderly woman entered through a side door, her arms spread wide in a gesture of welcome. She explained that the downstairs rooms were once a restaurant, before the pandemic forced her to close. But there was nowhere else to eat in the village, until the tourist season started next month.

'You are welcome to use the kitchen,' she said, indicating a large room at the back of the house. 'Otherwise, I don't know how to help.'

Upstairs were four bedrooms, none of them the same size. Because I was alone, I was given the smallest, with a single bed pushed into the corner. Its walls were a sea-green colour, the paint split in the gaps between each plank to expose the bare timber beneath. White curtains had been drawn across the window – the evening light diffuse as it seeped through the lace – and a candle was placed on a dressing table, alongside books about Wittgenstein in English and Norwegian.

My host's name was Mara. As I scanned the books on the table, she explained that this was the room where Wittgenstein slept. 'On his last visit to Norway, he stayed here too. He wanted to come back to Skjolden before he died, but in the end he was too sick.'

The room was no shrine, yet it was easy to imagine the philosopher occupying this simple space. Though built in the late nineteenth century as a hostel for mountain climbers, when Wittgenstein came to Skjolden it was an occasional hotel, run by a teacher named Anna Rebni. Because she spoke both English and German, Wittgenstein stopped here often for tea on his way back from Skjolden, and when the cabin was too cold he would lodge here as well.

Mara claimed the room was little different during Wittgenstein's stays. An embroidered cushion for the chair, a knitted spread for the bed, and a dressing table that could be used as a desk. In fact, it resembled a cell from one of the monasteries where I had stayed: plain without seeming stark, simple without being bare. As if Wittgenstein was seeking one final refuge where he might end his life.

After Mara left me alone, I walked to the edge of the lake. When I scanned the sheer mountains enclosing the valley, I spotted three waterfalls like white scars across wrinkled foreheads. Then I spotted the cabin on the opposite shore, a tiny building perched on a shelf of stone, with granite slopes on either side and knots of woodland where the ground was not too steep. From this distance it resembled a treehouse, or some child's plaything dropped among the clusters of birch and pine.

Following Wittgenstein's death, the cabin was inherited by a local friend named Arne Bolstad. In 1958 he dismantled the building, winching the materials down the hillside and dragging them across the frozen lake. Then the house was reassembled in the village, the walls clad in fibre cement and the door painted a dark shade of red. This was where Arne lived with his wife, Anny, who one overcast day noticed a figure standing in the kitchen with a drawn face and sunken eyes – unspeaking, as the dead often are in dreams. When she turned on the light the figure disappeared, and after that no more ghosts haunted their home.

Except for the stone foundations, little trace remained of Wittgenstein's cabin. But at some point a pole was erected by the lakeside, hung with the red and white stripes of the Austrian flag. Then, in 2019, the house in the village was dismantled once more, carried across the water and rebuilt on the original site. That was the cabin I had come to see.

Returning to Eide Garde, I sat at the dressing table and looked through the books. From the window I could see the evening sun descending behind the Børesteinen Mountains, and soon darkness was draped over the landscape like a heavy cloth, the village houses becoming creases and folds in the fabric. Then I lay on the bed and watched twilight fill the room, shadows creeping from the corners and consuming each piece of furniture. Finally I fell asleep, untroubled by a single sound.

As Wittgenstein died, his thoughts travelled back to Skjolden. Curtains of forest drawn across mountain slopes, the pine boughs textured like velvet. Inland fjords turning turquoise from their silted water, shading to deep green where the mountains were reflected. A wooden cabin balanced above a lake, like the ark cast ashore after the floodwaters receded.

Five times in his life Wittgenstein came to the fjords. First, in the years before the war, when he tried to solve all the problems of philosophy. Second, in 1921, when he visited with a family friend and volunteered to work in the lemonade factory. Third, in 1931, this time accompanied by Marguerite Respinger, the woman he briefly hoped to marry. Fourth, from the summer of 1936 to the winter of 1937, when again he worked on philosophy. Fifth, in the autumn of 1950, when already he was dying.

Wittgenstein was often lonely during these stays, or depressed by the solitude he had sought. But he kept returning to Norway, convinced he could work better here than anywhere else. In the years before the Second World War, he spent many months in the cabin, completing an early draft of the *Philosophical Investigations*. He also prepared a long confession for his family and closest friends: moments of cowardice when serving on the front, the mistreatment of pupils while teaching in Austria and the ways he had hidden his Jewish heritage. These were the sins he needed to share.

Philosophical insight and moral improvement were linked in Wittgenstein's mind. His notebooks from this period contained the line: 'Whoever is unwilling to descend into himself, because it is too painful, will of course remain superficial in his writing . . . If you are unwilling to know what you are, your writing is a form of deceit.' However, what Wittgenstein sought was not an intellectual solution but emotional relief – the kind of forgiveness offered by faith. On the boat back to Bergen, he even wrote the words 'And faith is faith in what is needed by my *heart*, my *soul*, not my speculative intelligence. For it is my soul with its passions, as it were with its flesh and blood, that has to be saved, not my abstract mind.'

Wittgenstein struggled to believe, yet he kept trying all the same, because if religion was true then salvation might be possible. What salvation meant was hinted in the philosopher's first and only public lecture, delivered soon after his return to Cambridge, where he detailed a pair of personal experiences on which his morality was grounded. The first was a sense of '*wonder at the existence of the world*'; the second was a sense of feeling '*absolutely* safe'. He went on: 'the first of them is, I believe, exactly what people were referring to when they said that God created the world; and the expe-

rience of absolute safety has been described by saying that
we feel safe in the hands of God.'

A sense of wonder and a sense of safety. These were the
two elements that mixed to make Wittgenstein's faith. And
these were the two things he discovered in Norway.

Towards the end of 1949, Wittgenstein was diagnosed
with prostate cancer. He was sixty years old and had recently
resigned from Cambridge to dedicate himself to writing.
Though he had no home or income, on learning the news
he began planning his return to Norway. In the autumn of
1950, he made the journey at last.

When Wittgenstein came back to Skjolden that final time,
he wanted nothing more than a holiday. He was accompanied
by Ben Richards, a medical student who was the closest
companion of his final years. By this point, Wittgenstein had
almost abandoned philosophy, but during these weeks the ability
to write returned. He began wondering whether he might stay
at Skjolden long enough to complete one final project.

The early autumn was warm, yet the days in the cabin
were difficult. Wittgenstein agreed with a young man at
Eide Garde that, if he needed help, he would hang a white
sheet from the balcony and someone would row across the
lake to rescue him. In the end it was Richards who caught
bronchitis, meaning he had to be moved to a nursing home,
while Wittgenstein went to live with Anna Rebni. But he
made plans to return before the year was out, even booking
a ticket for 30 December.

CONCLUSION

'If I can't work there I can't work anywhere,' Wittgenstein explained in a letter, hoping for enough quiet to finish the fragments of philosophy later collected in *On Certainty*. Perhaps he also hoped to die at Skjolden and be buried in the village graveyard. However, by Christmas he was so unwell this plan had to be abandoned.

Once it was clear Wittgenstein would never return to Norway, he asked a friend called Fr Conrad Pepler to find him somewhere to live. The priest proposed a Dominican priory in Leicester, where he could take part in the household chores and otherwise be left to work. Wittgenstein agreed to join the brothers for his remaining years, but come January he was so sick this plan was abandoned too. Instead he moved into the house of his Cambridge doctor.

These abortive attempts to withdraw fill me with pity. They suggest Wittgenstein was still searching for that safety, that wonder. But in the end there was no blue room, no view over the fjord, no evening light lasting late in the sky. Wittgenstein died at his doctor's house during the final days of April, his friends asking Fr Conrad to perform the last rites.

In his letters and journals, Wittgenstein refers to the cabin as his house. Perhaps all this time he was seeking a place that he need never leave. Somewhere to shelter from history, or recover from tragedy, or find clarity in the face of confusion. A still point in the turning world. A home to call his own.

★

273

If Wittgenstein wanted to leave his life behind, Jones wanted to hide away. Long before his death, he had withdrawn almost entirely, making his bedroom into a studio and living his last years surrounded by art.

In 1965, Jones was interviewed in this makeshift studio by the BBC. The opening shots set the scene in black and white: a palette, an ashtray and a bottle of white spirit strewn across the desk, along with dozens of paintbrushes bursting from a jug, resembling flowers grown wild with spring. The bed piled with books, the desk covered with painting materials, and the tiny table that served as an easel, a set of watercolours open on one side. Paper pinned to a wooden board with words drafted across its surface, the letters coloured in different shades like the play of light over trembling water.

This room was part of the residential hotel in North Harrow where Jones lived for the final decade of his life. Monksdene was the hotel's name, and he occupied a bedsit on the ground floor: a dismal space with French doors opening onto the garden and hoarded newspapers hidden out of sight. This was where he spent each day, the shelves muddled with carvings and crucifixes to form a miniature altar.

The next clip from the interview showed Jones preparing to work, fluttering round the room like a bird. Then he settled at the tiny table, his body balanced on the lip of the armchair and leaning over the wooden board. When he bowed down to paint, he might have been a monk at prayer, working with complete concentration.

Jones was seventy years old at the time. He wore a tweed coat and a tie for the cameras, the cuffed shirt a little too clean for painting. His hair still fell in a fringe across his forehead, so that he resembled a schoolboy dressed for a special occasion. And he dipped his head whenever he spoke, turning his eyes from the spotlights and causing the camera to zoom closer to catch his expression. At times he seemed to brush it away with the cigarette held in the fingertips of his left hand.

One wall was hung with a pale sketch of the hills surrounding Capel-y-ffin, another with a sketch of the sea from Caldey. The largest artwork was a painted inscription propped behind his chair, made for the chapel of a Carmelite convent in Presteigne (the mother superior had turned the work down, calling it 'too esoteric'). For a while the camera remained fixed on the lower half of this image, the same words written in Latin and Welsh, interspersed to form a single sentence. HOSTIAM + PVRAM HOSTIAM + SANCTAM / ABERTH PVR ABERTH GLAN / HOSTIAM + IMMACVLATAM / ABERTH DIFRYCHEVLYD.

Jones began working on the inscriptions during the Second World War. At first they were painted as gifts for friends, marking a birthday or a saint's day. They were never intended for exhibition or sale, and the finished images share something of this private quality, the broken quotations giving a sense of the echoing languages inside Jones's mind.

Each inscription was assembled out of fragments of text

borrowed from the Gospels, the mass, *Le Morte d'Arthur* and the poems of Celtic mythology. Jones would arrange the letters in pencil, before washing the page with an opaque pigment of Chinese white. Then he would paint the words with faint patterns of colour: crimson and emerald, bright black and dirty gold.

At this point, Jones was being prescribed a powerful mix of stimulants, depressants and sedatives. The side effects were no less powerful: sometimes lethargy and confusion, other times anxiety and insomnia. Poetry and watercolours were too tiring now, and eventually he could work on nothing more difficult than the painted inscriptions. But these inscriptions were as sublime as anything else he created, their mix of picture and text, of Welsh mythology and Catholic liturgy, weaving together the frayed strands of his career.

Jones had lived among stonemasons at Ditchling, and his later engravings were embellished with text. He was also inspired by the carvings on the first Christian catacombs and the manuscripts made by medieval monks. However, when I look at these inscriptions, I am reminded of the Chapel of St Illtyd on Caldey Island – of the stone that stands in the corner of that chapel, carved with Latin and Ogham script, asking the passer-by to pray for the soul of some forgotten saint. And I am moved by the idea that, in his final decades, Jones remembered again those years between the wars, when he withdrew to Wales and discovered his own calling.

Five years after this interview, Jones suffered a stroke, his mouth becoming slack in one corner. The next day he tripped on a tear in the carpet and broke the ball at the top of his femur. First he was taken to hospital, then to a nursing home run by nuns. Over the next few months his movements became painful and his eyesight started to fail, until it was impossible for him to leave the home, dying three days short of his seventy-ninth birthday.

Retreat need not only mean withdrawing from the world. For Jones, art was what connected him to place, to people, to the past. Nearing the end of the BBC interview, he explained that his work was nourished by the experiences of his life, from his stays in Wales to his years as a soldier.

'And so,' the interviewer asked, 'living here in this room – your studio and living room – with all these things about them, you're making your own world in the middle of this one?'

'It's the only way I can do it,' he replied, for a moment turning back towards the bed. The inscription was almost visible on the wall behind, its words taken from the Canon of the Mass and a Welsh poet of the fourteenth century. As if written as an epitaph for this devoted life, carried to its lonely conclusion.

This pure sacrifice,
This holy sacrifice,
This perfect sacrifice.

Weil's end was perhaps the most wretched of the three. She died far from home and even farther from her family. In the last letter she wrote to her parents, from a sanatorium bed in the Kent countryside, she made no mention of the fact that that she was mortally ill. For all her commitment to truth, she wanted to spare Selma and Bernard one final pain. In this, of course, she failed.

That letter arrived with her parents a few days after she died. At the time the Weils were living in New York; later they spent several years in Brazil, before finally returning to Paris in 1948. The family flat occupied the top two storeys of No.3 Rue Auguste Comte, a grand apartment block constructed between the wars. Its heavy Flemish furniture had been stolen when the Germans occupied the city and the building's masonry scarred by bullets during the Liberation.

Their daughter's bedroom was on the sixth floor, on the left as you entered the property. Shelves of books, a wooden lamp and a desk that was long enough to lie on. The window looked out over the city: the ordered expanse of the Jardin du Luxembourg and the mismatched towers of Saint-Sulpice, as well as the distant domes of Sacré-Coeur, adrift above the horizon. Here she could stand for hours on end, tracing the outline of avenues and boulevards, or else counting the sculpted buildings at her feet.

The desk was the one item of furniture that remained in the flat, too large for anyone to take away. This was where Selma and Bernard now worked, sitting at opposite ends of the table, their daughter's notebooks lying open between them. Weil had given her Marseille journals to Gustave Thibon, but the rest were kept in a cupboard in the corner of the room. Each morning her parents would take one of the journals from the cupboard, transcribing the contents into accounting ledgers purchased from New York. The notes and jottings, the crossings-out and corrections, every word their daughter had written in her childlike hand was copied out again.

Their beds were mattresses laid on the ground. Their chairs were garden furniture bought in Brazil. Their lunch was taken at midday, consisting of an egg, a potato and a portion of *fromage blanc*. Electricity was still being rationed, along with bread and coffee and sugar, but when tired they would snack on *croquignole* biscuits bought from a local bakery. The rest of the time they transcribed the journals, as if this tender task could extend their daughter's life for a few minutes more, or answer at last the mystery of her death.

Of course, they knew all the details of her final days. How she began working for the Free French in December 1942, writing reports on the reorganisation of France, though nobody took seriously her plan for the parachuting nurses. How she lived in a garret in Holland Park, refusing to heat the room and sleeping no more than three hours a night. How, one Wednesday morning in spring she was absent from work, and when a friend visited the flat she was found collapsed.

Weil was taken to Middlesex Hospital and diagnosed with tuberculosis in both lungs. At this point she was wearied to stooping silence, her long skirt brushing against the floor and its hem becoming threadbare. All the same, the doctors hoped she would be cured in a couple of months, given complete rest and enough to eat. Instead, her condition grew worse and worse, until she was moved to a sanatorium in Kent.

Grosvenor Sanatorium stood to the north of Ashford, surrounded on three sides by pines. It was a Victorian villa built from red brick, with a pair of modern pavilions to house the patients. Weil had a double room all to herself, its windows looking out over meadows, yellowed by the late-summer light.

When Weil arrived on 17 August, she called it 'a beautiful room to die in'. The nurses kept encouraging their patient to eat, but it was a trial for her to consume more than a few mouthfuls. At one point, she asked whether a French chef could be hired to prepare her favourite potato purée; at another point, she insisted that she could not accept food while the citizens of France were starving. A week after arriving at the sanatorium, Weil slipped into a coma and died before the end of the day.

In Weil's final hours, she resembled one of those emaciated saints celebrated by the Church. Like the medieval mystic Catherine of Siena, who starved to death at the age of thirty-three, or the modern saint Thérèse of Lisieux, who died of consumption at twenty-four. The sanctity of these saints did not come from their technicoloured visions of the divine, but their willing embrace of pain. With their pale faces and famished bodies, they proved that nothing of this world could satisfy the hunger for God. Yet there was a terrible ease to the martyrdom they sought, because even though it demanded the ultimate sacrifice, that sacrifice was made only a single time. Harder perhaps are the decades of quiet devotion and the daily campaign against doubt.

Weil was buried in the corner of a nearby cemetery reserved for Catholics. An inquest blamed her death on 'cardiac failure due to [. . .] starvation and pulmonary tuberculosis'. The coroner concluded, in the traditional language of the law, that 'The deceased did slay and kill herself while the balance of her mind was disturbed.' A local newspaper was much more blunt, running the headline 'DEATH FROM STARVATION. FRENCH PROFESSOR'S CURIOUS SACRIFICE.'

Few people who knew Weil believed her death was deliberate, and her writing condemned the act of suicide. Yet she talked about starvation with a strange fascination, as if hunger could somehow make space for the divine. 'The eternal part of the soul feeds on hunger,' she wrote in her notebooks while living in New York. 'When we do not eat, our organism consumes its own flesh and transforms it into energy. It is the same with the soul. The soul which does not eat consumes itself. The eternal part consumes the mortal part of the soul and transforms it. The hunger of the soul is hard to bear, but there is no other remedy for our disease.'

Weil never specified the disease hunger could cure. However, her American notebooks return several times to Christ's cry upon the cross: 'My God, my God, why hast thou forsaken me?' She argued that the anguish of the cry came from the lack of any answer, sounding in a silence that can offer no response. For Weil, the moment of abandonment was also the moment of understanding, when Christ knew at last the nature of God's love. 'The instant of death is the centre or object of life . . . the instant when, for an infinitesimal fraction of time, pure truth, naked, certain and eternal enters the soul.'

Truth, for Weil, was the highest value. As she neared her own death, she hoped to encounter it at last, stripped of all disguises and cleaned of all deceits. The truth towards which her whole life formed a painful pilgrimage. The truth that only the dead may know.

Now Selma and Bernard tried their best to comprehend. Sitting in their daughter's room, two decades of thinking and writing were written out again, her deepest thoughts and most deranged ideas copied down with infinite care. Over the following decade, almost all those words were published in France, the name of Simone Weil becoming known across Europe and America.

Selma at one end, Bernard at the other, bent over their long black notebooks. A photograph of their daughter, taken in America, hanging on the wall in between. Below was a trunk patched with stickers from New York, São Paulo and

Switzerland, and a vase of flowers placed on top. No sound but the faint scratching of their pens, the hushed stirring of their breath, and the silence that marked the loving labour of their work.

When I woke next morning, mist was rising off the fjord. Yesterday, the crests of the hills were splayed with snow, but now the clouds had sunk from the sky and smudged the summits with vapour. The colours had also faded, as if the landscape were seen through a sheet of gauze: the dense browns of the rockface, the deep blues of the forest, and the faint imprint of the landscape on the stilled surface of the fjord.

At nine o'clock I collected the key from the village Co-op and drove the length of the lake. Then I parked in a camp-site at the far end of the water, where sets of wooden cabins stood empty and waiting for summer, before following a footpath along the eastern edge of the lake, through putty-coloured fields and regular rows of planted pine. A gentle rain was falling, dampening the acoustics of the valley, but I could still hear the cascades rushing down from the summits, mixing with the morning's drizzle to form a faint static.

From a distance the water had the pitted grey of old pewter. Nearer, it was a pane of ageing glass, revealing the smooth stones that cobbled the lakebed. Fallen trees were gathered at the water's edge, the bark torn from their trunks, and their whited branches knitting together to block the bays.

Soon the track grew rocky, passing over broken boulders

and climbing up from the shore. At first I tread carefully along the rubbled path, but then I started pacing faster over the knuckled fists of stone. A rope bannister was fixed to the hillside, and, when I gripped it with both hands, I could heave my body higher like someone taking part in a tug-of-war. The closer I came, the quicker I climbed, my breath harsh, my strides wide, my hands beginning to burn, until I glimpsed the shingle roof and casement windows of the house. Finally I reached the granite ledge on which the cabin was built, hauling myself up the final few metres and then squatting on the ground, waiting for my breath to calm.

The sound of pouring water. Clouds of midges wheeling through the air. Heart beating deep and then beginning to slow. And the key fitting the lock, the door falling open, the smell of warm dust and dry wood from within.

Inside, the layout was simple, with a bedroom, a sitting room and a kitchen, as well as a pair of metal stoves to keep the place warm. The walls were timber, the furniture too, planed and treated but otherwise left bare. Souvenirs associated with the philosopher had been put on display: the canvas rucksack hanging near the door; the enamel tea set laid out for two; the brass candlesticks, brass oil lamps and brass alarm clock beside the bed, as well as a German copy of Tolstoy's *The Gospel in Brief*.

These mementos were arranged in a haphazard fashion, with laminated labels written in Norwegian, their corners starting to fray. Otherwise, the house had none of the weathered texture of somewhere old, no warped wood or sagging rooftiles. Nor did it have the pristine finish of a modern museum: the wax candles burned down to melted stubs and dead flies dropped along the window frames. Doubtless the winter days were cold, but there was little penitential about this place, and I could imagine the pleasure Wittgenstein took in his solitary existence: lighting a fire in the stove, sweeping the dust from the floor, and muttering to himself as he moved between the rooms, trying to break free from the boundaries of his own mind.

Upstairs was an attic space with a pitched ceiling. A door opened onto the balcony, fixed twelve storeys above the shore. The scenery was mirrored in the level grey of the lake: acres of forest plunging beneath the water, continents of cloud streaming across the surface, and the sky fathoms deep at my feet. The mountains surrounding the lake created an immense sense of stillness, and there was something forgiving about their presence. A landscape too large for any human failing, indifferent to the little vanities of our lives.

The rest of the cabin shared this settled calm, with everything kept at a distance and heard from far away. But it was not a lonely setting, and as I stood on the balcony the village felt close enough to reach out and touch. Here was anonymity without exposure, solitude without isolation, companionship without obligation. Here was the sense of protection a child might feel, knowing their mother was sitting next door, listening to every movement they made.

Looking at the last days of Wittgenstein, Jones and Weil, it's difficult to decide whether they should serve as a model or a warning. All three spent their final hours alone, without friends or family beside their beds. All three kept working to the very end, and all three died with that work unfinished – their deaths, like their lives, seeming to echo.

I once hoped that, by writing about these three, I might come to resemble them more closely. I also hoped that, by recreating their retreats, I might learn the secret of their unique lives. Instead I learned the cost of their originality – for themselves and the people who loved them. Because Wittgenstein's desire to be perfect resulted in misery, Jones's longing for solitude left him isolated, and Weil's wish to sacrifice herself led to suicide. Total devotion was not a life without compromise, but the neglect of everything except the one cause that mattered. Suffering was not the price that genius must pay, but the accidents that risked disrupting all their work.

At the beginning of this book I had a simple question: how much should a writer remain in the world and how much should they withdraw? No single life can solve that question, but the biographies of these three offer some hints. Retreat can play a precious part in the early stages of a career, preserving creative and intellectual talents as they emerge. For Wittgenstein, retreat was the mirror that exposed his faults, for Jones the blank page that he coloured with new work, and for Weil it was the absence that allowed her to encounter the divine. But, even when retreat is a route towards originality, it's not the destination. If withdrawing means an intake of breath, at some point you have to exhale.

Christ fasted for forty days and nights and then walked out of the desert to explain what he had seen. Withdrawing was never the purpose, but a preparation to enter the world once more. Similarly, though Wittgenstein, Jones and Weil dreamed of joining a religious community, they sought their solitary callings in the confusion of society. Their work found most value when it was read by other people; their retreats found most meaning when they finally returned. This is the reason we remember them today.

When I started these journeys, I expected to feel at home in each isolated setting, yet I missed my life much more than I expected. The promise of retreat is that we find our true selves, unhampered by the compromises of company, but I suspect there is more truth in the character that emerges through encounter. Withdrawing was no substitute for love, nor the wild possibilities of experience. Retreat was no lesson in how to live.

Standing on the balcony of the cabin, I understood at last that retreat and solitude did not mean the same thing. Wittgenstein came to Norway seeking freedom from society, but living among the inhabitants of Skjolden he joined a curious kind of community. In fact, all three of these biographies had half-hidden figures in the background – the colleagues and companions, the family members and friends – who made it possible for Wittgenstein, Jones and Weil to withdraw. As the shared solitude of the monastery carried the monks through their lonely calling, so these webs of unseen support held aloft their unique lives.

Turning to leave the cabin, I recalled an image from one of the books on the dressing table at Eide Garde. The book described how, during the coldest months of the year, children would skate on the frozen lake after school. Though the winter sun never lasted long, they kept playing on the lake until their cries were sounding in the darkness. The ice was marbled with pockets of methane, released from the matter decaying on the lakebed, and sometimes the children would hold a naked flame to the icecap, breaking the seal with a hammer or spade and causing the gas to flare from beneath. Perhaps there were evenings when Wittgenstein watched this display from his cabin: watched the skaters drawing spirals on the face of the water, becoming threads of spun silver in the metallic sheen from the moon; or watched the children huddled round a flickering torch, until the cold was flashed with fire and the lake began to burn. And perhaps, as he stood by the window and stared down into the shadows, what he saw was not the vast emptiness of the landscape, but the sparks of presence that peopled this place. Torches starring the ice and the skaters' expressions lit with wonder. A pillar of trembling flame glimpsed for an instant and then gone. As if others could fill our lives with light, or even set the night to blaze. As if a miracle was nothing more than the darkness made to dance.

# Acknowledgements

I am grateful to the communities of Stift Klosterneuburg, Caldey Abbey and Abbaye Saint-Pierre de Solesmes for welcoming me into their homes. I am also grateful to the priests, pilgrims, and guests who shared the reasons for their retreats with me.

The writing of this book has been generously supported by a Genesis Foundation Emerging Writer award (2021), a SOA Work in Progress award (2021), and an Oppenheim-John Downes Memorial Trust award (2023). I am also deeply grateful to the organisers and patrons of Gladstone's Library, Hawthornden Castle, Hawkwood College, and Tyrone Guthrie for offering me writing residencies in recent years.

Special thanks to George Prochnik for his interest and encouragement at an early stage of this project. Thanks also to Chloë Aridjis and Henry Hitchings, for all their guidance and advice. My agent Zoë Waldie and my editor Kris Doyle have both been wonderfully supportive from the start. For everything else, I want to thank my loving family.

# ENDNOTES

## INTRODUCTION

'What is necessary, after all, is only this . . .'
Rainer Maria Rilke, *Letters to a Young Poet*, trans. Charlie
  Louth (Penguin, 2011), p.26

'the most perfect example . . .'
Bertrand Russell, *The Autobiography of Bertrand Russell: 1914–1944*
  (Bantam, 1969), p.132

'above all a person in search . . .'
Fania Pascal, 'Wittgenstein: A Personal Memoir' in Rush
  Rhees (ed.), *Recollections of Wittgenstein* (Oxford University
  Press, 1984), p.44

'a work of genius'
T. S. Eliot, 'Introduction' in David Jones, *In Parenthesis* (Faber,
  1961 [1937]), p.vii

'the greatest book . . .'
W. H. Auden, *A Certain World* (Viking, New York, 1970),
  p.373

'the only great spirit . . .'

Albert Camus, letter to the mother of Simone Weil, 11
    February 1951

'having a heart that could beat . . .'
Simone Pétrement, *Simone Weil: A Life*, trans. Raymond
    Rosenthal (Pantheon Books, 1976), p.51

# PART ONE

'Tomorrow perhaps I shall be . . .'
Brian McGuinness, *Wittgenstein: A Life: Young Ludwig
    (1889–1921)* (Penguin, 1990), p.240

'What do I know . . .'
Ludwig Wittgenstein, *Notebooks 1914–1916* (Harper &
    Brothers, 1961), pp.72e-73e

'Not how the world is . . .'
Ludwig Wittgenstein, *Tractatus Logico-Philosophicus*, trans. C. K.
    Ogden (Routledge & Kegan Paul, 1949 [1922]), pp.186-7

'I was longing for . . .'
Paul Engelmann, *Letters from Ludwig Wittgenstein with a Memoir*
    (Blackwell, 1967), p.35

'I have sunk to . . .'
Ibid., p.33

'the most serious book . . .'
Maurice O'Connor Drury in *Recollections of Wittgenstein*, pp.78

'I think that . . .'

# ENDNOTES

Ludwig Wittgenstein, *Letters to Russell, Keynes and Moore,* ed. G. H. von Wright (Blackwell, 1974), p.10

'I said it would . . .'
Ray Monk, *Ludwig Wittgenstein: The Duty of Genius* (Penguin, 1991), p.91

'quiet seriousness'
Brian McGuinness, *Wittgenstein: A Life,* p.188

'Being alone here . . .'
Ray Monk, *Ludwig Wittgenstein: The Duty of Genius,* p.96

'hermit's life'
Ibid., p.89

'he was in a heightened state . . .'
Hermine Wittgenstein in *Recollections of Wittgenstein,* p.3

'It all started . . .'
Ludwig Wittgenstein, *Letters,* p.82.

'Deep inside me . . .'
Ray Monk, *Ludwig Wittgenstein: The Duty of Genius,* p.97

'this book virtually . . .'
Ibid., p.116

'God with me.'
Ludwig Wittgenstein, *Nachlass* (University of Bergen, online), 29/05/1916
https://wab.uib.no/nachlass/bemerkung/Ms–103,15v%5B2%5D_linear.html

'To pray is to think . . .'
Ludwig Wittgenstein, *Notebooks 1914–1916*, pp.72e-73e

'would have preferred . . .'
Ray Monk, *Ludwig Wittgenstein: The Duty of Genius*, p.159

'If you and I . . .'
Maurice O'Connor Drury in *Recollections of Wittgenstein*,
  pp.79

'The dead don't talk.'
Brian McGuinness, *Wittgenstein: A Life*, p.294

'So [. . .] I see that . . .'
Ray Monk, *Ludwig Wittgenstein: The Duty of Genius*, p.191

'You remind me . . .'
Hermine Wittgenstein in *Recollections of Wittgenstein,* p.4

'the humiliation is . . .'
Paul Engelmann, *Letters from Ludwig Wittgenstein*, p.19

'Not from my despair . . .'
Ibid., p.33

'I'm too stupid . . .'
Brian McGuinness, *Wittgenstein: A Life*, p.286

'the one good thing . . .'
Paul Engelmann, *Letters from Ludwig Wittgenstein*, p. 29.

'How things will go . . .'
Brian McGuinness, *Wittgenstein: A Life*, p.292

'suicide is the greatest piece . . .'
Arthur Schopenhauer, *Studies in Pessimism: A series of essays*,
    trans. Thomas Bailey (George Allen, 1913), p.43

'If suicide is allowed . . .'
Ludwig Wittgenstein, *Notebooks 1914–1916*, p.91e

'I have had . . .'
Paul Engelmann, *Letters from Ludwig Wittgenstein*, p.33

'I know that to kill . . .'
Ibid., pp.33–5

'The inmost kernel . . .'
Arthur Schopenhauer, *Studies in Pessimism*, p.45

'Of this I am certain . . .'
Maurice O'Connor Drury in *Recollections of Wittgenstein*, p.88.

'When shall we . . .'
Brian McGuinness (ed.), *Wittgenstein in Cambridge: Letters and
    Documents 1911–1951* (Blackwell, 2008), p.122

'I said it depended . . .'
Ibid., p.51

'Life can educate one . . .'
Ludwig Wittgenstein, *Culture and Value*, ed. G. H. von Wright,
    trans. Peter Winch (Blackwell, 1980), p.86e

'Do not seek delight . . .'
Leo Tolstoy, *The Gospel in Brief,* trans. Isabel Hapgood
    (University of Nebraska Press, 1997), p.75

'In fact I am . . .'
Paul Engelmann, *Letters from Ludwig Wittgenstein*, p.33

'An ethical totalitarianism . . .'
Ibid., p.109

'passionate purity'
Brian McGuinness, *Wittgenstein: A Life*, p.290

'I had felt in his book . . .'
Brian McGuinness (ed.), *Wittgenstein in Cambridge*, p.112

'expanded from the foundations . . .'
Ludwig Wittgenstein, *Notebooks 1914–1916*, p.79e

'It is clear that ethics . . .'
Ludwig Wittgenstein, *Tractatus Logico-Philosophicus*, p.183

'the point of the book . . .'
C. G. Luckhardt (ed.), *Wittgenstein Sources and Perspectives* (Cornell University Press, 1979), p.94.

'We feel that even if . . .'
Ludwig Wittgenstein, *Tractatus Logico-Philosophicus*, p.187

'There is not a single philosophical . . .'
Ludwig Wittgenstein, *Philosophical Investigations,* trans. G. E. M. Anscombe, P. M. S. Hacker and Joachim Schulte (Wiley-Blackwell, 2009 [1953]), p.57e

'There are, indeed, things . . .'
Ludwig Wittgenstein, *Tractatus Logico-Philosophicus*, p.187

'*Wittgenstein passionately believes . . .*'
Paul Engelmann, *Letters from Ludwig Wittgenstein*, p.97

'Either my piece is . . .'
Brian McGuinness, *Wittgenstein: A Life*, p.292

'laboratory of the apocalypse'
Karl Kraus, *Die Fackel*, 10 July 1914, p.2.

'unless all the devils in hell . . .'
Paul Engelmann, *Letters from Ludwig Wittgenstein*, p.37

'A short while ago . . .'
*Wittgenstein in Cambridge*, p.123

'a beautiful and tiny place'
Paul Engelmann, *Letters from Ludwig Wittgenstein*, p.39

'happy in my work at school'
Ibid., p.39

'I do need it badly . . .'
Ibid., p.39

'I had a task . . .'
Ibid., p.41

'One night, while he was a teacher . . .'
Ray Monk, *Ludwig Wittgenstein: The Duty of Genius*, p.199

'I felt totally annihilated . . .'
Genia Schönbaumsfeld, 'Kierkegaard and the *Tractatus*' in Peter
    Sullivan and Michael Potter (eds.), *Wittgenstein's Tractatus:*

*History and interpretation* (Oxford University Press, 2013),
   p.63

'It is not easy to have a saint . . .'
Alexander Waugh, *The House of Wittgenstein* (Bloomsbury,
   2009), p.155

'She understood that he had . . .
Leo Tolstoy, 'Father Sergius' in *The Kreutzer Sonata and Other
   Stories*, trans. David McDuff and Paul Foote (Penguin, 2008),
   p.258

'I have resolved to remain . . .'
*Wittgenstein in Cambridge,* p.157

'The edifice of your pride . . .'
Ludwig Wittgenstein, *Culture and Value*, p.26e

# PART TWO

'a great marvel'
Thomas Dilworth, *David Jones: Engraver, Soldier, Painter, Poet*
   (Vintage, 2019), p.48

'The Break'
David Jones, *The Anathemata* (Faber, 1972 [1952]),
   p.15

'pretty hit and miss . . .'
Thomas Dilworth, *David Jones: Engraver, Soldier, Painter, Poet,*
   p.87

# ENDNOTES

'tawny-red'
Thomas Dilworth, *David Jones Unabridged* (University of Windsor, online, 2022), p.355
https://collections.uwindsor.ca/scholcomm/David-Jones/David-Jones-Unabridged-20220407-final.pdf

'every inch'
Thomas Dilworth, *David Jones: Engraver, Soldier, Painter, Poet*, p.87

'very thrilling . . .'
René Hague (ed.), *Dai Greatcoat: A self-portrait of David Jones in his letters* (Faber, 1980), p.34

'a new beginning . . .'
David Jones, 'Autobiographical Talk' in *Epoch and Artist*, (Faber, 1973) p.29

'subsequent watercolour thing . . . developed.'
Ibid., p.30

'mother, bed-companion, helpmate . . .'
Eric Gill, *Autobiography* (Devin-Adair Company, 1941), p.254

'I had a thing . . .'
Thomas Dilworth, *David Jones Unabridged*, p.369

'an immense amount of tearing up . . .'
Rene Hague (ed.), *Dai Greatcoat*, p.44

'where lithosphere and watersphere . . .'
Thomas Dilworth, *David Jones Unabridged*, p.357

'The wise love . . .'
Ibid., p.356

'of its nature crystalline . . .'
Theodore Baily 'Stained Glass Yesterday and To-Day' in *Pax:
The Quarterly Review of the Benedictines of Caldey* (No.65,
September 1922), p.240

'We *all* know that God alone . . .'
Rene Hague (ed.), *Dai Greatcoat,* pp.44–5

'I think he would have . . .'
Thomas Dilworth, *David Jones: Engraver, Soldier, Painter, Poet,*
p.102

'What you do in religion . . .'
Ibid., p.103

'was sore wounded and alone . . .'
Thomas Dilworth, *David Jones Unabridged,* p.410

'He had taken . . .'
Jonathan Miles, *Try the Wilderness First* (Seren, 2018), p.124

'The Contemplative, who looks . . .'
Jacques Maritain, *Art and Scholasticism* (Charles Scribner's Sons,
1962), p.57

'I don't want to wake up . . .'
Thomas Dilworth, *David Jones Unabridged,* p.570

'You're not going to make . . .'
Ibid., p.986

# ENDNOTES

'turns away from reality . . .'
Sigmund Freud, 'Formulations on the Two Principles of
  Mental Functioning' in *Standard Edition of the Complete
  Works of Sigmund Freud* (Hogarth Press, 1958), Volume XII,
  p.224

'I still think about it . . .'
Thomas Dilworth, *David Jones: Engraver, Soldier, Painter, Poet*,
  p.54

'long professed'
David Jones, *In Parenthesis*, p.44

'serving their harsh novitiate'
Ibid., p.70

'silence peculiar to . . .'
Ibid, p.1

'quality of the monastic . . .'
Ibid., p.217n

'in stalls'
Ibid., p.98

'the uneven pulse of the night–antiphonal'
Ibid., p.99

'I suppose at no time . . .'
Ibid., p.xi

'I did not sleep . . .'
Thomas Dilworth, *David Jones: Engraver, Soldier, Painter, Poet*, p.158

'masterly inactivity.'
Rene Hague (ed.), *Dai Greatcoat,* p.112

'I sometimes wonder . . .'
Thomas Dilworth, *David Jones Unabridged,* p.629

'I have been in the presence . . .'
Ibid., p.1293


## PART THREE

'I stretched out on my back . . .'
Simone Pétrement, *Simone Weil: A Life,* p.274

'The only way into truth . . .'
Simone Weil, *An Anthology* (Penguin, 2005), p.90

'Desire is impossible . . .
Simone Weil, *Gravity and Grace,* trans. Emma Crawford and
    Mario von der Ruhr (Routledge Classics, 2002 [1952]),
    p.94

'Society is a cave . . .'
Simone Weil, *Gravity and Grace,* p.165

'You could not be born . . .'
Ibid., p.177

'whole existence was blotted out . . .'
Simone Weil, *Seventy Letters,* trans. Richard Rees (Oxford
    University Press, 1965), p.140

'I was suffering from . . .'
Simone Weil, *Waiting for God*, trans. Emma Crawford (Putnam
    & Sons, 1959 [1951]), p.68

'The contact with affliction . . .'
Ibid., pp.66–7

'In this state of mind . . .'
Ibid., p.67

'There the conviction . . .'
Ibid., p.67

'Although I only heard . . .'
Simone Pétrement, *Simone Weil: A Life*, p.278

'One sets out as a volunteer . . .'
Simone Weil, *Seventy Letters*, p.109

'an angel'
Simone Pétrement, *Simone Weil: A Life*, p.344

'an artist, a scholar . . .'
Louis Allen, 'French Intellectuals and T. E. Lawrence,' *Durham
    University Journal* (1976), p.60

'Who knows the whole extent . . .'
Ibid., p.61

'There, alone in the little . . .'
Simone Weil, *Waiting for God*, pp.67–8

'Nothing is more beautiful . . .'
Simone Pétrement, *Simone Weil: A Life,* p.304

'Through joy, the beauty . . .'
Simone Weil, *Waiting for God*, p.132

'beauty is eternity here below . . .'
Simone Weil, *Simone Weil Reader*, ed. George A. Panichas
 (David McKay, 1977), p.172

'The Passion of Christ . . .'
Simone Weil, *Waiting for God*, p.68

'Solesmes stands alone . . .'
Joris-Karl Huysmans, *The Oblate*, trans. Edward Perceval
 (Dutton, 1924), p.3-4

'I need to die . . .'
Bernard Doering, 'Loneliness and the existent: The dark nights
 of Pierre Reverdy and Jacques Maritain' in *Maritain Studies/
 Etudes Maritainiennes* (1988) 4, p.13

'The Hebrew tradition . . .'
Simone Pétrement, *Simone Weil: A Life,* p.304

'devil boy'
Ibid.*,* p.330

'a subjective *War and Peace.*'
Charles G. Bell, *The Half Gods* (Houghton Mifflin Company,
 1968), blurb

'As for Simone Weil, I met her at Solesmes . . .'
Ibid., p.viii

'a candle-lighted storeroom'
Ibid., p.297

'the hypnotic pulse . . .'
Ibid., p.301

'grass rippling . . .'
Ibid., p.299

'angel boy'
Simone Pétrement, *Simone Weil: A Life,* p.330

'the truly angelic radiance . . .'
Simone Weil, *Waiting for God,* p.68

'revulsion and a fortunately invincible feeling . . .'
Simone Pétrement, *Simone Weil: A Life,* p.221

'Your loving son, Simon'.
Sylvie Weil, *At Home with André and Simone Weil,* trans.
   Benjamin Ivry (Northwestern University Press, 2010), p.62

'the most beautiful poem . . .'
Simone Pétrement, *Simone Weil: A Life,* p.330

'Often, at the culminating point . . .'
*Waiting for God,* p.68

'At a moment of intense . . .'
Simone Weil, *Seventy Letters* p.140

'in my arguments about . . .'
*Waiting for God,* p.69

'Lear is broken by the external world . . .'
Simone Pétrement, *Simone Weil: A Life,* p.330

'This tearing apart . . .'
*Waiting for God*, p.124

'intermediaries'
Simone Weil, *Gravity and Grace*, p.94

'Every separation is a link.'
Ibid, p.94

'I feel an ever-increasing sense . . .'
Simone Weil, *Seventy Letters*, p.178

'fairy-tale house'.
J. M. Perrin and G. Thibon, *Simone Weil as we knew her*, trans.
  Emma Crawford (Routledge, London, 2003), p.117

'I don't know whether . . .'
Simone Pétrement, *Simone Weil: A Life,* p.415

'At times the very first . . .'
Simone Weil, *An Anthology*, p.41

'the rarest and purest . . .'
Simone Pétrement, *Simone Weil: A Life,* p.462

'Simone's true plan . . .'
Sylvie Weil, *At Home with André and Simone Weil*, p.154

'the Catholic liturgy . . .'
Simone Weil, *Waiting for God*, p.49

'I feel that it is necessary . . .'
Ibid., p.54

ENDNOTES

'There was in her a moral . . .'
Simone Pétrement, *Simone Weil: A Life,* p.459

'We must leave . . .'
Simone Weil, *Gravity and Grace,* p.13

'Relentless necessity, wretchedness, distress . . .'
Ibid., p.32

'To be a witness [. . .] means to live in such a way . . .'
Madeleine L'Engle, *Walking on Water* (Lion Publishing, 1982),
    p.27

'Every time I think . . .'
Simone Pétrement, *Simone Weil: A Life,* p.466

'I would be very happy . . .'
Françoise Lemarchand, 'Quelques précisions sur les rencontres
    de Simone Weil à Solesmes en 1938' in *Cahiers Simone Weil*
    (1983) VI, 2, p.17

# CONCLUSION

'Whoever is unwilling . . .'
Ray Monk, *Ludwig Wittgenstein: The Duty of Genius,* pp.366-7

'And faith is faith . . .'
Ludwig Wittgenstein, *Culture and Value,* p.33e

'*wonder at the existence* . . .'
Ludwig Wittgenstein, *Lecture on Ethics* (Wiley & Sons, 2014),
    p.47

'*absolutely* safe . . .'
Ibid., p.47

'the first of them is . . .'
Ibid., p.47

'If I can't work there I can't work anywhere . . .'
Ray Monk, *Ludwig Wittgenstein: The Duty of Genius*, p.574

'too esoteric'
Thomas Dilworth, *David Jones Unabridged*, p.355

'And so [. . .] living here . . .'
David Jones interviewed by Saunders Lewis (1965, online), 22:38
https://www.youtube.com/watch?v=psQkOT7eNwE

'a beautiful room . . .'
Simone Pétrement, *Simone Weil: A Life*, p.535

'cardiac failure due to . . .'
Ibid., p.537

'The deceased did slay and kill . . .
Ibid., p.537

'Death from starvation . . .
Ibid., p.537

'The eternal part . . .'
Simone Weil, *First and Last Notebooks*, trans. Richard Rees
　　(London, 1970), p.286

'The instant of death . . .'
Simone Weil, *Waiting for God*, p.63

# Select Bibliography

The secondary literature on Ludwig Wittgenstein is large, and that on David Jones and Simone Weil growing quickly. *The World Within* would not have been possible without the outstanding biographies by Ray Monk, Thomas Dilworth and Simone Pétrement. For anyone interested in the lives of this book's subjects, those three are an excellent place to start. Other sources are listed below, but they represent only a small selection of the available material:

Allen, Louis, 'French Intellectuals and T. E. Lawrence,' *Durham University Journal* (1976)

Anson, Peter, *Abbot Extraordinary: A Memoir of Aelred Carlyle, Monk and Missionary, 1874–1955* (Faith Press, 1958)

Anson, Peter, *The Benedictines of Caldey* (Burns, Oates and Washbourne, 1940)

Atkinson, James, *The Mystical in Wittgenstein's Early Writings* (Routledge, 2009)

Auden, W. H., *A Certain World* (Viking, 1970)

Baily, Theodore, 'Stained Glass Yesterday and To-Day' in *Pax: The Quarterly Review of the Benedictines of Caldey* (No.65, September 1922)

Banks, Ariane and Hills, Paul, *The Art of David Jones: Vision and Memory* (Pallant House Gallery, 2015)

Bell, Charles G., *The Half Gods* (Houghton Mifflin Company, 1968)

Bergeron, Katherine, *Decadent Enchantments: The Revival of Gregorian Chant at Solesmes* (University of California Press, 1998)

Combe, Dom Pierre (ed), *The Restoration of Gregorian Chant: Solesmes and the Vatican Edition*, trans. Theodore N. Marier and William Skinner (Catholic University of America Press, 2003)

Dilworth, Thomas, *David Jones Unabridged* (University of Windsor, online, 2022) https://collections.uwindsor.ca/scholcomm/David-Jones/David-Jones-Unabridged-20220407-final.pdf

Dilworth, Thomas, *David Jones: Engraver, Soldier, Painter, Poet* (Vintage, 2019)

Doering, Bernard, 'Loneliness and the existent: The dark nights of Pierre Reverdy and Jacques Maritain' in *Maritain Studies/Etudes Maritainiennes* (1988)

Engelmann, Paul, *Letters from Ludwig Wittgenstein with a Memoir* (Blackwell, 1967)

Freud, Sigmund, 'Formulations on the Two Principles of Mental Functioning' in *Standard Edition of the Complete Works of Sigmund Freud* (Hogarth Press, 1958), Volume XII

Gill, Eric, *Autobiography* (Devin-Adair Company, 1941)

Gray, Nicolete, *The Painted Inscriptions of David Jones* (Gordon Fraser, 1981)

Hague, René (ed.), *Dai Greatcoat: A self-portrait of David Jones in his letters* (Faber, 1980)

Hala, Dom Patrick, *Solesmes: les écrivains et les poètes (1833–1954)* (Éditions de Solesmes, 2011)

Harris, Alexandra, *Romantic Moderns: English Writers, Artists and the Imagination from Virginia Woolf to John Piper* (Thames & Hudson, 2015)

Huysmans, Joris-Karl, *The Oblate*, trans. Edward Perceval (Dutton, 1924)

Jones, David interviewed by Saunders Lewis (1965, online): https://www.youtube.com/watch?v=psQkOT7eNwE

Jones, David, *Epoch and Artist* (Faber, 1974)

Jones, David, *In Parenthesis* (Faber, 1961 [1937])

Jones, David, *The Anathemata* (Faber, 1972)

Kraus, Karl, *Die Fackel*, 10 July 1914

L'Engle, Madeleine, *Walking on Water* (Lion Publishing, 1982)

Leigh Fermor, Patrick, *A Time to Keep Silence* (John Murray, 2004 [1953])

Lemarchand, Françoise, 'Quelques précisions sur les rencontres de Simone Weil à Solesmes en 1938' in *Cahiers Simone Weil* (1983)

Luckhardt, C. G. (ed.), *Wittgenstein Sources and Perspectives* (Cornell University Press, 1979)

MacCulloch, Diarmaid, *Silence: A Christian History* (Penguin, 2014)

Maritain, Jacques, *Art and Scholasticism* (Charles Scribner's Sons, 1962)

McGuinness, Brian (ed.), *Wittgenstein in Cambridge: Letters and Documents 1911–1951* (Blackwell, 2008)

McGuinness, Brian, *Wittgenstein: A Life: Young Ludwig (1889–1921)* (Penguin, 1990)

Miles, Jonathan, *Backgrounds to David Jones: A study in sources and drafts* (University of Wales Press, 1990)

Miles, Jonathan, *Try the Wilderness First* (Seren, 2018)

Monk, Ray, *Bertrand Russell: The Spirit of Solitude* (Vintage, 1997)

Monk, Ray, *Ludwig Wittgenstein: The Duty of Genius* (Penguin, 1991)

Perrin, J. M. and Thibon, G, *Simone Weil as we knew her*, trans. Emma Crawford (Routledge, London, 2003)

Pétrement, Simone, *Simone Weil: A Life*, trans. Raymond Rosenthal (Pantheon Books, 1976)

Preston, Paul, *We Saw Spain Die: Foreign Correspondents in the Spanish Civil War* (Constable, 2009)

Rhees, Rush (ed.), *Recollections of Wittgenstein* (Oxford University Press, 1984)

Rilke, Rainer Maria, *Letters to a Young Poet*, trans. Charlie Louth (Penguin, 2011)

Russell, Bertrand, *The Autobiography of Bertrand Russell: 1914–1944* (Bantam, 1969)

Schopenhauer, Arthur, *Studies in Pessimism: A series of essays*, trans. Thomas Bailey (George Allen, 1913)

Segnit, Nat, *Retreat: Adventures in Search of Solitude, Silence and Renewal* (Vintage, 2022)

Solemes, Abbaye Saint-Pierre de, *Gregorian Chants* (RCA Victor, 1930): https://www.youtube.com/watch?v=sKm54iQ1i-M

Spalding, Frances, *The Real and the Romantic: English Art Between Two World Wars* (Thames & Hudson, 2022)

Sullivan, Peter and Potter, Michael (eds.), *Wittgenstein's Tractatus: History and interpretation* (Oxford University Press, 2013)

Tolstoy, Leo, *The Gospel in Brief,* trans. Isabel Hapgood (University of Nebraska Press, 1997)

Tolstoy, Leo, *The Kreutzer Sonata and Other Stories*, trans. David McDuff and Paul Foote (Penguin, 2008)

Vincent, David, *A History of Solitude* (Polity, 2020)

Waugh, Alexander, *The House of Wittgenstein* (Bloomsbury, 2009)

Weil, Simone, *An Anthology* (Penguin, 2005)

Weil, Simone, *First and Last Notebooks,* trans. Richard Rees (Oxford University Press, 1965)

Weil, Simone, *Gravity and Grace*, trans. Emma Crawford and Mario von der Ruhr (Routledge Classics, 2002 [1952])

Weil, Simone, *Seventy Letters*, trans. Richard Rees (Oxford University Press, 1965)

Weil, Simone, *Simone Weil Reader*, ed. George A. Panichas (David McKay, 1977)

Weil, Simone, *The Need for Roots: Prelude to a Declaration of Duties Towards Mankind* (Routledge, 2001)

Weil, Simone, *Waiting for God*, trans. Emma Crawford (Putnam & Sons, 1959 [1951])

Weil, Sylvie, *At Home with André and Simone Weil*, trans. Benjamin Ivry (Northwestern University Press, 2010)

Wittgenstein, Ludwig, *Culture and Value*, ed. G. H. von Wright, trans. Peter Winch (Blackwell, 1980)

Wittgenstein, Ludwig, *Lecture on Ethics* (Wiley & Sons, 2014)

Wittgenstein, Ludwig, *Letters to Russell, Keynes and Moore*, ed. G. H. von Wright, (Blackwell, 1974)

Wittgenstein, Ludwig, *Nachlass* (University of Bergen, online): https://wab.uib.no/nachlass/bemerkung/ Ms-103,15v%5B2%5D_linear.html

Wittgenstein, Ludwig, *Notebooks 1914–1916* (Harper & Brothers, 1961)

Wittgenstein, Ludwig, *Philosophical Investigations,* trans. G. E. M. Anscombe, P. M. S. Hacker and Joachim Schulte (Blackwell, 2009 [1953])

Wittgenstein, Ludwig, *Tractatus Logico-Philosophicus*, trans. C. K. Ogden (Routledge & Kegan Paul, 1949 [1922])

Zweig, Stefan, *The World of Yesterday,* trans. Anthea Bell (Pushkin Press, 2009)